Cheriton Fitzpaine

A Sense of Community

Village gathering outside Cheriton Rectory, unknown date

Cheriton Fitzpaine

A Sense of Community

Elly Babbedge

2016

Published in 2016

Copyright © Elly Babbedge 2016

A CIP record for this book is available from the British Library

ISBN 978-0-9935357-0-3

Printed and bound by Short Run Press Ltd, Exeter

This book is dedicated to Charles and Iona Cole

Contents

Preface

'… before the beginning and after the end …'

T.S. Eliot Burnt Norton

Anyone who attempts to research and write a parish history will never complete it. The details you find along the way will no doubt increase knowledge about past residents, but what you find is what you find, and what you don't come across will stay lurking in dark attics and deep chests, smiling wryly at your continuing ignorance. I started my research in March 2015 with a blank piece of paper and a hopeful heart, and I had no idea at all what I would uncover about the village where I live. Everyone else was an expert and I knew relatively little, but I was acutely aware that Cheriton Fitzpaine is a different community with a particular sense of warmth, acceptance and self-sufficiency, and I wanted to know where that very strong sense of community had come from.

A year later I find myself in possession of some astounding facts, figures and theories and my head is full of inter-connecting family trees. As a genealogist I have traced most of the key families back and forwards in time to establish lease-land ownership, and lines of succession. As a researcher I have tried to provide some historical background to make sense of villagers' attitudes and actions. As an archivist I have attempted to locate primary and secondary sources, held in a variety of repositories. There is enough to share now, but it is not the end of the story of Cheriton Fitzpaine. There is more waiting to be found out from earlier periods of history and more waiting to be added now that I have reached the end of my research.

And I am always aware that in some details, I may be wrong … I seek to give delight and hurt not.

A sense of Community

Social and psychological features define a community. These features are the 'taken for granted' values and beliefs that evolve in any community. It is 'the way we do things around here'; it is the 'who we are' as a unique group; it is the 'what you are expected to do' when you join us. Psychological community is so much more than a political or geographical area: it is a myriad of groups, all interconnected, each with their own place within the whole. How a community chooses to react to threats and crises can tell a lot about its underlying values and belief systems and can shine a light upon those who hold positions of power and decision making. Such crises can cement the qualities and characteristics that will become part of the community's distinct history, and therefore, part of its future identity. This research set out to discover who and what shaped the community of Cheriton Fitzpaine, a self-contained, mid-Devon parish.

Elly Babbedge
2016

Acknowledgements

Devon parish records reproduced with the kind permission of Devon Archives and Local Studies Services.

With thanks to friends living in the parish who have encouraged and supported me; to the staff at the Devon Heritage Centre, the Somerset Heritage Centre, the Plymouth and West Devon Record Office, and The National Archives; to Robin Whittaker with whom I trained at Aberystwyth; to Eleanor Hartnoll, Carol Foan, Edie Blackburn, John and Sarah Tricks, Paula Mossman, Brenda Fowler, Louise Earle, Barbara and Gordon Smith, Geraldine de Sancha, Geoff Yeandle, Sheila Handy, Peter and Jan Ashby-Crane and many others; to the Mid Devon Rights of Way Officers; to the Ordnance Survey; to Elizabeth Trout at the Mills Archive; to Elizabeth Fisher of Grampound Museum; to the Fareham Local History Society; to Todd Grey and John Booker, and to the late Charles H. B. Cole of Upcott Barton, who was as passionate about the past as I always will be.

A Period of Lunacy – Herman Taylor

How Cheriton reacted to both physical and mental illness in the community is enlightening. It says a lot about the values and beliefs shared by villagers at the time, and we are left wondering how many elements have filtered down through the years to the present day? The story of Herman Taylor 1681 gives a clear illustration.

Herman Taylor married Catherine Tom in 1704 and they had four children: Ann 1706, Herman jnr 1715, John 1717 and James 1720. He was not wealthy and in 1716 he received the sum of 6d. from Daniel Tucker's Bequest for the Poor along with several other deserving parishioners, but he seems to have supported himself and his family well enough.[1] He must have been able to support his family by working because he was not recommended for further money from Tucker's fund until 1722.

In the Accounts for 1722–3 however it appears that things had gone very wrong for the Taylor family. Herman fell sick with an undisclosed illness. Officials were not able to offer him effective medical care and they decided to refer his case to Dr Lewis Southcombe at Rose Ash near South Molton. Herman and Catherine were both taken for a consultation with the rector-cum-doctor fifteen miles away at a cost to the parish of 3/6d.[2]

Dr Lewis Southcombe was the second in what was to become a long line of Southcombes who were Anglican rectors in that parish. He had a special interest in medicine and mental health, and in particular melancholy, a condition of deep sadness and lethargic behaviour that could lead to periods of delusion, and sometimes to the temptation of suicide. It is more than likely that Southcombe was familiar with the writings of Robert Burton who had published his book,

LEWIS SOUTHCOMB
(rector in 1675).

LEWIS II
(1736).

The Anatomy of Melancholy in 1621. Burton suggested that a healthy diet, sleep, music and 'meaningful work', combined with talking with a friend, could cure melancholy. This is a familiar approach to us today but in the seventeenth and eighteenth centuries, these ideas were radical and untested.

Southcombe had studied in London and Oxford and was a man somewhat ahead of his time, taking a real interest in the human condition. He was rector in a small rural Devon parish where members of his family were the local benevolent patriarchs. As a cleric he argued for a 'concord' between individuals, their church and their Bishop, and in a sermon written in 1735 based around the teachings of St Paul, he stated his belief that: 'there is nothing that more conduces to the Happiness and Prosperity of any society than a perfect Harmony and Concord amongst its Members …'[3]

In the 1723–4 Overseers' Accounts Herman Taylor was supported with parish relief for a period of 5 months and 2 weeks @ 14/- per month; one of his children was supported for 3 weeks @ 18d. per week; and his wife, in her necessity was awarded 3/6d. Herman was provided with a coat and shoes at parish expense (possibly in readiness for his journey to Rose Ash) and a parishioner was paid 6d. to shave him. This indicates that he was either physically incapable of shaving or perhaps could not be trusted with a sharp razor because of his state of mind. All evidence collected points towards the fact that Herman Taylor was severely depressed and a danger to himself.

Another set of Accounts submitted to the Overseers for the same year, 1723–4 has the following entries which indicate that the problem was now serious enough to warrant professional treatment rather than just advice from Dr Southcombe:

Paid towards Hermon Taylor 6 weeks @ 9/- per week

For carrying money for Hermon Taylor 2/-

For Hermon Taylor's quarters at ash £1.1s.0d.

For going to see Hermon Taylor 2/-

The journey from Cheriton via Black Dog and Witheridge to Rose Ash would have been a lengthy and perilous one. Retracing the route by car in the Autumn of 2015, it still presents as a challenging and protracted journey, so for a man who was mentally disturbed, not knowing where or why he was travelling, it would have been gruelling. Arriving at the vicarage, Herman would have been disorientated and exhausted so being met by Southcombe, a kindly and understanding practitioner would have made all the difference.

Rose Ash Church, South Molton

His 'quarters at ash' may well have been in the new Rectory itself, completed in 1718, or perhaps in the surrounding courtyard buildings where Dr Southcombe could keep a close eye on his patient. This treatment was not cheap for the parish. The doctor was paid £10 for his 'physick' or medicine, and £1.14s.6d. towards Herman's care.

Although little survives about Dr Lewis Southcombe and his approach to patients, something of his family's philosophy in life does appears in a book entitled, 'Peace of Mind and Health of Body' published in 1750. Both he and his father, also called Lewis were men who were not afraid to stand up and be different. Lewis snr had been deprived of his rectorship as a non-juror when he refused to swear the Oath of Allegiance to William and Mary in 1688. A man with a sensitive conscience, he had come to the conclusion that the Oath was an unlawful one, and that the prayers he was directed to lead in church for William and Mary were therefore 'immoral.' He admitted openly that he had refused to read the Services appointed for Fast-days and Thanksgiving-days by the government, and that he had omitted all names in ' State Prayers' in the Prayer Book. In his defense he pointed out that he had invited another clergyman, with a clear conscience about such things, to take his place.[4] Like many clerics who objected at this time to the Oath, he was deprived of his living until the death of King James II in 1701.

Lewis Southcombe snr's burial entry in the parish register was annotated by his son and confirms that he was a passionate and committed man:

> 'he has been the most vigilant incumbent of the parish and most faithful in-structor of his flock for above 57 years'

Lewis jnr is said to have been 'garrulous and lively' in his writings and he certainly departed from a long tradition of Anglican preachers with his views on the subject of mental incapacity. Rather than seeing this as a manifestation of the devil, he viewed extreme cases of insanity as a medical problem like any other disease that only doctors could cure. He rejected all the 'moral' treatments and torture practiced in Bedlam and other specialist institutions, and refused to attach any stigma to the worst cases of insanity. He did not hold the insane person responsible any more than if he had a fever, and held the opinion that madness could proceed from either 'a wounded spirit' or a 'disordered body'.[5]

When he was treating Herman Taylor at the Rectory, Lewis jnr was in his

From a portrait held by the parishioners of Rose Ash in their Vestry (by kind permission of the Churchwardens)

40s whilst Lewis snr was in his 60s and still running parish affairs. The two men must have talked together about Taylor and his progress. Having studied 'physick', Lewis jnr was well known to have rejected 'all those Means which tend to the giving of Pain and Uneasiness … such as Blisters, Seatons, Cupping, Scarifying, and all other Punishments of the like kind'. Such 'tormenting Means' had sometimes 'rendered a very curable Disease, either incurable, or been the Occasion of protracting the Cure longer than otherwise the Nature of the Case would have required.'[6]

So, although no journal or commentary survive, there are strong clues as to how Herman Taylor would have been treated.

A third set of Cheriton Accounts concerning Herman for the year 1723–4 make for disturbing reading:

> For bringing home Hermon Taylor from Spark Down and cutting his hair and shaving his beard and cleansing the rest of his body £2.2s.6d.
>
> For keeping Hermon Taylor 18 weeks 3 days @ 3/6d. per week
>
> Hermon Taylor's wife in her distress several times 14s.9d.

So, Herman had gone missing – not for a day or two but for some considerable time, and villagers had been alerted to search for him, knowing that he was not in his right mind and a danger to himself. He had lived all his life in the north of the parish where there were wooded valleys and deep ravines that he knew well. He managed to remain hidden for quite some time, and when he was discovered he required 'cleansing' so he must have been living rough for a few weeks. He was found on Spark Downs which lie to the south of Grantland Hill between Buildings Cross and Beer Ash Cross. They belonged to Marshay Farm but backed onto both North and South Coombe Farms where there are still well stocked streams and ponds.

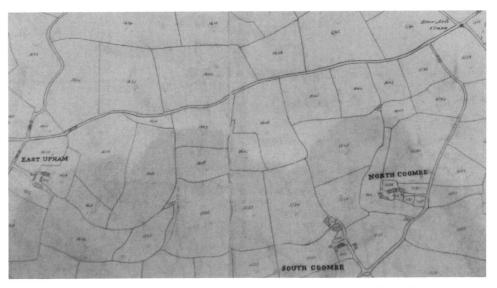

Sparks Downs are marked 606–610 in the centre of this image of the Tythe map

Taylors and Chownes Farm (called Chownes by 1840) may have been where Herman Taylor grew up. It lay off Watery Lane beyond Higher Claw on the extreme western border of the parish. Little Trundlemoor and Tapps have since disappeared, but Trundlemoor Copse still exists.

During Herman's disappearance Catherine was left at home with four children, wondering whether her husband would be found dead or alive, but there was sympathy and support for her from the community in her distress and the parish issued her with payments:

Hermon Taylor's children 4 months @ 10/- per month £2.13s.9d.

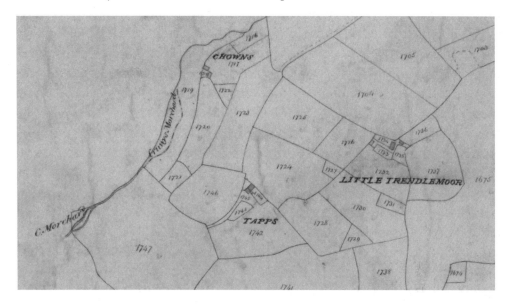

It was Richard Gibb who found him living rough on Spark Downs near Marshay Farm and fetched him back to the village where he was cleaned up and given back some dignity with a new waistcoat and breeches costing 9s.9d., and two changes of clothes and stockings costing 7s.3d. Clearly he showed no threat to the village, only to himself.

Accounts dated April 22nd 1724 record:

> the sum of 16/- for Hermon Taylor 'during the time of his lunacy'
>
> 6/- for Hermon's child, for 4 weeks.
>
> Taylor's child 5 months @ 4/- per month £1.

Herman Taylor's boy who was being clothed and given shoes and stockings at the parish expense was probably James, aged four.

In the midst of this crisis a new baby was conceived and Robert, son of Herman Taylor was baptised at Cheriton Fitzpaine July 10th 1724, perhaps marking a new beginning and future hope for Herman and Catherine Taylor.

These three concurrent accounts for the financial year April 1723 to April 1724 do not allow us to construct a time-line of the events. Did the Southcombe treatment come first, or was it the period of living rough that ended up with the

7

Rose Ash treatment? Whichever the case, this was not a cure for Herman Taylor and he continued to show signs of significant mental illness.

Parish officials met to discuss the case in Vestry and they decided that they could not give up on Herman and his family just yet. There are no reports of violent behaviour from him or of any need to restrain him, but it is clear that his symptoms were severe and protracted. He was in a state of extreme distress and could not be left to live a normal life in the community. All parishes had their share of eccentrics and people who were once termed 'odd' or labelled 'village idiots', but Herman's suffering seems to have been of a different order. Why were parish officials prepared to take so much care over him?

The 1724–5 Accounts record that Overseers and Churchwardens decided to try another approach for the Taylor family, and one of them rode over to Silverton to speak to Dr Sprague about his case. William Sprague was Silverton's parish doctor at the time and he probably lived in the house in Fore Street now called 'The Spragues', often treating villagers from as far away as Cheriton Fitzpaine. It would have taken the best part of a day to travel there and back for a consultation

The Spragues, Fore Street, Silverton

with him or to collect a 'physick' for a patient, so he was only consulted when no remedy could be found in the village.

As a result of this consultation, Herman was then taken for treatment to Silverton and this time there is no mention of his wife being involved. John Heard was paid for 16/- for looking after him during his 2 months of treatment, and Dr Sprague received £14 for 'curing Herman Taylor for a mallancholy disorder.' As a more traditional parish/workhouse doctor, the harsher known treatments were almost certainly metered out to Herman and this must have resulted in a noticeable change in his demeanour. Whether he was cured or not is a matter for conjecture.

After his return from Silverton, Taylor and his family were still supported financially in Cheriton Fitzpaine. In 1725 the parish outlaid another 7 months and 2 weeks relief money for his support and in 1727 he was once again considered deserving of a handout of the sum of 1/- from Fugar's Legacy Fund for the Poor.

Overseers had been prepared to outlay around £50 in total to see Herman Taylor through these difficult months – about half of what they normally spent on the entire parish in a whole year. This 'period of lunacy' has been quoted by R R Sellman, and passing references have been made to it in later publications on madness, but the exploration here serves to provide a much fuller picture of the events surrounding Herman's illness and the way that the local community supported him.[7]

Expenses appear in the Accounts at this time for several villagers 'waking' for days and nights. 'Waking' or 'keeping' usually referred to the practise of nursing patients who required twenty four hour care because they were very sick indeed and probably about to die. The total period concerned covered nine days and twelve nights and involved seven different people giving their time to the Cheriton officials. Mary Colwell co-ordinated the shifts and provided their refreshments:

Grace Colwells charges submitted to the Overseers of the Poor 1725:

Mary Gisson for waking 3 days and nights 3s.6d.

For wood 2/6d, for candles 6d.

Mary Mare for watching 3 days and 3 nights 3s.6d.

For several things 7½d.

John Cruwys for waking one night 1/-

William Cruwys for waking one day and one night 2/-

Robert Hewish ditto 2/-

Robert Sunders for waking one day and 2 nights 3/-

William Maunder for waking one night 1/-

For bread and for beer 3s.5d.

A final entry in the 1725 accounts shows that 4/- was paid out for 'the 2 weeks that Herman Taylor was sick', so the above 'waking' shifts must have been organised to care for him.

There is also an entry with no further explanation which reads, 'paid Taylor's bill £1.0s.9½d.'

There is no way of knowing what this was about, but if Herman died it may have been something to do with funeral expenses, even though there is no burial entry for him in the Parish Register or mention of a grave being dug or a shroud prepared as was usual in the Overseers' accounts. There is no burial entry for him in the Cheriton parish registers or in any of the surrounding parish registers. Did he perhaps take his own life? Was he therefore precluded from a Christian burial? Where was he buried?

Anyone who has been touched by his story will also ask 'What happened to his family after that?' There can be no resolution for his case, but the overall impression is that parish officials in Cheriton Fitzpaine went more than the extra mile for one of their number, in a vain attempt to help him in his period of lunacy. The chances are that he eventually found a way to take his own life and was buried in un-consecrated ground somewhere in the north of the parish.

There was only one Catherine Taylor in the parish at that time so a marriage entry for Catherine Taylor to William Ackerman February 15th 1729 may offer an answer to one of the questions. Herman must have been known to be dead. It seems that the misfortunes of the past few years had not attached any stigma to Catherine and that she was still considered to be marriageable material, and had not been driven away or socially ostracised or labelled by the community. Ackerman was not a local man and most families with that surname hailed from Honiton, so he may have been in Cheriton on business or because he had heard of the treatment and final plight of Herman Taylor and had taken an interest.

Catherine Ackerman certainly did not remain in Cheriton with her new husband. What happened to her is not yet known.

Herman Taylor's background – What led Herman to this period of lunacy?

He was the youngest of at least six children born to Andrew and Margery Taylor (nee Pierce) who married in 1663. The children were Joane 1664, Richard 1668, Andrew 1674, Alice 1675, Robert 1677 and Herman 1781. He grew up with both parents in his life until Margery was buried in woollen in 1696 when he was fifteen years old and his father Andrew died either in 1691 or 1697 – there are two Andrew Taylors recorded in the registers. Herman's father was a man of some standing in the parish who paid Poor Rates on a property on northside and in 1682 (the year after Herman's birth) he took his turn as an Overseer of the Poor, submitting a detailed set of Accounts at the Vestry meeting. Andrew was given money for clothing an apprentice in 1680 and again in 1684 and was promised re-imbursement of the sum of £1.3s.4d. in 1682 when he paid out money to Katherine Upham to look after Nicholas West's child Mary on behalf of the parish. Katherine Upham had refused to carry out her promised duty to look after the baby. That same year he made up the parish rate by paying 2/- out of his own pocket when insufficient money was collected. Andrew Taylor was a local boy with parents Francis and Alice Taylor, also from the village, but his wife Margery Pierce was an in-comer from Newton St Cyres. The Taylor family was well-established and well-respected in the locality, helping others and being in a position to make decisions for their fellow parishioners. Perhaps this had something to do with the great care that was taken over Herman when his mental health failed in the 1720s. What caused his deep depression will remain unknown, but his decline was rapid and severe.

To invest in a 'new-fangled' and as yet untried medical treatment was unusual and risky, and could well have been a mark of respect or fondness for the family. When the approach did not cure him, parish officials did not withdraw their care and concern and instead decided to lay out even more parish money on a traditional treatment. One wonders whether every member of the Vestry committee was happy with the decisions made and the risks taken, but there was obviously a majority decision made.

At the same time that Herman was undergoing his experimental treatment with Southcombe at Rose Ash, other parishioners continued to be referred to more conventional doctors for their treatment. In the light of this, the choice made for Herman was even more considered and deliberate.

In the 1732–4 accounts:

> Paid the doctor concerning Frances Martin £1.1s.0d.
>
> For Frances Martin diet and other things £2.0s.6d
>
> For carrying her to abide with the doctor 2/-
>
> For meat drink washing lodging and attendance for Frances Martin £1.10s.0d.

In the 1736–7 accounts:

> Paid John Hewish for a horse three times to ride to Dr Sproagues
>
> Doctor's bill 3s.6d.

A few years earlier Herman's older brother Richard, the parish sexton, had also received good care. Records show that in 1713 the Churchwardens paid him 2/-. to stand at the doors of each pew to ensure that only the rightful title holders sat in them. In 1719 he had become too ill to be cared for in the village and he was taken to Dr Salter in Clyst. A man was paid to ride with him and to have dinner the first day at Clyst. Then there were parish expenses of 7/- for house room, fire and bedding for Richard and 18s.6d. for his diet and attendance. Richard died leaving five children Jacob 1704, Richard 1708, John 1711, Thomas 1713 and Sarah 1717.

That same year a villager called Ann Weston fell ill and a horse was hired to carry her to Dr Richards at Silverton at a cost of 1/- (Richards was William Sprague's predecessor.) Dr Richards was paid 10s.6d. for curing Ann and further money was paid out to the tune of 1/- for keeping her and 3s.6d. for her since she came home.

The following year Dr Richards had 10/- for curing Thomas Westron and a Mr Frank received 4s.6d. for 'physick' for John Hookway.

In 1721 Mr Caleb Lowdham was paid £1.1s.0d. for curing William Taylor's son of a rupture, so parish officials obviously had a range of medical experts to call upon according to the ailment.

Treatments were not always successful however, for poor John Hearnden/

Hardin seems to have died of complications after breaking his shoulder. We are not told what sort of accident he suffered and the broken shoulder might have obscured more serious internal injuries which were not mentioned. He had been receiving poor relief for several years but the parish had managed to find him some work in Sandford and Stockleigh. In 1713–14 he was badly injured:

> For bringing him from Sandford 1/-
>
> to Richard Taylor and William Hill to fetch John Hearnden from Stockleigh and keeping him overnight 2s.6d.
>
> For fetching John Hearnden's bed from Stockleigh
>
> Cloth for making a bed tye, pillows and a coverlet
>
> For setting his shoulder £1.1s.6d.
>
> John Hardin's diet when his shoulder was set 3s.6d.
>
> bleeding of Hardin 1/-
>
> for a fillet to bind up his arm after he was bled 1½d.

But then things took a turn for the worse and Hearnden passed away:

> For stretching forth John Hearnden 2/-
>
> for a coffin for John Hearden 2/-, digging his grave 1/-, for washing his cloth

As was common, in order to offset some of their expenses, officials gathered together all of John's worldly goods and clothing and sold them off:

> Received for John Hearnden's goods 11s.7d.

In 1728 parish officials again contacted Dr Sprague at Silverton to treat a parishioner traditionally:

> for going to Silverton to consult with the doctor about Camp by the order of the parish 2s.6d.
>
> for going to Dr Sprague to get quarters for Camp by the parish order 2/-
>
> for the hire of a horse for Camp to ride to Dr Sprauge 1/-
>
> for the hire of a horse to carry him under the doctor 1/-

John Pope for going there with him twice 1s.6d.

to Camp's wife in her necessity 2s.6d.

With Dr Richards and Dr Sprague so far away in Silverton something needed to be done to decrease expenditure. Silverton was a 9 mile ride away and it took the best part of a day to get there and back for consultations. Then there was the hire of horses and the day rate for an official's time all to be added to the doctor's bill itself. In 1789 it was decided to secure the position of a dedicated parish doctor who would be on call at times of need and would live in Cheriton Fitzpaine. Mr Turner was duly invited to serve as parish doctor for a salary of £3.3s.0d. per anum with extra expenses. He was referred to as the 'parish doctor, surgeon and apothecary'.

1804 to admission of George Wotton at the Asylum £2.11s.9d.

Expenses conveying him there 10/-

To the treasurer of the Asylum for him £6.15s.0d.

George was the son of Isaac Wotton and Elizabeth Cruwys and was forty one when admitted to the Asylum.

Alternative medicine and treatment

Being a rural area there is evidence that parishioners put a great deal of trust in home-made remedies when they fell ill. Herbs were grown in most gardens and tried and tested potions were still administered in the home. The farm at Yeo even had a large herb garden which was mentioned in deeds for the property in the early eighteenth century. People did not appear to be too wary of those purporting to have special skills, particularly if other villages recommended them as being successful. One such example is that of Widow Wreford who was officially employed by parish officials:

1803 to Widow Wreford for 'striking John Sharland for the King's evil' 3/-

Widow Wreford was feted as an expert in the neighbourhood and possibly carried with her references from the parishes she operated in. She went on to receive payment for a similar treatment in nearby Sandford village as late as 1809. The King's evil or scrofula was the term used for lymphadenopathy of the neck, usually as a result of an infection in the lymph nodes. It could be caused by tuberculous, with the underlying condition being malnutrition. The signs were usually a swelling on the neck and discolouration of the skin, and treatment in the early 19th century would have been to lance and drain the abscess, leaving a sizable scar. Some practitioners may have done no more than 'touch' the site of infection whilst incanting words.

1717/18 Mrs Frank for curing Keen's wife of an ague 5/-; widow Frank for bleeding Mary Lizwill and curing her head 5/-

1731/2 Mrs Cooksley for medicines for John Smith 4/-

1732 Mary Heart for curing Grace Upham's eyes 3/-

1762/3 Mrs Gubb in part for curing Mary Shapcott 10s.6d.

And Doctor John Dyer, who lived at West Burrough was paid for curing Elizabeth Wellington's leg in 1741/2, whilst Margaret Littlewer was cured of the itch and 'struck'.

Another entry shows that village officials dutifully carried out the requirements asked of them by Government:

1808 for inoculating 17 poor children £1.14s.0d.

On April 10th 1807 The House of Commons had passed a resolution (60 votes to 5) concerning small pox inoculation after considering the Report of the Royal College of Physicians of London.

What can be concluded from these illustrations of medical care in Cheriton Fitzpaine over the course of 100 years? Were those who held the power and decision making just being conscience in their duties? Were they carrying out treatments as economically as possible with parish funds in mind? Were they negligent at times? Were they trusted by their parishioners? There is no doubt that extra care was taken over individual cases and that sometimes large amounts of money were spent in an attempt to reach a good outcomes. Certain values and mind-sets can be identified from the evidence of the actions of those who held authority in Cheriton when there were crises to deal with.

This was a community that trusted its officials and understood at some unspoken level that each one of them would be treated fairly and with a certain generosity of spirit. With that sort of modelling from those who held positions of power and decision making, it is not surprising that the community as a whole was accepting of mistakes and misfortunes.

Was there a future for Herman Taylor's children?

Herman Taylor's son John 1717 stayed in the village and married Mary Hedge, baptising children Mary 1739, Richard 1745, Sarah 1745, Elizabeth 1751 and John 1754. The Quarter Sessions for 1753–4 document a dispute between Mary Taylor the wife of John Taylor and four people all accused of beating her up. One might immediately imagine that this was connected in some way to prejudice or resentment around Herman's lunacy, but as John was in no way implicated, it was probably just a disagreement fuelled by drink. Two of the attackers in turn accused Mary of assaulting them: Mary wife of William Brewer a cordwainer and Joseph Brewer, a tailor. The other couple were Robert Brewer a white bread maker and his wife Mary. Amazingly, Mrs Taylor gave birth to another child in 1754, shortly after the case was heard.

This case is one of a surprisingly few Cheriton disputes taken to Quarter Sessions for a verdict. There was generally little discord in the community as most disagreements were sorted out amicably at the time.

The story of Herman Taylor illustrates the extraordinary lengths to which Cheriton officials were prepared to go to care for an individual in the throes of mental turmoil. It says a lot about the values and beliefs shared by villagers at the time, showing a lack of prejudice towards those who were different and demonstrating a considerable capacity for care towards individuals.

References

1. Cheriton Fitzpaine parish registers
2. Cheriton Fitzpaine Overseers of the Poor Accounts
3. Lewis Southcombe 2 sermons 1735 4131M/F18-19
4. Plumptre, E.H. 1821–1891, The Life of Thomas Kenn D.D. Bishop of Bath and Wells. 1889

5. Scull, Andrew. Social Order/Mental Disorder: Anglo-American Psychiatry in Historical Perspective. 1989
6. Ditto
7. Sellman, R.R. Cheriton Fitzpaine: Notes from the parish records and other sources 1978, and Porter, Roy. Mind-Forg'd Manacles 1987 p 120

Saunders Tenement – a house worth fighting for

The house, originally built in the 16th century is one of the oldest in the village and it stands at the junction of Back Hayes Lane and the main road, close to the old Poor House. Originally a three or four roomed cross-passage house it has two closed trusses at the western end, and its smoke-blackened roof indicates that it was once a single storey hall house with a central fire. Like several other surviving farm-houses in the parish, cross beams and ceilings were added in the 17th century and chimney-stacks and hearths were constructed. Unlike some however, Saunders does not retain its oak and plank muntin passage screen or have any decorative carpentry of note. (Listing NGR: SS8681906202)

On the fireplace in the room at the western end of Lower Saunders there are elaborate but crude carvings depicting a four-leafed clover, a fleur-de-lys, the date 1706 and the initials 'L' above and 'M H' below.

There were no marriages that year between couples with the same initials; the house did not change hands that year, and no children were born. In fact from before 1691 through 1706 and on to 1727 a man called Morrish Hewish lived there with his wife and children: John 1686, Abraham 1687, William 1689, Elizabeth 1692, Richard 1694, Jane 1696 and Mary 1698. He had married Elizabeth Oxenham at Puddington in 1685. The significance of the carved date is not yet evident but it is just possible that the 'M H' stands for Morrish Hewish.

Morrish and Elizabeth probably moved into the house as newly-weds, and early surviving rate lists certainly place them there with their first three children in 1691.

Fireplace in the western room of Lower Saunders

1691 Morrish Hewish paid Poor rates on Saunders

1704 Morrish Hewish paid 1s.6d. Church rate on Saunders

1723 Morrish Hewish of Saunders wrote a will that has not survived

1731 Hugh Payne paid rates on Saunders

1744 William Hewish paid 2/- Church rate on Saunders

Morrish was the first son of John Hewish and his wife Elizabeth Morrish from whom he got his unusual forename. In 1660 when a toddler he was a beneficiary in his grandmother Joane Morrish of Stockleigh Pomeroy's will.[1] The Hewish family was well established in Cheriton but in later years also held leases on

properties in Stockleigh, namely Frogpool farm which may have found its way into the family through the Morrish/Hewish marriage.

After Morrish and his wife had passed away, a new ninety nine year lease on Lower Saunders was drawn up by the Lord of the Manor, John Harris of Hayne, Cornwall. William Hewish yeoman, the third son of the marriage paid the necessary fee but he did not name himself as one of the three lives in the lease.[2] Instead, the lease was to run for the three young lives of:

> William Hewish jnr 1727, his son
>
> Abraham Hewish 1726, his nephew and
>
> Andrew Hewish 1731, another nephew.

Abraham and Andrew were the sons of William's eldest brother John Hewish, 1686. It was a straightforward transaction such as many families made at the time, and was intended to provide an income and inheritance for the three boys when they grew up. William had another older brother Abraham but he had no children.

After his parents' demise, William Hewish lived at Lower Saunders with his wife Ann Melhuish whom he married in 1720 at Puddington north-west of the village. William and Ann were described in the Puddington register as being 'both of Cheriton Fitzpaine' at the time of their wedding, but Ann may have been born there and been related to the Ferdinando Melhuish who married there in 1713 and the Joan Melhuish who married in 1716. Puddington had not had a marriage for two years and as William's mother Elizabeth Oxenham had come from Puddington herself, the couple may have decided to hold their wedding there rather than in Cheriton.

Once settled back in Cheriton they had three little daughters Rebecca 1721 (died), Ann 1723 and Mary 1725 (died) and then their only son William jnr was born 1727. The signing of the lease in favour of the boy and his cousins however was to sow the seeds for a tragic story to unfold some twenty years later.

We learn about the tragedy in 1806 in Alexander Jenkins' History and Description of The City of Exeter:

> 1752 An Act was this year passed, for the more speedy execution of murderers, and delivering their bodies to the Surgeons to be anatomised; the first person executed on this act in Exeter, was Mr Huish, a gentleman of some fortune, who had served an apprenticeship in the city, with Mr Arundel, a capital serge-maker; but turning out very wild and undutiful to his parents (who lived at Cheriton Fitzpaine,) he was accused of poisoning his father, and beating his mother to death; the first of these crimes he was acquitted of, on his trial. But found guilty of the second, for which he was executed at Heavitree Gallows, and his body sent to the Devon and Exeter Hospital, where it was anatomized; his bones remained there in the cupola, for many years (a striking example to all parricides) 'till they mouldered into dust.[3]

Writing only fifty years after the event, Jenkins gives us one of the few brief reports that survive about the murders, but in doing so he muddled up the court judgements, stating that William Hewish was found guilty of his *mother's* death, when in fact he was acquitted of that charge. The Assize records would give a full account of proceedings of course, but like so many, they do not survive for that year. Officials often destroyed them when they ran out of storage space and only a few have been deposited in the National Archives. A letter in a newspaper of the time however does offer a little extra information, referring to an eight hour trial on 28th March, when to everyone's surprise William was found not guilty of his mother's 'deliberated' murder. It reports that the following day there was a nine hour trial, after which William was sentenced to death for the murder of his father, by poisoning. The date given for execution was April 2nd 1753, but the disposal of his body had not as yet been made public.

'Thursday last our Assizes ended here, when William Hewish who had the day before (to the surprise of everyone) been found not guilty of the deliberated murder of his own mother. Was convicted on another indictment of the deliberated murder of his own father, (horrible! most horrible!) and received sentence to be executed this instant, according to the Statute. However, as it is left to the discretion of his Lordship the judge, not only to order the disposal of his dead body, but (if he sees fit) to respite execution for a few days, we were not certain til early this morning, that this very day is fixed on for his execution. As to the disposal of his body, is not yet public. Three others received sentence of death, viz, Thomas Bennet, John Williams and John Slocombe, all for horse-stealing, two to be transported viz, Edward German and John Kitchen, three burnt in the hand, five whipt and four acquitted. Hewish's trial the first day lasted eight hours and the last about nine hours.'

Sherborne Mercury and Western Flying Post 2nd April 1753

Jenkins' recount revealed that his body was anatomised for use at the Exeter Hospital in line with the new Act.

A double murder is an unusual event, especially when both parents are involved. For it to happen in a peaceful, tucked-away village in mid-Devon, renowned for its supportive and caring community, is almost unbelievable, and with no apparent mention of it in the ensuing years and no obvious prejudice shown towards surviving family members, the story deserves further investigation.

The first intriguing fact is the evidence in the parish registers:

William Hewish snr was buried on December 26th 1752

Ann Hewish was buried on December 16th 1751

So the two deaths did not occur at the same time, nor even in the same year, and if William was thought to be guilty of his mother's murder in 1751 he was certainly not tried for it or even arrested as a suspect, and continued to be a free man. That year he had taken his turn to act as Churchwarden and Overseer of the Poor for the parish, and had submitted a very efficient set of signed accounts.

The Assize sat in early 1753.

William's father died as a result of poisoning – neither a fool-proof nor speedy method of killing someone, and generally speaking, not a method chosen by men. He was buried the day after Christmas in 1752, a time when William and his sisters would have been celebrating the festivities with their father. Because the Coroner had been called to examine the body on this occasions, the death probably took place a few days *before* Christmas. The Coroner's report does not survive but evidence that he submitted his expenses for visiting Cheriton does.[4]

Suspicions must have been raised as a result of the visit and sometime afterwards William must have been arrested and taken to Exeter to stand trial. There is some confusion over the actual dates of his incarceration but in February 1753 he saw a solicitor to take out Letters of Administration, favouring himself as the sole beneficiary of his father's estate. As outlined by the Cornell Legal Information Institute, 'The letters authorize the administrator to settle the deceased person's estate according to the state's intestate succession laws.' William snr had died unexpectedly, intestate, and William jnr was aware that because of the other lives mentioned on the lease, he would have to share his inheritance of Lower Saunders tenement with his two cousins. He was seeking to revoke the terms of the lease to cut Abraham and Andrew out and was prepared to put forward a release fee for this to happen. William was not married and had no children himself so this was not the action of a man about to die who wanted to secure property for his descendants in his absence, but rather indicates that he felt he had a future himself and wanted to ensure that he had a house to live in. At this time he also drew up his own will, but this has not survives, being a casualty of the Exeter bombings in World War II.[5] William's attempt to carry out the transaction however did him no favours in the public's eye.

When he was brought to trial for his mother's murder (one newspaper report says February, another says March) he was found not guilty after eight hours of evidence and deliberation, indicating that this was not a straightforward case of guilt. Everyone in attendance, according to one report was said to be surprised at the verdict, but those passing judgement were clearly not entirely satisfied by what they heard on the day, and William was found not guilty of her *deliberated* murder. Perhaps the word 'deliberated' points towards some measure of culpability? William is reported to have said that he felt that he *deserved* punishment for the way he had treated his mother in the past, but he pleaded not guilty to murder.

If other news reports are to be believed, Ann Hewish died some while after a beating from her son. If this evidence was put forward in the court perhaps

23

there was uncertainty as to whether the beating was her actual cause of death, and whether William had any clear intention to kill her. Ann may of course have died from completely unrelated medical issues that were neither diagnosed nor treated at the time. What remains is the likelihood that these two often argued together and that William was a young man with a temper.

Lower Saunders stands at the centre of the village on a busy corner of the Churchtown loop where Back Hayes Lane meets the main road. It is next to the Poor House and not far from the church and many villagers would have passed by or been working nearby during day light hours. It was reported to the court that William could be 'very wild and undutiful to his parents', which sounds more like the description of an unruly teenager than a man in his mid-twenties. One is left wondering about the root cause of such behaviour. Was his father prone to violent outbursts? Were both parents disappointed with their son's life-choices? Was his mother over-indulgent or too controlling? Was William more than a bad-tempered offspring?

Strangely no local newspapers featured the details of the trial, but this report appeared in Manchester Mercury in 1753:

> 'Bristol, April 7 William Hewish condemned at Exeter for poisoning his father, was executed on Saturday last, agreeable to the late Act of Parliament at the gallows. He owned he had beat his mother in a cruel manner several time, once in particular before his father, who said when he had almost strangled her, Sirrah! Wilt thou murder thy mother before mine eyes? To which he replied, I must do it, by G-d, He had been often heard to say, when one reprehended him for misusing his mother. That she was a Hell-born old whore, and that if he had 100 weight of gunpowder he would blow the old Hell born B---h to Hell. He denied the poisoning of his father, but acknowledged he deserved death for his barbarous usage to his mother.'

Newspapers have always wanted to sell copy. Witnesses have often got caught up in the moment and remembered what they thought they ought to. But confusing detail is revealed in the Derby Mercury dated March 6th 1753:

This report starts unpromisingly with a glaring error, for William could not possibly have been tried for his mother's murder in October 1751, two months before her burial. The writer in Derby takes a similar sensational approach to

At the Affizes at Exeter, in October 1751, one Huifh was tried for the Murder of his Mother, and after eight Hours Trial was acquitted; though there was very ftrong Evidence againft him, of his beating, kicking, and dragging her about by the Hair of her Head, and frequently declaring he would kill her : She having alfo told feveral People before her Death, that her Illnefs was occafioned by a Blow with a Bar on her Stomach. On Thurfday laft the fame Perfon was tried at the Affizes for poifoning his Father, in December laft, and after a Trial of feven Hours, found guilty, and ordered for Execution on Saturday. He was a genteel young Fellow, and extremely well dreffed on his Trial. He robbed his Mafter when Apprentice, fled, and afterwards had the Benefit of the laft Pardon. If he had been acquitted of the above Offence, he would have been indicted for Forgery.

that of the Manchester writer, giving verbatim reports of what William said and gruesome details about the act of murder. Neither of these men would have been present at the Exeter trial and news of it would have travelled like Chinese whispers to the north via London and Bristol. Why then were none of these details present in newspapers in Devon and Somerset? The only reference to the trial was in a letter to the editor of The Sherboune Mercury and Western Flying Post (see above) that told in a matter of fact way that William Hewish was found not guilty of the deliberated murder of his own mother, but was convicted on another indictment of the deliberated murder of his own father.

Back home in Cheriton Fitzpaine there was nothing committed to paper about the Hewish trials. In 1753 when William was under suspicion, Rev Spettigue took out a caveat to prevent him from holding the office of churchwarden that year at the request of the parishioners and after the hanging, one respectful note in the Overseers of the Poor Accounts for 1753 makes a passing reference:

'By cash of James Chamberlain being an arrears received for Saunders tenement, not charged in his account for last year, 7s.6d.'

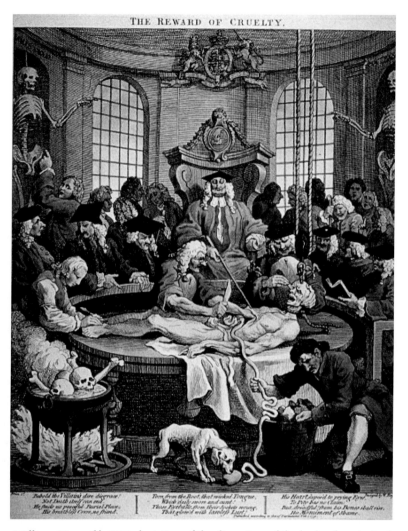

William Hogarth's 1751 depiction of the dissection of the body of a criminal

Perhaps William snr did point the finger of blame when he himself was in the throes of dying from poisoning; perhaps neighbours felt that the co-incidence of two unnatural deaths in one family must be down to the 'wild child' that was William; perhaps the Coroner alerted the authorities after his visit to the village. Whatever the case, William was sentenced to death after the double murder trial and was hung at Heavitree gallows on April 2nd.

The Derby report stated that William was 'a genteel young fellow and extremely well dressed on his trial' and also that 'he robbed is master when apprentice, fled, and afterwards had the benefit of the last pardon.' Had he not been found guilty of murder at the trials it was claimed that he would have been indicted for 'forgery'.

The little information that survives about William is conflicting. His demeanour at the trials as 'a genteel young fellow' certainly suggests that he knew how to behave in society, and evidence in parish records shows that when aged only twenty four in 1751 he had served as both Overseer of the Poor and Churchwarden for the village for the entire year, taking on the role of a responsible member of the community. It was a demanding task to represent the Overseers and the Church and he would have needed a good measure of maturity to carry out these two roles. His set of detailed Accounts submitted that year are prefaced with the words: 'William Hewish jnr Overseer of the Poor and Churchwarden for Saunders acting as a substitute for Mr Philip Western alias Westron of West Burrow.' He signed the accounts as follows, in his own hand:

'I William Hewish do make oath that the aforesaid Accounts are true accounts to the best of my knowledge. William jnr sworn by me 17th April 1751'

William, 'a gentleman of some fortune' was working as a farmer in Cheriton and not pursuing the career his parents had chosen for him in Exeter. He had been apprenticed for several years to Alexander Arundell master serge-maker, but things had gone wrong and he had left, accused of theft. No doubt his parents were disappointed that he had thrown away the opportunities they had offered him in the nearby city and there may have been family frictions about the matter, but he seemed to have been leading a useful life back in Cheriton. Going about his daily business in the parish he would have been well-known as coming from a respected family. His close Hewish relatives lived at Pool Barton, and family members were in possession of many leases in the parish. Beneath his exterior of respectability however William was also capable of erratic behaviour.

His former master, Alexander Arundell would certainly have been called upon to bear witness at William's trials, especially since he had lived and worked alongside the young man for some considerable time before the petty crime alluded to in the Court. What sort of evidence was he likely to give? Little is known of Arundell of St Thomas the Apostle, Exeter save that he left a will dated May 22nd 1757, proved two years later and administered by Rev Mr John Harrington and Rev Mr John Walrond.[6]

The will reveals that he was separated from his wife, for whom he made extra provision, and that he had no children of his own. His bequests showed that he was a practising Presbyterian who attended the 'Bow meeting' in the city for he left money to the congregation there. He owned and lived in two adjoining houses in St Mary Major and left these to his nephews Sampson and George Downing. After bequests to enable young Protestant dissenters to be educated in academic learning, he left the bulk of his estate and the income from a mortgaged property in Clyst St George to Arundell Phillips, his sister's grandchild. Alexander's ambition was that the boy, born in 1744, should become a Presbyterian or Protestant Minister, and he went into meticulous detail as to what was to happen to the money if Arundell Phillips was or wasn't to have children of his own. As it happened the boy did go on to marry and baptised several children into the Presbyterian Church: Maria 1776, Charlotte 1778, Jane 1779 and John 1780.

Many wealthy merchant families in Exeter at that time were Presbyterian. They preferred a simpler form of worship to that of the established church and believed that the congregation rather than the building itself constituted the Church. Alexander would have attended meetings in a converted house in Smythen Street (which was then a continuation of Stepcote Hill). The present day St George's Presbyterian Meeting House in South Street was not built until 1760, a few years after his death. Because of the choices that dissident tradesmen made, members of the official Church often shunned them, and they were known to be strong-minded in their beliefs. Alexander would have been just such a man. He was a skilled manufacturer and an astute businessman and it would have been quite an accolade to secure an apprenticeship with him. He was also someone who wanted to make life right and fair for young people and he would have been a strong influence upon William jnr.

When he bequeathed his two houses to Sampson and George he stated that he wanted them to hold them as, 'tenants in common and not as joint tenants.' This meant that they would legally own different shares of the property and that one part of the property would not automatically go to the other owner if one of them died. It also ensured that they could each pass on their individual share of the property in their own wills. There must have been a reason for him to add this particular detail, and knowing the young William Hewish as he did, he would have been aware of the problems that his young apprentice felt he had around sharing an interest in Lower Saunders with his cousins. The terms of his will effectively safeguarded each of his nephews' inheritance.

Hewish is said to have robbed his master and fled and that as a result he was likely to have been tried for forgery. He may then have stolen lengths of cloth from Arundell and tried to pass them off as his own in the marketplace, a crime, but not a heinous one, and Arundell may have spoken up for the good character of his young apprentice at the trial.

Serge was made from a combination of the long fibred wool that was used to produce worsted, and the woollen yarn that was produced from a shorter and softer fleece. The cloth was ribbed diagonally giving it a front and a back and it was both lightweight and hard-wearing. Fleeces from sheep reared in Devon and Somerset were particularly prized by the serge-makers. Friday Serge Markets were held weekly in front of The Bear Inn in the city but many bolts of cloth were exported via the Exeter Basin and the port of Topsham and they fetched good prices. Tuckers Hall was built by the Exeter woollen merchants and it still survives in Fore Street.

Tuckers Hall, Fore Street, Exeter

When William had rushed to draw up Letters of Administration dated February 27th 1753 to gain control over his estate and to exclude his cousins Abraham and Andrew, his Uncle John took immediate actions to block him. Then just two years after the hanging, Abraham Hewish died leaving Andrew Hewish as the sole living leasee of Lower Saunders. Things were not going to be straightforward for him either however.

Growing up, Abraham and Andrew Hewish had heard rumours about their rights to Saunders but had never known the truth. They had often asked their father John about the deeds: 'with tears in their eyes they often prayed to have sight of it', but this was always denied them.[7] Abraham died in 1755 before the truth could be known and Andrew was left very much in the dark. The two were in fact co-tenants of the property according to the unrevoked lease.

When William jnr was hung, his Uncle John had seized the property, paying off the £30 owing on the lease to the Rev Arthur Harris as landlord. He then felt that he was rightfully able to receive all rents and profits that came from the tenement and in his 1766 will, he stated his clear wish that all profits from Saunders were to be for the benefit of his daughters Sarah, wife of William Wotton and Mary, widow of Thomas Wellington. Andrew was to act as co-trustee with Edward Hewish esq of Pool, his close relative.[8]

Edward, a very wealthy man had inherited Pool from his father but was living in Cornwall at the time of John's death. Under instruction from Edward, a local family friend, William Bellew esq of Stockleigh English visited John's home and took away all deeds and papers relating to Saunders. With Edward's blessing he then managed the estate himself, (Andrew claimed later that he did this 'fraudulently'.). When Edward returned to live in the village, Bellew handed the documentation over to him, but Andrew was still kept ignorant of his rights over the property. As co-trustee of his father's will he was even persuaded by Edward to formalise John's intentions by applying for a new lease on the tenement favouring his sister Sarah and her husband William Wotton for the yearly rent of £12.12s.0d. With this in place Edward eventually allowed Andrew to have sight of the original lease and at last, in 1772, he learned that he was the surviving named tenant. He immediately demanded his share of all past rents and profits on Saunders, but the family argued that it had never been worth much and that no income had been taken over the years. Offended and incensed, he had no alternative but to take the matter to Court to resolve it, and in 1772 he registered a complaint in the Chancery Court to gain what was rightfully his.[9]

Inevitably Andrew Hewish won the case and Saunders Tenement was at last his. One can only imagine the damage done to family relationships over the years, but at least he had managed to secure the property for his son, John. Andrew had married Sarah Stabbick in 1756 and produced Mary in 1757 (who married John Brewer 1779) and John in 1761 (who was married three times and produced ten children). They had been living in Cheriton Barton house and farming the 123 acres attached to it whilst the subterfuge around Saunders was going on. The lease of that property had been held his sister Mary and her husband Thomas Wellington, but when Thomas died young in 1758, Mary was unable to farm the land herself with young children to care for and it appears that Andrew moved into the farmhouse to run the estate. After the court case he secured Lower Saunders for his son's future, taking on a John Adams as an apprentice there in 1781 and paying Land Tax on the property.[10] Andrew died just a couple of years later in December 1783.

Lower Saunders must have been a house worth fighting for!

Edward Hewish of Cornwall and Cheriton Fitzpaine

Edward was the only surviving son of Mr William Hewish and his wife Rebecca, daughter of Nicholas Hicks the rector of Cheriton Fitzpaine from 1675–1719. He was heir to the prestigious Pool estate, but as a young man he spent many years away from the village living with his Uncle John Hicks in Cornwall. Hicks had amassed an extraordinary fortune in and around Altarun near Launceston, and although married, he had no children of his own and looked upon Edward as a son and heir. When his uncle died in 1760 Edward inherited a large portfolio of property both in Cornwall and in Devon, and as executor had the task of distributing many other properties to relatives on his mother's side of the family.[11] Cousins Elizabeth and Mary Hicks were major beneficiaries and smaller bequests were made to unmarried cousins Rebecca and Elizabeth Hewish and to nephews William and John Davenport.

Nicholas Hicks had produced John as his eldest son in 1682 with other children being Elizabeth 1679, Rebecca 1680, Nicholas 1688 and Thomas 1690, and although John as an adult looked upon Cornwall as his home, he left a sum of money in his Will to the poor of Cheriton Fitzpaine where he grew up.

Edward Hewish too looked favourably upon Cornwall but eventually returned to Cheriton and became actively involved in the dispute over Saunders Tenement. He claimed back the paperwork from Bellew and tried to keep the peace between all parties. He was a well-respected man and when he died in 1778 an article in The Exeter Flying Post confirmed the fact:

'On Saturday last died at Cheriton Fitzpaine, in the county of Devon, Edward Hewish esq sincerely lamented not only by his family, but by a numerous connection formed on the basis of an active integrity. The faithful discharge of a confidence reported in him by departing friends, made glad the hearts of widows and orphans, who prise his memory, and his many and just arbitrations speak the universal loss of a once valuate member of society.'

His will proved in 1779 mentions his unmarried sister Rebecca Hewish, his unmarried cousins Elizabeth and Mary Hicks, and Ann jnr, 'the daughter of Ann Hewish' and her husband Thomas Cotton, Alderman of Exeter in 1753.[12]

Thomas and Ann Cotton's son James 1756 was a cleric and from his Cornish estate Edward bequeathed the Rectorship of Linkinhorn to him. James left Exeter and took up the position in Cornwall, naming one of his children *Edward Hewish* Cotton after his generous benefactor.

Cousin Elizabeth Hicks remained a spinster all her life, dying in 1797 and passing her moiety of Pool Barton and Brindiwell to the same James Coffin. She is mentioned in these leases held in private hands:

> 28.9.1795 copy lease for a year for 5/- for moiety of Pool Barton or farm in the occupation of Mrs Elizabeth Hicks and Samuel Pridham also Little or Lower Wolland or Dallys now in the possession of John Cross or his undertenants

> 4.1.1807 Lease and Release for a year for 5/- The Barton House now called Poole formerly in the possession of William Hewish esq, afterwards Edward Hewish and now and for many years in the possession of Elizabeth Hicks and Samuel Pridham as tenant to Eliz Hicks and then James Coffin

Like her cousin Edward, Elizabeth remembered her close relatives when she died, leaving East and West Hayne together with a cottage to Ann Cotton jnr, who by that time had married John Adams, a goldsmith of Exeter. She also left her Cornish property to her 'cousin' William Newcombe of The Bank of England, being the grandson of her Uncle William Newcombe. To her other cousin, Robert Lydstone Newcombe she left more of her Cornish property. Elizabeth Paine, a cousin was left an income out of the moiety of Pool, and the trio of Elizabeth Newcombe, Sarah Manley the daughter of William Manley and Elizabeth Bellew of Stockleigh English were also remembered in her will.[13]

Rebecca Hewish 1730 also remained a spinster all her life and died in 1797, passing on her share of property to the same Hicks sisters. She also left South Down tenement in Cheriton and itemised valuables including a silver spoon with the inscription 'A D. R H. 1722'. Could 'R H' have been Rebecca Hicks or Rebecca Hewish? 'A D' remains a mystery, although the spoon probably commemorated a betrothal or a christening in the family.[14]

Tainted or unfortunate?

It seems remarkable that Andrew Hewish was caught up in his cousin, William's scandal through no fault of his own. Why was he not mentioned in his father's will? Why was he denied knowledge of his inheritance until the facts were revealed to him and he was forced to take his case to court?

Being of about the same age, he would have grown up knowing his cousin William well and he may even have stood as a character witness for him at the murder trials. Was it this that alienated him from his father? As young men the two of them would have shared confidences and Andrew may have known and understood the triggers that led to William's erratic behaviour. Did the two of them share similar traits? Was Andrew quick-tempered or erratic?

Nothing has been found to indicate that Andrew was other than a hard-working farmer, and a responsible member of the Cheriton community, but recent research has uncovered something alarming about his descendants.

Just two generations later, the Hewish family was to exhibit signs of mental instability.

Andrew's son John Hewish was a resilient character living to the age of eighty, marrying three times, and fathering ten surviving children:

Sarah 1786 and Charity 1788 from his marriage to Faith Melhuish in 1782

John c1792, Andrew 1794, Richard 1804, Edward 1807 and Elizabeth 1811 from his marriage to Elizabeth Cockram in 1789 and

Abraham 1813, Robert 1816, and (Mary) Ann c1820 from his final marriage at the age of fifty one to Betty Westcott in 1812

He provided well for all his children, which was a measure of his success as a famer and a landowner. Some of his wealth came from his first marriage into the Melhuish family, but he had a good head for business and managed to increase his property portfolio throughout his life. One of his sons Robert 1816 only aspired to be a farm labourer and lived all his life with family members, but others had very successful careers. John, the eldest and therefore Andrew's eldest Hewish grandson farmed successfully at Holes in the village for many years marrying Elizabeth Cockram and producing Maria, twins Edward and Merina, Elizabeth, Hannah, Lucinda and Emma, introducing some exotic new names to the parish. But in later life, John was not able to cope and in 1875 his family had to agree to him being committed to the Lunatic Asylum in Exeter. He was by then an elderly man but his behaviour had proved too challenging to manage at home. When he died soon afterwards his daughter Emma was his sole executor. This could have been a case of dementia, but one is mindful to put it into the context of what happened next.

Two months later his daughter Emma Hewish married local man Thomas Cole and together they farmed at Barnshill. They put Holes Farm up for sale and ploughed the profits into their new venture. Theirs was a close and happy marriage shattered by a devastating development when Emma was diagnosed with a brain tumour about ten years later. She struggled with erratic behaviour and the farm was a dangerous and busy place for her to be whilst of unstable mind. She too could have been committed to the Asylum, but Tom fought against the idea and instead made private arrangements for her to stay with a Mrs Bradford in Shobrooke. There she was watched day and night and kept as safe as was possible, with Tom visiting her regularly. In 1886 however she attempted suicide by cutting her throat with a knife she had concealed from Mrs Bradford. After a search another sharp knife was found. The doctor attended and she was saved but it was said that she continued to suffer great pain and anxiety as a result of her growing tumour. Emma was eventually moved to Exeter, possibly to the Asylum, and passed away in 1887 aged fifty one. Tom Cole was heartbroken and was persuaded to sell up and move away to start a new life farming in Oxfordshire. With one daughter he married a second time but died a widower in 1925. Significantly, he was not buried in Oxfordshire and his last wish was to be brought back to Cheriton and put into his beloved Emma's grave at the west end of the churchyard. It was not thought proper to include his details on her stone, but his 'In Memoriam' card at the time read:

In ever loving memory of THOMAS COLE who died March 3rd 1925 aged 77 years.
Interred at Cheriton Fitzpaine Churchyard, Saturday, March 7th 1925.
For ever with the Lord.
Peace Perfect Peace

The third tragedy struck the Hewish family just three years later.

Emma's sister Maria was a corset maker and she had married her distant cousin Richard Hewish a master tailor and moved away to Upton Pyne where they ran a small business from their home at Rose Cottage. They had two children whilst there, Emily 1856 and Ben Hewish 1860. Richard was a skilled craftsman and with Maria's support he was able to take on two apprentices, Alfred Speare from

Upton and James Bolt from Morchard Bishop and their future looked good. In the winter of 1873 however Richard died suddenly, the coroner was called and an inquest was held into his death. The note in the Upton Pyne burial register simply says, 'drowned'. There are no further details and one might suppose that like so many others he was a casualty of the River Exe or the River Creedy, close to Rose Cottage. A nine year old girl had drowned in the village years before when her mother sent her to draw water from the river and she slipped into the fast-flowing current, and before the century was out the vicar of Upton Pyne himself, Rev Gibbons would suffer the same fate when his bicycle slipped off a foot-bridge leading into the village.

Three years later Maria married again, becoming the wife of a widower called Moses Corner who farmed at Pryor Court House, Broad Clyst. Moses was not a blood relative to Maria but he was her late husband's uncle, and therefore brother to her mother-in-law Elizabeth Hewish (nee Corner). His signature at the time of the marriage is almost unreadable showing that at the age of seventy he was already somewhat infirm.

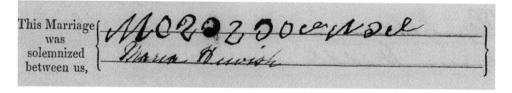

Maria left Upton Pyne to keep house for her new husband and the following year her daughter Emily married an outfitter called Henry Dorrington. Ben, her brother signed as a witness to the wedding ceremony. Shortly after that Ben Hewish made his way to London where he worked as a warehouseman, living in 1881 in a hostel in Five Foot Lane, St Nicholas Olave's. John Strype mentioned the area in his Survey of London:

'Five Foot lane, so called, for that the West end was but five Foot broad. It hath its chief Entrance out of Thames street, and with a turning passage leads into Fish street hill. It hath another passage out of Bread street hill, by St. Nicolas Olave's Churchyard; and another into Old Fish street, through Star Court, which is but small.'

Ben's mental health began to deteriorate and in October 1888 he was admitted to the Exeter Lunatic Asylum. His admission notes give him as a linen draper who had worked for some years for Passmore and Co, merchants of Exeter and then for Cooks at St Paul's churchyard. He had left some months earlier and returned home, unwell. His case notes reveal some interesting facts. Firstly, in his family history it was stated that 'both his grandfathers were queer'. This is an alarming fact since Maria's father John Hewish yeoman farmer and Richard's father John Hewish, master tailor were both descended from the same man, albeit several generations before. Secondly, when physically examined it was reported that Ben had extremely large pupils that reacted hardly at all to light and that he walked rapidly, dragging his left foot. He was excited and grandiose and talked about going to Australia 'next week' and he boasted about having served in the telegraph corps in India, China, Australia and Afghanistan, none of which was correct. He was agitated and noisy at night but not violent. Of below middle height he had a small head, brown hair, medium complexion, thin lips and a sharp, pointed nose.[15]

He was 'discharged on trial' from the Asylum at Exminster on March 6th 1889 and he died in 1890 aged only twenty nine, leaving an estate worth £88.6s.8d to his mother Maria Corner as next of kin

So in this unfortunate family, John Hewish of Holes Farm was committed to the Exeter Lunatic Asylum as an elderly man in 1875, his daughter Emma developed a brain tumour, became unbalanced and died in 1887, and his grandson Ben died a lunatic aged twenty nine in 1890. Three generations of the family were similarly affected. Each was considered to be mentally unstable: two, using the medical terminology of the time were dubbed 'lunatics' and were 'committed' whilst the other was cared for privately with a twenty four hour watch and suffered greatly until her death. These were all descended from William Hewish' cousin Andrew and It seems more than a co-incidence that their erratic behaviour and violent outbursts mirrored those attributed to William. William proved himself to be an intelligent young man who was perfectly able to understand moral and social codes, but as he got older he was unable to control his anger. In the light of Emma's medical diagnosis, could William too have been suffering from a prefrontal cortex brain tumour? Is it possible for certain families to have a predisposition to develop such tumours, or is it just a cruel co-incidence?

The whole tragedy of two unexplained deaths, of the Saunders property dispute, and of mental instability in a family, cannot fail to touch us. We learn so much from the past and yet there remain so many questions. What looked at first like a straightforward, heinous double murder culminating in execution may turn out to have been a miscarriage of justice.

Other members of the Hewish family

Most of Andrew Hewish grandchildren from his son John did well for themselves, with the majority marrying in the village and bringing up their own families locally. In the 1841 census Richard Hewish 1804 (from John's second marriage) was a vetinary surgeon and farmer of 14 acres living at Lower Saunders. Ten years later he was still living there with John Melhuish 1836 a farm servant and Richard Melhuish, 1822 a shoemaker, both related to him through his father's first marriage. Unmarried and successful, Richard often offered hospitality to family members and in 1861 widowed Mary Melhuish was his housekeeper with John Melhuish 1836 described as a carter and Henry Melhuish 1853 as a lodger. In 1865 the ninety nine year lease taken out on Lower Saunders when Andrew's father John snr died in 1766 expired. The property was then advertised as:

'Lot 1 a dwelling house, cottage and walled and other gardens, courtyard, barn, stable and other outbuildings and about fourteen acres of rich meadow, pasture and arable land and about one acre of orchard.'

Richard Hewish was able to renew the lease and ten years later he was still there with Mary Melhuish his housekeeper. By this time his younger half-brother

Woolmers Plymouth and Exeter Gazette 9th Jan 1841

EMIGRATION.

The following interesting communication has been sent to Mr J. B. Wilcocks, the Austra ian Emigration Agent in this city, by Mr Richard Hewish, Veterinary Surgeon, of Cheriton Fitzpaine the brother of the writer, a very respectable individual, who proceeded to New South Wales in the Australian Packet Ship "*Lady Raffles*," and is now settled about twelve miles from Melbourne, Australia Felix; it is satisfactory to find the letters of Emigrants of all classes affording equally gratifying statements of the advantages to be derived by Emigrating to the fine colony of Eastern Australia.

"Melbourne, June 15th, 1840

DEAR BROTHER,—I again write, since I hear you did not receive my first letter sent by a sailor. I have been in this about three months—wages in this place are very high, it has only been inhabited about four years; it is now about the size of Crediton—men here are better than money—any man can get a pound a week, even a common farmer's labourer, and rations; which is 12 lbs. of beef, ditto of flour, ¼lb of tea, 2lbs. of sugar per week, but that is only in a cert in place or so where they have made waste, it is in general as much as you please;—any tradesman can make a fortune here. I am told the three best trades are publicans, butchers, and bakers. I should thank you to read this to Mr. R—s, and let him write to Misses — of Plymouth directly. If they or any one else think of Emigrating, they cannot go to a better country for getting money than this is. Wm. N— D—, and O—, A—, and others—the wages for all their trades is 12s. per day—blacksmiths 14s. per day. We can get beef and mutton at moderate prices—beef 6d. per lb. mutton 5d., york 10d—the meat is as good as in England; here is one butcher here kills thirty bullocks per week—the same man kills 170 sheep per week from 60 to 100lbs. each. Shearing season is now drawing nigh—the price for wool is £1 per hundred—the land here is very heavy. If a man had the ready he could buy a section of land (640 acres) from £1 to £1 10s. per acre, and costs about £20 clearing—a man can do very well with £400 or £500, take out the squat er's license, that is to go into the bush—buy a lot of cattle, milk, and make butter and cheese—you can get all sorts of garden produce any where in the bush, This is the best place in the world for getting money. I hope to build a p ace convenient for those I have named to come out, and will do all I can for them if they do come they will not be deceived in me—I do not wish them to come, it can be of no benefit to me—I wish it entirely for their good—and should feel pleasure to be of service to my fellow creatures; they shall not want a shilling as long as I have one; and, thank God, I have plenty of everything this word can afford. Tell Mr. P— I called on Mr T—; Mr. and Mrs. T— were well, and the correctness of every thing that has been said about Mr. T— may be depended upon; he has nearly 2,000 head of sheep and cattle, and in seven years he will be worth more than all the other parts of the family. John, my dear fellow, you can do nothing like coming here; with what you can bring, you can do just as you please, and lead a gentleman's life here—you can go into the bush and live as cheap as at home—banking interest is 10 per cent—there is plenty of room to range in the country—my master made £1,400 of bush hay in one year, • •

Your affectionate brother,
E. HEWISH."

Robert Hewish 1816 had lost both parents, and as an un-married and unskilled farm labourer he was taken care of by Richard. Robert had lived a sheltered life with his father John who was described as 'a yeoman of Independent means', and his mother Betty, 'an annuitant'. Betty was widowed in 1842 and died in 1866.

Other sons from the three marriages became tailors and set themselves up in business in and around Cheriton but Abraham Hewish 1813 bucked the family trend and became a school teacher. The eldest child from the third marriage he taught first of all at Broadclyst School near Exeter and then moved with his wife to Garsington in Oxfordshire. He later moved to Hitchen in Hertfordshire to take up another teaching position.

Andrew Hewish 1794, the second son from John's second marriage married Mary Brewer in 1825 and when widowed, he married Elizabeth Melhuish in 1833, running a successful 257 acre farm called Warbrights in Stoodleigh near Tiverton.

Edward Hewish 1807 emigrated to New South Wales before his father's death and wrote a letter to his brother Richard dated June 15th 1840 from his home twelve miles outside Melbourne. Richard had it published in the newspaper the following year as there was much interest shown in successful emigration at the time. Edward had sailed on the Australian packet ship Lady Raffles.

Edward had been in the region for a matter of months but reported that he had plenty of everything and that any tradesman could make a fortune by settling there, even a labourer could earn £1 per week, enough to by 12 lbs of beef, 12 lbs of flour, ¼lb of tea, and 2lb of sugar. The best trades to have were that of publican, butcher and baker and as it was coming up to the shearing season he pointed out that a man could earn £1 per 100 fleeces and that land was only £1 to £1.10s.0d. per acre. No doubt hearing these facts other villagers were tempted to cut their ties with Devon and make the exciting voyage to Australia. The tailoring branch of the family, descended from Andrew Hewish and Rebecca Esworthy, recognised that their skills would be needed in the new world and James Hewish 1814 and his wife Maria Wright 1811 took their two babies Emma and John to Melbourne at about this time, settling successfully and having seven further children to help colonize the area.

Charity Hewish of the first marriage married James Cockram in 1811 and less than a year later her father married his third wife, Elizabeth Cockram. These two were not, thankfully, brother and sister but were probably first or second cousins.

Sarah Hewish John's eldest child may have been the same Sarah who married William Tucker in 1815.

Mary Ann Hewish the youngest of all John's children lodged with her school teacher brother Abraham in Broadclyst, helping to look after his young children, but then returned to Cheriton and married Thomas Huckwell a gardener. When she had a family of her own, some of the names she chose mirrored those of her neices: Reuban, *Lucinda,* Elizabeth, *Merina, Hannah* and Alice. Thomas died in 1869 so Mary Ann Huckwell took her youngest daughter Alice (Snell) and went to live in Upton Pyne near her aunt Maria Hewish of Rose Cottage.

References

1. Will of Joane Morrish 1660 Stockleigh Pomeroy PROB11 298
2. Lease for Saunders tenement 1727 William Hewish mentioned in C12/1251/63
3. Jenkins, Alexander. History and Description of The City of Exeter (1806)
4. Coroners' expenses Devon Quarter Sessions records
5. During the Second World War bombing raids destroyed many of the wills held in the Exeter Archive
6. Will of Alexander Arundell of Exeter 1757 PROB11 834
7. C12/1251/63
8. Will of John Hewish 1766 Cheriton Fitzpaine, list entry only
9. Chancery Court papers 1772 Hewish C12/1251/63
10. Land Tax return Cheriton Fitzpaine. microfiche Devon Heritage Centre
11. Will of John Hicks 1747 Alturnon, Cornwall 189M-1/F2/14 copy will
12. Will of Edward Hewish Cheriton Fitzpaine 1779 PROB 11 1049
13. Will of Elizabeth Hicks Cheriton Fitzpaine 1791 SRO Index (A) MED copy will
14. Will of Rebecca Hewish Cheriton Fitzpaine 1787 1049M/FW20
15. 3769A H9/5 Medical Case Book Exeter Asylum

Religion and the Reynold family

The ancient family Motto for this distinguished family was:
'Jus meum tuebor', I will defend my right

One day in December 1537 Thomas Reynold arrived in the village of Cheriton Fitzpaine to act as rector of the parish, taking over from the Rev Alnethus Arscott. He would live in the hall house a stone's throw from the church behind the current Rectory and take charge of a flourishing farming congregation, well-versed in the ways of the Catholic Church. Reynold, a graduate of Corpus Christi College, Oxford was a man with a mission. There is no doubt that the community would be deeply influenced by him and what he stood for, for many years afterwards, and his time in the community would shape and impact many core values and attitudes held by its members.

Thomas Reynold, born in Devon c1490 grew up in a well-read, religious family and proved himself to be a prodigious student, entering Oxford University in his early teens and devoting his whole life to religion and learning. In his will dated 1559 he took great pains to distribute his many books and tracts to those who would appreciate them and to provide money for the poor in every place he had lived.[1] After University he trained as a priest, and in 1530 was appointed rector of his home parish of Pinhoe, which lies to the north-east of Exeter.

In 1537 the living of Pinhoe passed to his brother Michael Reynold, and Thomas moved out to Cheriton Fitzpaine in mid-Devon where he already had family ties. It is unclear who sponsored him, but in the early 16th century ownership of the Manor was in contention, with Star Chamber documents showing Humphrey Cadwoodley as plaintiff and William Kelly and others as

Cheriton Fitzpaine Church has a 14th century nave and 15th century aisles, porch and tower.
Dedicated to All Saints in the 14th century and known as St Mary's until 1850,
it has since been dedicated to St Matthew

defendants. The Manor had been held by the Stantons, and then passed through marriages to the Fitzpaines, the Asthills and then the Kellys. Whoever nominated Reynold must have known that he was a zealous Catholic with a burning desire to educate and broaden the minds of the young. He was to be made warden of Merton College, Oxford in 1545, chaplain to Queen Mary in 1553, Dean of Exeter in 1555, vice chancellor of the University of Oxford in 1556 and promissory Bishop of Hereford in 1558. The evidence of his will written in 1559 proved his generosity towards those in need or suffering and his commitment to educate more than the privileged classes. He was to die however in the Marshalsea prison on November 24th 1559, exiled for his Catholic faith, and deprived of his Bishopric by Queen Elizabeth 1.

With a man of such calibre arriving in Cheriton Fitzpaine it was inevitable that education would play its part in the community. Although there was no formal

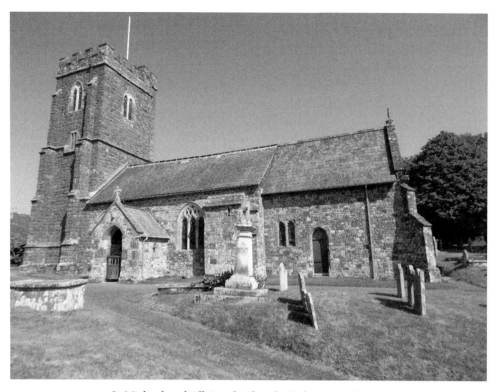

St Michael and All Angels Church, Pinhoe, near Exeter.

school in the village at the time, Thomas would certainly have sought to educate young men and boys, teaching them Latin and the scriptures, and ensuring that they understood the basics of their Catholic faith and fulfilled their commitment to God and the Pope. He had built up a substantial library of books and tracts and probably used the hall house or the Parvis to regularly tutor small group of young men. Single all his life, he never-the-less held the institution of marriage close to his heart and promoted true and lasting matches amongst the youngsters in his parish. In his will he left, 'some portion also towards the marriage of honest poor men and maidens'.

Thomas Reynold would have known his congregation well, and whilst in the village he would have been closely involved with their lives – spiritual, moral and agricultural. The son and grandson of yeoman farmers himself he knew all about crop rotation and grazing, husbandry and market prices, and could readily discuss and advise. He would have been able to read the landscape, the weather and the seasons as well as the next man, and his opinion would have counted.

*View of Cheriton Fitzpaine Church, arriving along the top road and
down past the Rectory hall house into the valley.*

Respected in the community, he was by all accounts the ideal country cleric:
learned, generous, caring, and in touch with his surroundings.

Cheriton was a relatively isolated parish, tucked away from major routes and
several miles from the nearest town, but surprisingly, the parishioners were all
too aware of what was happening in the wider world. It was the time when Henry
VIII was in dispute with papal authorities over his divorce from Katharine of
Aragon. Although Henry was not challenging doctrinal matters and he remained
a believer in core Catholic theological teachings, he had excommunicated
himself from the Roman Catholic Church and declared himself 'supreme leader'.
Church congregations throughout England would continue to worship as they
had always done, following the familiar rhythms of the traditional church
calendar and honouring the Catholic order of service. What would affect them
however was the demand that they swear allegiance to Henry, rather than to the
Pope. In Cheriton Fitzpaine, backwater though it was, folk were far more aware

than other rural congregations for they had first hand reports of some of their sovereign's unsavoury actions in far distant London. They knew about Henry's attacks on men and women in monastic orders. They knew how far their king was prepared to go to establish his supremacy over his people. They knew that lives were put in real danger.

Thomas Reynold their new rector had personal and bitter experiences to share with them on the matter.

In November 1534 King Henry had published The Act of Supremacy (26 Hen. VIII c.1), declaring that he was 'the only supreme head on earth of the Church of England', and that as king he would enjoy 'all honours, dignities, pre-eminences, jurisdictions, privileges, authorities, immunities, profits, and commodities ...' By the end of that year he had appointed Thomas Cromwell as his Vice Regent in spiritual matters and he sent him out to monastic establishments around the country to secure the allegiance of those in holy orders. When Cromwell arrived at Syon Abbey in Twickenham, he was aware of the strength of opinion held by some of the Briggentine monks there, but he was not fully prepared for his meeting with one charismatic cleric in particular by the name of Richard Reynold.

The seal of Syon Abbey depicting King Henry V

Richard Reynold felt so strongly about his loyalty to the Pope that he was prepared to give up his life for his Catholic faith, refusing point blank to recognise Henry above God and the Pope, and continuing to voice his opinion that Katharine of Aragon was still the true Queen of England. He was thrown into the Tower of London on April 20th 1535 and the King had to meet with his advisors to discuss how best to deal with Reynold. Considering the heightened nature of the situation, Henry had no other alternative but to set legal proceedings in motion against the abstainers.

Letters in Henry VIII's archive document Reynold's trial as a recusant and describe how this great preacher, highly educated in Latin, Greek and Hebrew, and a close friend of Thomas More, steadfastly refused to pledge his allegiance to

Blessed Richard Reynold of Syon

the king.[2] He was further accused of inciting others to refuse the Oath, and as a well-respected religious leader, this Bridgettine monk was considered to be a real threat to the Crown.

Reynold had to be made an example of and he was condemned to death. On May 4th 1535 he was dragged through the streets of London with four others towards Tyburn, and a horrible death. Contemporary reports record that the crowds were shocked to see that the monks were still wearing their religious habits as they were dragged through the streets.[3] Eye-witness reports reveal that Reynold was forced to watch his three brethren hung, drawn and quartered before him, as he waited for his own torture to begin. It was said that he preached steadfastly throughout, offering courage to the men as they died. In his turn he was hung, castrated, drawn and quartered and finally hacked to pieces. Parts of his body were then displayed in prominent places in and around the city of London. He died, unbroken in spirit. Many years later his bravery was recognised and he was canonised and known thereafter as 'the Angel of Syon', something of a folk hero.

Strype wrote to Pole in 1535 that when Starky was sent to hear the reasons why the men, including Thomas Reynold would not sign, that 'they sought their own death, and of it none could be justly accused but themselves.'[4]

Hung, drawn and quartered at Tyburn[5]

So how was Thomas Reynold, rector of Cheriton Fitzpaine connected to Richard Reynold, the Angel of Syon?

Richard's family background has been explored by scholars but remains unresolved to this day. It would be interesting to piece together all the facts from extant records to see if the picture can be clarified:

Richard was born in Devon in 1492 and the suggestion is that he was from Pinhoe to the north-east of Exeter.[6] Both Richard and Thomas Reynold certainly shared distinctive family traits of intelligence, steadfastness, passion and religious zeal, and the family name that they shared was not a common one in the area. The forename Richard was passed down in Thomas' family from generation to generation and indeed, he had a brother, father and grandfather so named. Thomas Reynold was also born about 1490 into a family of Devon yeomen farmers who held substantial lands in Pinhoe.

Richard the Martyr and Thomas the scholar were each sufficiently well-educated to attend University and both became learned clerics – Richard graduating from Cambridge and Thomas and his close family, from Oxford. In his 1559 will Thomas mentioned that his mother's maiden name was Martin and there were Martins in the Pinhoe area at that time. One historian, the Rev. John Prince, went so far as to write in his unpublished notes at the end of the 17th century that Thomas Reynolds was actually born not in Pinhoe, but in the 'family home in Cheriton Fitzpaine in 1490', and was the second son of Richard Reynold, gentleman farmer of that parish.[7]

Scholars have questioned Prince's accuracy in the published version of his Worthies of Devon, but the unpublished notes in which he refers to Thomas' birthplace being Cheriton Fitzpaine have not yet been held up for authentication, and the document remains virtually unseen. Prince was writing fairly close in time to the actual events and he collected much of his material about the family from a Rev Crocker, who had married a Sarah Reynold.

There is real uncertainty as to whether Thomas was born in Cheriton Fitzpaine or in Pinhoe, but Pinhoe seems the most likely, with Thomas moving to Cheriton in 1537 to join family members who were already established there when he became rector of the parish. His brother John was certainly already farming in nearby Sandford with his wife and daughters in 1524.[8]

Martyr Richard Reynold's place of birth has been explored by Dom Hamilton who favours the idea that he was from Pinhoe.[9] He noticed that local landowning families from Pinhoe acted as benefactors to Syon Abbey where Richard was a monk, and referred to the evidential incidence of the forename 'Richard' in the family. Furthermore, he identified the Thomas Reynold who was listed in Syon records 'as a man who did not receive a pardon from the king', as the same Thomas Reynold who was rector of Cheriton Fitzpaine, later became Dean of Exeter etc.

There were several close ties between the parishes of Pinhoe and Cheriton and further evidence appears in Thomas Reynold's 1559 will where he left bequests to his four brothers: John Reynolds of Sandford, with his wife Elizabeth and three daughters including Jane; William Reynolds of Cheriton Fitzpaine with his daughters including Agnes; Michael (in holy orders) who had succeeded him to the living of Pinhoe, and Richard of Cheriton Fitzpaine with daughters including Joan and Margaret and sons Hieron, Edmund, William, James, John and Nicholas. This categorically places many members of the family in the village of Cheriton in the mid sixteenth century.

Of Richard Reynold's sons, Nicholas Reynold was the only one of Thomas' nephews not to take up Holy Orders and he retained land in Pinhoe which he farmed. All the remaining nephews followed their uncle to Oxford University. Thomas Reynold's will is detailed, and amongst many bequests he left his brother Richard of Cheriton Fitzpaine the sum of £5 to buy a holding or other necessities, and his second best bed.

Richard Reynold, Martyr of Syon was certainly not a brother to Thomas, but he may have been a first or second cousin. The two branches of the family were closely entwined and there were strong links between Pinhoe and Cheriton.

One can only imagine the horror and vitriol that the Reynold family back in Devon would have experienced when Richard was martyred. They may even have been present at his very public execution, standing amongst the crowds of onlookers at Tyburn. Public hangings were a popular spectacle and there is no way with such a high profile court case and outcome that the Devon Reynolds would have not known about it. Surely Thomas Reynold travelled to Tyburn to witness his relative's zealous courage and sacrifice, praying perhaps for a last minute reprieve?

Family members must have struggled with their beliefs, their loyalties and their emotions in the turmoil of such cruelty and perceived injustice, especially the young nephews who would have been old enough to form their own opinions by then. It seems however, that as a result, this family was galvanised into maintaining and strengthening their commitment to continue following a pure Catholicism in the ensuing years.

When Thomas became rector in the village, it was less than two years after Richard's martyrdom and he must have brought with him a burning resolve to be a scrupulously fair and Christian leader of his new flock.

Thomas was one of five sons and four daughters fathered by Richard Reynold, farmer of Pinhoe: sons Richard, Thomas, Michael, William and John, and daughters Joan, Margaret, Alice and one other. He graduated from Merton College Oxford in 1521/2 and embarked upon a memorable career as an educationalist and cleric. He was appointed Canon of the 11th Prebend in Westminster; was vice chancellor of Oxford University; was made Dean of Exeter, and acted as Queen Mary's domestic chaplain. His brothers William, John and Richard were yeoman farmers like their father, but his other brother Michael was also a cleric. It was Thomas who was to be the most zealous about maintaining the family's religion; it was Thomas who came to Cheriton to preach and educate the young; it was Thomas, himself childless, who most influenced five of his nephews to follow him to Oxford University and into careers in the Catholic faith, and it was Thomas who died for his beloved religion in 1559.

After a period of respite from 1553 to 1558 when Catholic Queen Mary ruled the country and looked favourably upon him, Thomas was himself faced with an Oath of Allegiance to the new Protestant Queen Elizabeth in 1559.[10] He refused point blank to sign and was thrown into gaol for his refusal. This swift action on Elizabeth's part may well have been fuelled by memories of Richard Reynold's actions in 1535 and the way that her father had resolved the matter. An elderly man by this time, Thomas wrote his will on November 20th 1559 whilst in Marshalsea prison and he died a few days later. He was not hanged, he was not martyred, but he did die for his beliefs, and Cheriton folk would have been well aware of this fact.

As a village Cheriton Fitzpaine has always been keenly Royalist but in the 16th and 17th Centuries the community also fought hard to maintain its traditionally Catholic approach to worship.

The Reynold family living in Cheriton Fitzpaine

Richard's eldest son Heiron alias Jerome wrote a will in 1570 in which he mentioned that he had been born and baptised in Pinhoe, clarifying that his branch of the family must have moved from Pinhoe into Cheriton sometime after his birth in 1533, after his uncle's arrival as rector in 1537 and after the Lay subsidy roll of 1543, but well before 1559. Because Thomas was made warden of Merton College Oxford in 1545 it is feasible that his brother Richard moved then with the nephews and nieces to help support his work in Cheriton church whilst he was absent. Hieron his eldest child would have been about 12 years old at the time, spending a few years in the village before travelling up country to attend Oxford University in his teens. His nine younger siblings would have spent their childhood years in Cheriton Fitzpaine, playing in the fields, making friends with local children and helping their father with stock, ploughing and harvest. This begs the question 'Where did they live?' and there are two possibilities: either

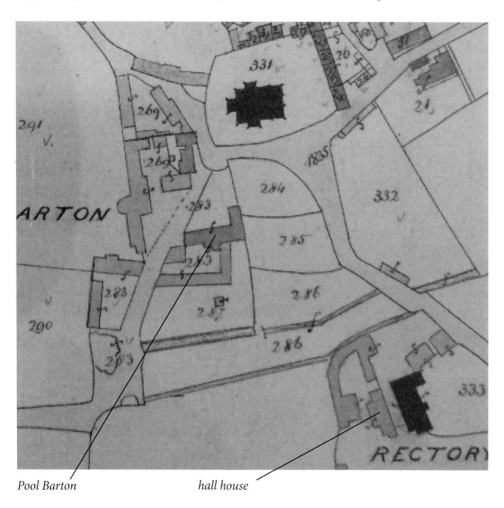

Pool Barton   hall house

Three room and cross passage plan

View from the churchyard of late 15th early 16th century Pool Barton house with later external chimney stacks at the front. Late 17th century extension at right angles juts forward to the left. A late 16th early 17th century kitchen-cum-service block lies at right angles, to the rear.

Ovolo-moulded ceiling beams in the main room at Pool

that they lived in Thomas' hall house-cum-Rectory a little way up Church Hill, or that they shared a house with Richard's younger brother William Reynold who had moved into the village a little earlier (between 1524 and 1543). The hall house-cum-Rectory is coloured grey, and stands to the right of the black building numbered 333 on the 1840 Tythe map, in the bottom right hand corner of the frame on page 51.

William Reynold was living at nearby Pool Barton, an imposing 15th century hall house, standing directly opposite the church. It is numbered 283 on the 1840 Tythe map.

It is probable that the Lake family built Pool Barton house which can be dated in part to the late 15th century, possibly 1490. John Lake was living at Pool in 1524 when the Lay Subsidy Roll was drawn up but by the time of the next Lay Subsidy in 1543, the owner was William Reynold. On the cross passage screen the initials 'G L' have been carefully carved which may indicate a George Lake as the original owner, and given the dates, this might have been John Lake's father.

The lettering is similar in dimensions and style to initials carved on one of the church chests in St Matthew's Church.

Thomas Reynold took up his position as Rector in Cheriton in 1537, and it was probably through him that his two farmer brothers William and Richard heard about the potential of the fertile farmlands and well-stocked streams in the valley. The moment that Pool Barton lease was put up for sale by John Lake, William Reynold would have been the first to step forward and purchase the flourishing farmstead.

Originally built to a three room and cross passage plan with an inner room to the right (western end), it was enlarged by a member of the Reynold family when a kitchen/service wing was added at right angles to the rear in the sixteenth century. This service block boasts external pigeon holes similar to those at Stockadon farm in the east of the parish and a substantial inglenook fireplace and adjoining smoke chamber. When the main hall house was floored, well-carved ovolo-moulded oak beams were installed, running lengthways across the ceiling and these are remarkably similar to the highly carved ovolu-moulded beams in Stockadon. It is believed that these may be ship's timbers from Exeter or Topsham. At the rear, a late sixteenth century spiral staircase with oak treads connects the lower floor of Pool to the three chambers above.

When Thomas Reynold's will was published in 1559 an opportunity pre-sented itself for Thomas left Richard the sum of £5 to 'buy himself a holding or other necessities.' With his demise, a new incumbent was appointed to Cheriton, meaning that Richard and his family had to vacate the hall house which served as the Rectory. Thomas knew that he was dying in Marshalsea and would not have wanted his brother made homeless with so many children. It seems probable that this was the time that Bowdell, a less imposing, south-facing hall house was built at the east end of the village. It too was a three room cross passage house but with an inner room to the left and slightly smaller overall dimensions. 'New' build-ing techniques and local knowledge about weather conditions, watercourses and land-fertility meant that this house could be positioned with due thought at the entrance to the village, taking advantage of the lie of the land. Surrounded by foliage now, the house still makes a statement, standing directly in the face of the traveller as he descends Lag Hill and approaches the village around a right hand bend. It is the first thing you see as you approach Cheriton Fitzpaine down a very steep hill.

The £5 bequest from Thomas would not have been sufficient to complete the

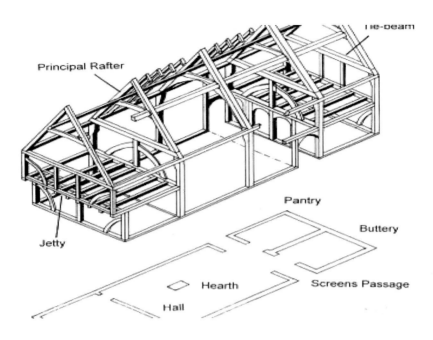

Three room and cross passage house with service rooms to the right

building project and it seems that Reynold looked to William Knapman, gent of Drewsteignton to put up half the money. Knapman was actively engaged in the land market between 1555 and 1565 and was building up a portfolio of property near Tiverton as well as around his home at Throwleigh.[11] Some years later when William Knapman was hanged for murder, his share of Bowdell was passed on as part of a considerable portfolio to his second son James Knapman. Soon after that James' mother also died and he may have decided to consolidate his holding by selling off some of them. He agreed to release his half share in Bowdell in 1620 and the next occupier, also named William Reynolds became the outright owner.

Bowdell is a well-crafted cross-passage house with spacious rooms and carpentry of a high standard. Now two dwellings named Bowdell and Buddle, it has a seventeenth century external chimney stack but is believed to have started life in the mid to late sixteenth century with an open fire and gallery, all of which fits well with the building date suggested by the documents. This is further supported by the understanding that it was rare for a hall house to be built in the area after 1570.

The Reynolds held Bowdell/Buddle for the next 100 years and a later William

Bowdell and Buddle were originally one large South facing hall house

The external chimney stack at the front was a later 17th century addition to Bowdell and an extension was built to the right sometime in the 20th century

Reynold signed as its owner in the 1641 Protestation returns. In the Returns both Buddle and Pool were listed as belonging to members of the Reynold's family, who by that date held substantial land in the parish and commanded considerable respect in the community.

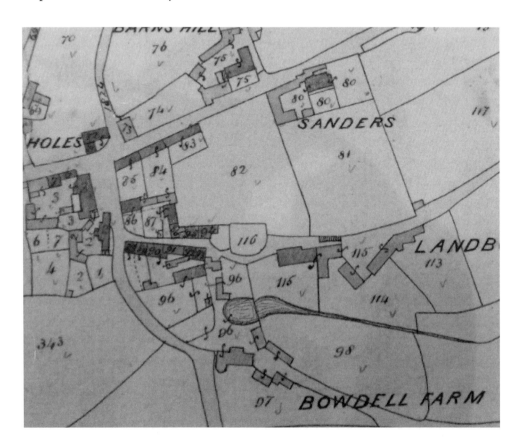

The Tythe map of 1840 shows Buddle number 96. At that time it was owned by non-resident landlord William Nation and tenanted by farmer John Melhuish jnr. Nation was a wealthy magistrate and landowner who had bought the property as a rental investment, along with Hannabeth and Landboat farms, living himself at 35, Southernhay, Exeter with his second wife and six children. His son William Hamilton Codrington Nation inherited most of his father's assets when he died in 1861. He in turn left them to a nephew who showed little interest in the role of landlord and sold each property to local families.

Thomas Reynold's bequests

Returning to Thomas Reynold's will, he left his brother Michael the priest a 'best black gown, a gilt standing cup and a best feather bed'. He left sums of money and other goods to his domestic staff in Westminster, Exeter and Ditcheat, Somerset, and numerous girls in the family were given money for their future marriages – one of these being Agnes Reynold, daughter of his brother William. He left money for the poor in places where he had served as a priest: Holsworthy, Pitt in Tiverton, Ditcheat, Cheriton Fitzpaine and Pyn, and bequests to help children from deserving families to gain an education. He also set out clearly his ambitions for his brother's boys, leaving the sum of £100 to each that followed him to the University of Oxford, together with surplices and a hood and scarlet gown lined with sarsenet (fine silk material) for the first to achieve a doctorate in whatever subject they chose. Unmarried and celibate according to Catholic tradition, Thomas Reynold was a thoughtful and generous man. He left many bequests including, 'to every bedred person within the City of Exeter and suburbs, 12d.' and he bequeathed a vast collection of books and educational material to scholars and libraries. Most significantly, he started the family's tradition of leaving money to those in prison, acknowledging their plight and perhaps his own as he sat in Marshalsea gaol, awaiting his fate in 1559.

'To every prisoner in the King's, City of Exeter and Bishop's prisons there, 2d.

To every inhabitant by foundation in the Almshouses of Wynnards, St Rocks Lane, St Andrews Chapel, the House in East gate Street, and the poor by the belluters gate, 4d.

In the general alms which I will to be given out of St Peter's Cloister, to every person, 1d.

To John Anthony of Exeter towards the bringing up of his children £6

To the poor of Cheriton Fitzpaine 40/-, Holsworthy 40/-, of Pitt in Tiverton 40/-, Ditcheat in Somerset £5, North Nubald in York, £4 and Pyn £4

My books to be given to my brother Michael, priest and my nephews Hieron, Edmund, William, James and John, joining to them my brother William's children if any of them prosper in learning

Towards the exhibition of my nephews Mr Hieron, Edmund, William, James and John, sons of my brother Richard, and other my brother William's children if they proceed in learning and come to the University of Oxford, £100

To John Brogden my scholar in Oxford, 10/-

To my nephews my surplices in order of age after they come to the University or me made priests, by the hands of Mr Walter Mugg, Richard Reynolds of Pyn and Thomas Jacob of Ditcheat whom I make my executors

The residue to be employed by my executors in bringing up poor children in virtue and learning and some portion also towards the marriage of honest poor men and maidens, and the relief of such as be already burdened by many children, and mainly of such as were in my cures.'

John Reynold and the King James Bible

John Reynold, another of Thomas' brothers had three daughters and farmed in the Sandford area as early as 1524. Because he did not have any sons with his wife Elizabeth, the Reynold name for his branch of the family died with him, but there was another member of the family named John Reynold. He was one of Richard's sons and a nephew to Thomas. And it was he who was to make an enormously significant contribution as a scholar and a cleric. But first it is important to look at the lives of his five brothers, the other nephews of Thomas Reynold:

Thomas' six nephews and several nieces grew up in the village with the eldest, Hieron (Jerome) Reynold being admitted to Corpus Christi College Oxford in 1548 and later moving overseas to Louvain in France. He died in England however and his 1570 will reveals that he was by then a 'physician of Winchester'.[12] He listed his brothers, his youngest sister Alice, his mother-in-law, but no children. Interestingly he carried on the Reynold's tradition of acknowledging those who were incarcerated by leaving money to various prisoners, and in so doing remembering his charismatic uncle's experiences in Marshalsea. He bequeathed the sum of 40/- to the prisoners in Oxford, Winchester, Hershe and Exeter prisons.

Edmund the third eldest nephew graduated in 1564 and became a fellow of Corpus Christi Oxford, amassing a substantial portfolio of properties in the city and dying a very rich man.

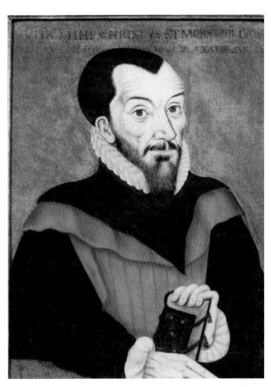

Portrait of John Reynold by an unknown artist

An angel in the church porch bears some resemblance to John Reynold

James the fourth eldest obtained an MA from Exeter College Oxford where he preached, translated and published.

Although all the nephews had a passion for learning and religion, two of them seem to have inherited the same zealous gene as their Uncle Thomas. It was William the second son (New College Oxford) and John the fifth son (Merton and Corpus Christi Oxford) who had an ardent love of debate and diatribe. Famously, the day came when the brothers had a bitter fall-out over their individual beliefs.[13] Bucking the family trend, William Reynold had decided to become a passionate Protestant, perhaps as an act of self-preservation, remembering the fate of his Catholic ancestor the blessed Richard Reynold, martyred for his beliefs. John Reynold argued long and hard with him about the family's long-held Catholic beliefs versus what he saw as a poor choice to practice Protestantism. So good was their inherent shared gift for public diatribe and dispute, backed up by doctrine that the argument resulted in each man being persuaded by the other's beliefs. They completely changed places with each other: John then becoming an ardent Protestant, and William reverting to traditional Catholicism. Recognising that he had thus made himself a religious outcast, William left for the continent and travelled to Rheims where he became a professor of Hebrew. He died a religious exile in Antwerp.

John Prince referred to the dispute in his entry for William Reynold:

> William Rainolds Doctor of Divinity, 2nd son of Richard Rainolds, Pinhoe. Attended Winchester School. Later became Fellow of New College, Oxford. Took Holy Orders 1567 a convinced Protestant and thereby entered into a bitter dispute with his brother John Rainolds, Fellow of Corpus Christi, a Romanist. The difference became "a fireball" between them. Paradox that the two brothers exchanged their religious positions. John adopted the Protestant faith, and William having turned Catholic, left the country and settled in Rheims where he became Professor of Hebrew. Later taught in Antwerp. Died a religious exile in Antwerp 1594.[7]

This falling out may have split the family in two, but without it John Reynold would not have gone on to achieve what he did. Having made a U-turn he now favoured the low-church and Calvinism. In 1604 he was the leading spokesman for the Puritan side at a conference held at Hampton Court which tried to reconcile the differences between the High-Church and Low-Church factions. In the past he had been scolded by Queen Elizabeth for his 'obstinate preciseness' and at the conference he raised his objections to the phrase, 'with my body I thee worship,' in the marriage service. He was answered by King James who told him:

> 'Many a man speaks of Robin Hood who never shot in his bow: if you had a good wife yourself, you would think that all the honour and worship you could do to her were well bestowed.'[14]

The conference failed to reach conciliation and the clergy were ordered to subscribe to a series of canons enforcing Anglican discipline. John Reynold then decided to do all that he could to make the scriptures more accessible to ordinary worshipers, persuading other scholars to join him in a translation of the bible into English. In 1607, a little while before the work was completed and published, and believing that he was suffering from no more than gout, John suddenly died of consumption. The Authorized Version of the bible, also known as the King James Bible was published in 1611. The New Testament had been translated from Greek, the Old Testament from Hebrew and Aramaic text, and the Apocrypha from Greek and Latin. John had been instrumental in leading the group of scholars who translated the Prophets.

A few years later Rev. John Prince wrote copious notes on John Reynolds in his Worthies of Devon.[15] He examined University records and talked with those who knew Reynold's contemporaries. He referred to his writings, his prodigious memory and his generosity towards scholars young and old and the fact that he was buried with due reverence in the inner chapel at Corpus Christi college, Oxford. In many ways, John was a carbon copy of his Uncle Thomas, putting as much verve and passion into Protestantism as his muse had put into Catholicism.

Rev. Prince lived from 1643 to 1723, and probably completed his Worthies manuscript in about 1697, less than a hundred years after John Reynold's death. He attributed some of the personal information that he included about the Reynold family to the Rev. Crocker who had joined the family when he married Sarah Reynold. A handwritten unpublished volume of his notes held by the Plymouth Record Office (373/2) adds tantalising details about John, his brothers, his father and his uncle Thomas Reynold.

Thomas Reynold held the living of Cheriton Fitzpaine from 1537 until his death in 1559 and as a professor of sacred theology he made a lasting impact upon his parishioners. One can infer from everything that is known about him that he was keen to educate the young and to care for the poor of the parish. His sermons would have been carefully prepared and enthusiastically delivered to the congregation. Being an ardent, traditional Catholic he would have been incensed at the martyrdom of Richard Reynolds in 1535 and acutely aware of the injustice metred out by the King. Hidden away in mid Devon he would have worked hard to ensure that his parishioners had all the facts at their finger-tips and were in a position to think rationally about what was happening in their country. Surely he would have taken the opportunity to promote a sense of religious harmony in the village. Certainly, after he left Cheriton for the parish of Ditcheat in Somerset in 1537 his brothers and nephews would have maintained his spirit of Catholicism, and maintained the role he had established as educator and benefactor. He held Cheriton until his death in 1559, but spent time in Ditcheat in Somerset, Pitt in Tiverton, Holsworthy, Exeter and Westminster, so his nephews in training for their future roles in the church may well have taken turns to prepare and deliver worship in Cheriton when he was absent.

The Prayer Book Rebellion

Edward VI came to the throne after his father Henry's death, ruling from January 1547 until 1553. As he got older he took a keen interest in religion and worked with officials to shape a Protestant church, renouncing Catholic doctrine and abolishing the Latin Mass, making services in English compulsory. He also put an end to the practice of clerical celibacy. Thomas Cranmer, Archbishop of Canterbury led the changes, promoting the use of The Book of Common Prayer.

During Thomas Reynold's time in the village there was unrest close to home for only a few miles away events of 1547 at St Andrew's Church, Sampford Courtnay were to have far reaching effects. The elderly rector William Harper, no doubt known to Reynold did not have the strength of will that Thomas did and as instructed by law he conducted the Whitsun service using the new Book of Common Prayer.[16] The congregation objected to the loss of their Catholic ceremony – the procession, the plain chanting, the altar lights, and the blessing and the Elevation of the Host etc. Parishioners gathered together and the mood turned hostile when a local farmer, William Hellyons tried to persuade them to obey the new law. A skirmish ensued and Hellyons was run through with a pitchfork on the steps of the parish rooms and killed. The angry crowd then hacked his body to pieces. Dissenters started massing in Sampford Courtnay and

Edward VI c 1550 by
William Scrotts

the movement grew. Then dissenters decided to march to Exeter and, gathering Catholics as they passed through villages, reached the wool town of Crediton in June 1549 under the banner of the Five Wounds of Christ. At the east end of Crediton the kings' men arrived and met with barricades across the road to Exeter. According to reports about the Prayer Book rebellion the confrontation in Crediton was a skirmish rather than a major battle but men were armed and many were killed or injured. Barns were set alight at the edge of the town and the king's army eventually broke down the barricades. Dissenters travelled on to Exeter and reached Clyst St Mary where there was then a major battle.

Mid-Devon parishioners were initially fuelled by resentment of the introduction of the new Prayer Book, but at the same time the farmers amongst them in the Crediton Hundred were being assessed for a potentially crippling Sheep Tax, and understandably dissent was widespread. It was feared that taxation would then spread to geese, cattle and crops and the future looked bleak. Assessments were to start in May 1549 and to be completed by November 1st that year. Beresford points out that Devon was one of five counties where

Symbols on the ceiling of Cheriton Fitzpaine Church porch

these assessments were actually carried out before the tax was abolished so the Sampford Courtnay dissenters would certainly have had some experience of this.[17] Those who were involved in Crediton's wool industry joined with sheep farmers in the surrounding areas to express their anger and distress at recent developments. Robert Trobrigge of Crediton was one farmer who had already been assessed.

In Cheriton it was virtually impossible for villagers to be unaffected by the Prayer Book rebellion, and some men must have travelled the five miles to Crediton that summer to take part in the uprising. There are no records to show that this was the case but logic dictates that it was highly likely.

Interestingly, in the ceiling of the entrance porch to Cheriton church there is a central boss depicting the five sacred wounds of Christ: two pierced hands, two pierced feet and a pierced heart.

During the English Reformation, this image developed a powerful symbolism beyond the devotion: Prayer Book rebels chose it as a powerful symbol to march under.

65

Prayer Book rebellion banner in Sampford Courtnay showing the wounds of Christ

In the floor of Cheriton Church there is a tombstone to James Courtney jun esq of Upcott Barton, northside, Cheriton Fitzpaine who was buried on the 8th September 1592. As a firm Catholic he had refused to subscribe to Elizabeth's Act of Uniformity in 1569 and had been penalised for it, suffering considerable hardship. It is difficult to believe that he would have turned a blind eye to the turmoil in Crediton, so close to his family home.

In the Reynold family many members were highly intelligent with prodigious memories and an obstinate preciseness. Gifted thinkers, writers and orators, with their deeply held religious beliefs, they stood out as extraordinary men and could not fail to influence those around them. Cheriton Fitzpaine had become the home of this illustrious and passionate family, and its community witnessed first-hand their attitudes, actions and beliefs. Parishioners saw how they chose to live, sometimes flying in the face of great adversity and risking their lives for their religion. This must have had an impact upon villagers who both respected and admired the family. Because of them, ordinary young men in the parish had the opportunity to learn how to read and write and received a basic education in Latin and the scriptures. The impact of this would last for more than a generation with men passing on to their children the skills they had learnt in literacy as well as in husbandry. Indeed, three or four generations later there was a surprisingly large number of men over the age of 18 who were actually able to sign their names in the 1641 Protestation Returns. This was unusual for the time and a tangible legacy of Thomas Reynold's residency in the parish.

Expectations of the community's moral standards, religious commitment and loyalty to one another would have been high under the Reynold family. These standards once set, may also have been passed on from generation to generation. As a stronghold of traditional Catholicism, tucked away in the depths of Devon, this was a special community to belong to.

Although later members of the Reynold family decided against careers in the church and moved away from the village, they certainly put their intelligence and single-mindedness to good use. Several became very successful businessmen. Andrew Reynold, vintner of Exeter left a considerable fortune including:

£325.10s.0d. in his purse and bills

£595.18s.0d. in his wine cellar

£208 due on the books

plate and wearing apparel

a cottage in Cheriton Fitzpaine then occupied by Matthew Kelland and another tenement

table boards in several Exeter pubs – The Eagle, Stars, Anchor, Lyon, Bell, Rose, Crown, Luce etc.[18]

The future of Reynold's hall house and The Rectory

The next rector to take on the Cheriton congregation was Thomas Williams 1559–1581. Later rectors included:

Diggory Nicholls 1581–3

William Clotworthy 1583–85

Thomas Barrett 1585–1633

John (George) Cowling 1633–39

Nathaniel Durant 1639–1662

William Harris 1662–1675

Nicholas Hicks 1675–1719

Arthur Harris 1719–1771

In the 1613 Glebe Terrier the Rectory House property is described as 'a Hall, parlour, buttery, two chambers with a study over the entrance near the hall and one kitchen, There is one stable with a hayloft over, two woodhouses adjoining, one gate house or portlodge with a gallery and four chambers adjoining, one barn, one sheep house or cowhouse with a house for a …'[19]

In 1649 the Glebe Terrier states that this same building was only used as a detached kitchen or bakehouse.[20]

By 1679 the hall house that served as the Rectory had been relegated to an outhouse, and a new two-storey building had been constructed in front of it. The 1679 Glebe Terrier inventory of the parsonage refers to it as something separate: 'one house which is commonly called the great kitchen,' implying that it had not been lived in as a house for quite a long time.[21]

The new main house now had its own integral kitchen chamber with a study over it, a wainscoted floor-boarded parlour, a hall floored with lime and sand and several other rooms. Perhaps as a 'great kitchen' it was still being used for special events in the parish, but having lost its original purpose it gradually fell out of use becoming a bake-house and then, just a barn.

Part of the rate levied to repair the church in 1696 was put toward renovating the barn and that year two masons and several officials signed their names to witness that:

'We whose names are underwritten do certify all persons whom it doth concern that the barn belonging to the rectory of Cheriton Fitzpaine is in very good repair and never better this twenty years or more both in walls and covering.'

Signed by Aaron Philp and William Oliver, masons, William Hewish snr, churchwarden, Richard Gibbs, Andrew Payne, Richard Parkhouse, Thomas Marshall, John Voysey, William Madge and William Hewish jnr. December 2nd 1696.[22]

The hall house is listed in its own right now as the 'Manor House Barn' being described as an original 16th century hall house with low partitions and an open fire.[23] The roof was entirely smoke blackened at the time of a report prepared by Keystone Historic Buildings Consultants in July 2002, suggesting that it was an early 16th century house which had never been floored – 'a rare and interesting survival of a mediaeval hall.' It has since been renovated and re-purposed.

In the 1726 Glebe Terrier the original hall house is referred to as 'a brewing house which consists of five bays of building'

The Manor House historic buildings entry dates the 'new' building as late 17th century, but the documentary evidence of the Terriers suggest that it was probably built in the early to mid-17th century for Rev Nathaniel Durant 1639– 1662.

What did the Reynold family do for the parish?

In the evolution of a community it is recognised that shared experiences feed into a shared history that can then influence its common future. It is known that shared attitudes and values create a common outlook which incomers must then accept and promote if they are to become full members of the community. Shared conflict and adversity work rapidly to deepen resolve and strengthen ties between members of a community. 'The way that we do things round here', becomes something of a mantra in any community that is functioning effectively. There is no doubt that the extraordinary Reynold family modelled clearly their compassion for the poor, their love of education, their generosity and their religious commitment. There is evidence that parishioners followed the example that the family set and built upon it in future years, maintaining a strong sense of community in the village.

References

1. Will of Thomas Reynold clerk Westminster 1559 MUR abstract vol 27, OM coll 8/36
2. Letters and Papers, Foreign and Domestic, Henry VIII, Volume 8, January-July 1535 (Originally published by Her Majesty's Stationery Office, London, 1885)
3. There are many publications reporting the details of the execution but a contemporary one can be found in, Chappell, Julie. Perilous Passages: The Book of Margery Kempe, 1534–1934 pp 117-18
4. Strype to Pole cited in 9

5. 16th century woodcut, origin unknown
   Rev Andrew Clark, M.A. (ed.): The Life and Times of Anthony Wood, Antiquary, of Oxford, 1632–1695, Described by Himself, Collected from his diaries and other papers: Vol. I (1632–63) Vol xix OHS 1891
6. R Meredith, The Reynolds of Pinhoe and Exeter (2011)

   William Reynolds' letter to Wood ref the Pinhoe Reynolds, published by Oxford antiquarian & scholar Rev Andrew Clark OHS 1891 XIX p. 303.

   'The Reynolds Family – their Association with Pinhoe', Devon& Exeter Daily Gazette March 8, 1911 (author anon, later confirmed as Rev Roger Granville).

   Biographical obit on Rev Roger Granville (1848-1911) Devonshire Association for the Advancement of Science, Literature & Art vol 43, pp. 39-40 July 1911

   Richard Aylmer, Finding people in the Reynolds Connection pp. 23-24

   Dom Adam Hamilton makes a case for the birthplace of Richard Reynolds in the final chapter of The Angel of Syon where he explores the connection made by Strype between Richard and Thomas Reynolds, Dean of Exeter, exempted as he was from a pardon. He points out that several benefactors of the monastery are Devon men including Edward Courtenay, Earl of Devon and the Kirkham family that they had close associations with the Reynolds in the Pinhoe area. He picks up the idea that the name of Richard is significant as it was belonged to Thomas' parents Richard and Edith Reynolds, his brother Richard, called by Wood, 'a sufficient farmer', and his grandfather Richard. His conclusions are that Richard angel of Syon was born in Devon in c1490 and was a close relative of Thomas Reynolds
7. Rev John Prince, The Worthies of Devon, Two un-published volumes of biographical material ref. 373/2 pp. 491-531 Plymouth and West Devon Record Office (John Prince (1643–1723), vicar of Berry Pomeroy and author of 'Worthies of Devon', 1701, had at his death further biographical material for which he could find no publisher. The unpublished work was acquired by Sir Thomas Phillips
8. Lay Subsidy Roll 1524
9. Hamilton, Dom Adam. The Angel of Syon : the life and martyrdom of Blessed Richard Reynolds, martyred at Tyburn, May 4, 1535. Sands and Co 1905
10. Act of Supremacy (26 Hen VIII c1) The Act of Supremacy (1 Eliz 1 c 1)
11. Andrew Knapman's family research can be found on genuki.ncl.ac.uk/DEV/DevonMisc/Knapman2014.pdf
12. Will of Jerome Reynold physician Winchester 1570 MUR abstract vol 27, PROB 11/53/68
13. Rev Andrew Clark, M.A. (ed.): The Life and Times of Anthony Wood, Antiquary, of Oxford, 1632–1695, Described by Himself, Collected from his diaries and other papers: Vol. I (1632–63) Vol xix OHS 1891

Wood, Anthomy. Athenae Oxoniensis: An Exact History of all the Writers … vol 1

14. Hampton Court Conference 1604 and John Rainolds cited in The *Dictionary of National Biography*

15. Rev John Prince, Danmonii orientales illustres; or, The Worthies of Devon. A work, wherein the lives and fortunes of the most famous divines, statesmen, swordsmen, physicians, writers, and other eminent persons, natives of that most noble province, from before the Norman conquest, down to the present age, are memorized … out of the most approved authors, both in print and manuscript … pub 1810

16. A comprehensive account can be found at, The Prayer Book Rebellion of 1549 – Part 1 www.devonperspectives.co.uk/prayerbook_rebellion_1.html

17. Beresford,M W. The Poll Tax and Census of Sheep 1549 can be viewed at www.bahs.org.uk/AGHR/ARTICLES/02n1a3.pdf

18. Will of Andrew Reynold, vintner Exeter MUR1 Vol 27 plus inventory

19. 1613 Glebe Terrier Cheriton Fitzpaine FUR/856-910 May 17.1613

20. 1649 ditto

21. 1679 ditto

22. Notes on Some Devon Parishes by Fursdon – 1696 Church Rate

23. www.britishlistedbuildings.co.uk/england/devon/cheriton+fitzpaine

Falling out with the Reynolds –
the Scutt-Reynold's dispute

Thomas Reynold's will written shortly before his death in Marshalsea prison in November 1559 makes reference to the fact that his niece Agnes Reynold was about to marry in Cheriton Fitzpaine.[1] He left her a generous bequest of twenty Marks with which to start her married life with Clement Scutt. Although never an actual coin, the Mark represented money to the value of two thirds of a pound and was used in higher level transactions such as land purchase and dowries. In total Agnes would have received about £15.10s.0d. from her uncle's estate on the occasion of her marriage. Agnes was the eldest daughter of his brother William Reynold and is the only one of his children named in the will so may have been a favourite. The boys are referred to as 'my brother William's children if they proceed in learning and come to the University of Oxford, £100'.

In contrast Thomas left his eldest brother Richard of Cheriton Fitzpaine the sum of £5 to buy 'a holding or some other necessities'.

£5 coin/medal struck in Queen Elizabeth's reign

The Scutts and the Reynolds were close neighbours, each holding leases on several properties in the parish and having a comfortable amount of disposable income. It was inevitable that there would be a marriage between these two illustrious families before too long and it was Clement Scutt who married Agnes Reynold in 1560, a short time after her Uncle Thomas' unfortunate death. For generations the Scutts had lived at Perryhays and farmed on the western slopes of the village. Their ancestors Richard, Thomas and John held a considerable amount of property in the 1524 Subsidy Roll, and as far back as 1454 a William Scutt had acted as one of the twelve jurors at the area court.[2] Peter Scutt left a will dated 1548 which has not survived, but he was most probably father to Clement and Andrew, passing his wealth to them. Andrew as eldest son inherited Perryhays and a moiety of Stckparks, whilst Clement as second son held other property in the parish.

Agnes' father William Reynold favoured the union of the two families and promised the couple an additional £100 together with a house, currently in the occupation of Joane Dalley, widow. It seemed like an auspicious start to a happy marriage.

Chancery Court records however tell a different story and it appears that there was a serious and prolonged falling out over money and property with proceedings commencing in about 1567.[3] Clement accused his father-in-law of going back on his promise and claimed in court that the £100 dowry had never been paid to them. This was an ambitious claim against an authoritative man, and Clement must have had the backing of his family to take the matter to arbitration. A reply from the father-in-law showed that he was not to be browbeaten for he completely refuted Clement's claim. Reynold was a serious man who ran his farm efficiently and he was very careful with his money. He stated in court that he recorded all his transaction in a note book, and since the marriage he had kept a 'book of reckoninge' listing everything he had given to support the young couple. He meticulously itemised every sum of money and the value of each animal that he had gifted Clement and Agnes since their wedding:

Given to the said Clement and Agnes:

Seven years ago 25s.8d. for wedding apparel and provisions for the wedding and £5

Four years ago, 4 nobles to buy of Thomas Towcker of Shobrooke one black oxen

At Christmas last, 19/-

Seven years ago, twelve steers and heifers each worth 40/- amounting to £24

In the last seven years threescore lambs each worth 20d amounting to £5

At the time of the marriage, ten ewes and wethers each worth 4/- amounting to 40/

One year ago 40/-

At the time of harvest…..to workmen for mowing and reaping and carrying the corn and hay in wages 40/- and in meat and drink for the workmen

Diverse other sums of money and cattle and sheep etc.

The whole amounting to £140.

William for his part felt that he had been generous towards the couple but one can have some sympathy with Clement, who would probably have preferred to take control of his finances as a newly married man, rather than being spoon-fed by his father-in-law. He seems to have accepted help readily enough however for seven years or so.

Six years ago £5 to buy of one Dodderidge of Poughill two oxen
Five years ago £3 to buy one oxen at St Lawrence's fair in Crediton

William saw no reason for Agnes and Clement to be wanting more from him as he felt that he had more than fulfilled the dowry promise made in 1560. During the seven years of their marriage the couple had their only daughter, Elizabeth Scutt.

Clement lodged a counter claim stating that everything his father-in-law might have given them in the past had been a gift given in good will and not the promised sum of money, 'being but trifles and of a small value.' Furthermore, the 'book of reckoninge' put forward as evidence by William was said to have been burnt, so his account of these transactions could not be proven in court one way or another. During and after the court proceedings life must have been very uncomfortable for all parties living in such close proximity to each other. Members of the extended families would also have been affected on a daily basis, William and Clement both taking the moral high ground.

Reynold remained a highly respected member of the community and he acted as a Presenter for the village when the 1569 Muster Roll was drawn up for the Queen. In each parish trusted landholders were given the task of listing all able-bodied men who could fight, and all who could provide cash and arms in the event of war. Clement Scutt was also invited to act as Presenter which meant that the two men had to work alongside each other, travelling from farm to farm to survey the population. Reynold and Scutt themselves each had goods valued at G7 which meant that in the event of war they would be required to provide a cash sum of £10-£20 together with one bow, a sheaf of arrows, one steel cap and one bill. Clement as a younger man would have been called upon to serve as an archer if there was a call to arms.

No will has survived for William Reynold but he died as an elderly man some-time in the 1570s. Clement died quite young in 1584 leaving his widow Agnes and daughter, Elizabeth Scutt. A sentence passed in 1590 appointed Clement's brother Andrew Scutt to manage affairs for Agnes and Elizabeth.[4] Significantly, no-one in the Reynold family was mentioned in the document.

In 1590 and again in 1594 Agnes Scutt made an appearance at the local court lodging a complaint against one Andrew Reynold.[6] Unfortunately no details are recorded and one is left wondering if it was a continuation of the dispute with her deceased father or a new fall out between Agnes and one of her brothers.

Her brother-in-law Andrew Scutt, gent of Perryhayes died in 1594 and his will was to have a lasting effect upon the village.[7] People living in the village today will know that he was a wealthy and benevolent man and it was his bequest that enabled the building of six almshouses at the east end of the village. It has been written of him that he was a generous man:

'Andrew Scutt, being in his lifetime liberal to the poor …'

He made provision for his widow Margery during her lifetime, but on her death, property and money were left to provide housing for the poor of the parish. Andrew Scutt's act of charity has lasted until the present day. His almshouses with their distinctive tall chimneys were built a few years later and are still standing as three private dwellings opposite the new entrance to the parish hall. Trustees were appointed first in 1606 which indicates that the almshouses were built sometime after that date.[5] One almshouse was added to the row at a later date.

Scutt stipulated that the almsmen and women chosen from villagers should be 'of good report, honest behaviour and godly conversation' and should be 'enjoined to repair to the parish church at all times of public prayer if they should be able to do so.' So although in later years only women were given homes by the charity it was Andrew's intention that both men and women should be considered.

The Charity Commissioners' report of 1911 gives a good summary of Andrew Scutt's 1594 wishes:

Andrew Scutt by his will, bearing the date 3rd May 1594, gave to the parish of Cheriton Fitzpaine, after the death of his wife, All his lands, for the erection and maintenance of six almshouses, for six poor people of the said parish, who were to have 6d. a piece weekly; and he appointed William Bodley, Parson of Shobrooke, executor in trust, of his will, to whom he gave all his lands in fee, as well in the county of Devon as in the city of Exeter, to the uses mentioned in the said will.[6]

The properties concerned included The Red Lion Public House in St Lawrence, Exeter together with gardens and land in St Sidwells and St Davids, Exeter. He also gave a half share or moiety of a tenement called Stockparks in Cheriton Fitzpaine to be kept for his widow Margery's lifetime and then sold to benefit the poor of the parish. Margery Scutt died in 1597and her executor was William Hewish. The other half share of Stockparks was held by Nicholas and

The almshouses at the east end of the village built with Scutt's bequest. There is a raised causeway running between the road and the front of the building

Mary Carpenter and their son Andrew of Poughill. Both moieties were granted by John Hayes, of Witheridge in 1571.

In 1740 the almshouses were in a poor state of repair and the Trustees called a meeting to activate a major renovation project. The two eastern floors were to be paved, the walls of the ground floor rooms and the chambers were to be plastered near to the stairs with good haired mortar, and the rest with 'hayed' mortar and lime. The roof over the chamber windows was to be lathe and plastered to the first panes and the foundations and quoins were to be footed up wherever they were defective. The stonework was to be pointed inside and out and the window sills mended. Rough casting was to be applied to the front and it was to be lime-washed. Water on the south side was to be conveyed off so as to not come into the houses. Glass was to be cleaned and window leaves and doors repaired. To keep off horses and carts, posts were to be placed at each end and at the middle of the causeway in front of the house.[7]

By 1823 The Red Lion Pub which stood in the High Street next to St Lawrence church had been converted to a baker's shop and was in the occupation of Thomas Couch, under a lease dated June 9th 1794, and it still provided in income for the charity. At that time the Cheriton almshouses were being regularly repaired at the annual cost to the Trust of £3 and were inhabited by six almswomen, each receiving a weekly wage of 1/6d. By 1788 the charity had accrued an excess of £40 in the hands of William Lake esq a former Trustee, and after expenses a decision was made to deposit some of it in 3% Exeter Bank shares. In 1823 the Charity Commissioners recommended that the money be deposited in a Savings Bank. The annual income that year was said to be £22.12s.0d.[8]

The leaseland of Stockparks, later part of the Pool Barton estate comprised one barn, one garden and certain parcels of land containing around 50 acres of meadow, pasture and furze ground. The lease was originally held by Andrew Scutt together with Perryhays farm, and it passed out of the family when Clement Scutt's daughter Elizabeth married into the Hewish family. The Hewishes thus inherited the Scutt/Reynold dispute and a Chancery Court action was taken out against defendants Andrew and William Hewish by one Richard Reynold of Pool.[9]

The terms of Andrew Scutt's 1594 will had stated that the lease on Stockparks was to be sold for the best price and invested to generate money for the poor of the parish, specifically 50/- per anum. The Hewishes had taken it upon themselves to keep the Stockparks lease for themselves and to sub-let it out well enough to generate the same amount of money. They witnessed that each year they had been paying five 'poor and impotent people' in the parish the yearly sum of 10/- a piece from the income, thus making up the required 50/- allocated in the will and keeping Stockparks as a whole parcel of land to safeguard Scutt's bequest for ever. This indeed seemed to be a better deal for the poor and it had been agreed in a sentence granted against the bequest to the poor by Annias Lampfield and Sir John Acland, MP of Broadclyst, enabling a friendly partition in favour of the wardens, overseers and officials and some other parishioners who were to pay Richard Reynold 10/- rent per year on Stockparks. Stockparks was immediately adjacent to Pool Barton and Reynold was farming it leasehold along with other lands that belonged to him. Reynold was not happy with the state of affairs and wanted to own Stockparks himself and secure it for the future as part of his estate. The Hewish defendants stated that Richard Reynold had shown malice in his actions and 'by many and diverse shifts was often times injurious to the poor', and wanted to get possession of the property himself 'at some trifling rent'. William and Andrew Hewish, the defendants claimed that this was 'to mark his malice and private grudge' against them.

The future of Stockparks

Lifeleasehold properties were common in the parish as in many Western counties, but whereas such a transaction in 1650 may have ensured a family security of tenure for approximately twenty one years, with improved life expectancy and the practise of renewing a lease within a family, tenure was in essence ninety nine years by the 1720s. In Cheriton Fitzpaine it was a strong tradition for the absentee Lord of the Manor to always renew lifeleasehold properties, allowing families complete freedom in how they farmed and giving the false impression that farmsteads were in fact owned by them for generations.

A lease on Stockparks was granted to Robert Vickary and his wife Olive. In 1614 the moiety was leased for 10/- per anum to Andrew Hewish on the three lives of Andrew himself and Agnes and Margaret the daughters of George Hole for ten shillings rent per year.

(N.B. An Olive Vickary born 1638 married one Andrew Hewish of Perry some years later, showing that the two families were interlinked for many years.)

1671 indenture re moiety of Stockparks held by Scutt.

The original moiety of Stock Parks was about fifty acres and in 1726 a deed in private hands shows that John Harris who held the manor of Cheriton was still leasing out part of of Stockparks to the Hewish family:

26.12.1726 35 acres called Stockparks leased for 99 years for £110.10s.0d

John Harris of Hayne to

Mary Hewish, widow

On the lives of Andrew Hewish, son and Sarah Hewish, daughter to commence from and after the death of Susannah Hewish

All corn and grain grown on the premises to be ground at Cheriton Mill

Witnessed by Arthur Harris and William Hewish

Later Stockparks was leased by the Tremlett family and then passed on by marriage to the Pridhams.

1.5.1779 All that messuage and tenement called Stockparks containing four closes of land late in the possession of Edward Hewish esq deceased leased for 99 years for 3 lives John Tremlett 19, Elias Tremlett 17 and Elizabeth Tremlett 13 for the consideration of £330

William Harris to retain the rights over timber, minerals, stone etc and Daniel Tremlett was to repair and maintain.

William Harris esq to

Daniel Tremlett, yeoman

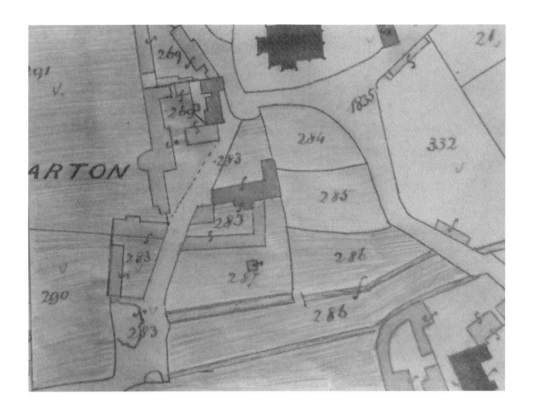

In 1807 Samuel Pridham was leasing Stockparks

By 1819 Samuel Pridham had managed to unite both moieties of Stockparks so that in 1840 the parcel comprised about 128 acres rather than 50 acres

In 1840 Plots around Pool Barton (283) were farmed and owned by Pridham whereas 284 and 285 were farmed from Cheriton Barton (269) by Pridham as a tenant farmer. Pridham also farmed Sutton farm.

Furse tenement

An additional almshouse called Scut's was built in 1717 at the entrance to The Hayes. This is managed today by the twelve Trustees of the amalgamated Cheriton Charities together with the open space behind it called The Hayes which was given as a village green for the 'sport and enjoyment' of the youth of the village by John Harris in 1648.

In 1717 Furze/Furse tenement was purchased with £200 from the charity bequest by Edward Dicker, yeoman of Upton Hellions on behalf of the twelve

Trustees of the charity.[10] It was acquired to bring in a guaranteed income for the charity and comprised a house, garden and 40-50 acres of land on northside. The rents and profits from the estate were to be used to support the needy in the parish. These rents were referred to as Poor's money. The property appeared on the 1840 Tythe map:

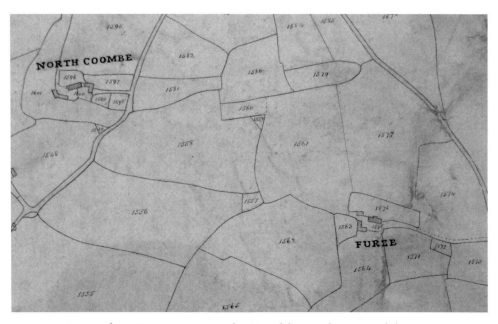

Income from Furse tenement in the East of the parish supported the poor.

References

1. Will of thomas Reynold clerk Westminster 1559 MUR abstract vol 27, OM coll 8/36
2. Court Rolls for the Manor of West Budleigh
3. Chancery Court records C3/154/43
4. Sentence of Clement Scutt 1590 PROB 11/76/3
5. Trustees appointment 1606 – missing document
6. Will also cited in The Report of the commissioners Concerning Charities … vol 3
7. 1740 repairs to the almshouses, parish records
8. as 6
9. Chancery Court records C2/Jas/R16/11
10. 1717 conveyance Furse 2614A/PF8

John Harris, Church House and The Village Green

Church House was the parish hall of its day: somewhere for villagers to hold religious and secular meetings and the popular fundraising 'church ales' which were communal drinking sessions with various sports, plays and Morris dancing (banned under Oliver Cromwell and the Puritans) that raised funds for the church. Before the nave of the church was filled with seating, this would have been the place for some of these activities, and the need for a Church House generally arose in the 15th or 16th centuries. Cheriton's Church House was completed in 1642, which is unusually late. It has an impressive set of steps leading conveniently from the upper chamber into the churchyard and is thought to be the longest thatched building in England. On closer inspection it is comprised of at least three buildings with slightly different roof levels, and indeed at the time of the 1840 Tythe map both ends of the property were still being rented out as housing. There is evidence of these being leased out over the years when not needed to house pensioners themselves. The dwelling at the southern end was enlarged at one point to jut over the trim-tram path.

A Church House is almost always part of the Glebe and will be mentioned in Glebe Terriers. This is not the case in Cheriton because it was built on manorial land by Mr John Harris of Hayne House, Stowford who was a patron of the church as early as 1639 and who had inherited the manor of Cheriton Fitzpaine from his parents. When John's father Arthur Harris died in 1628 he left a vast fortune including ten manors and 4,200 acres of land in Cornwall and Devon, and when his mother Margaret (nee Davells) died in 1634 a further six manors were passed down in the family.[1] At one point the Harris's also owned St Michael's Mount, but by the early sixteenth century they had made their home at Hayne House near

Church House from the western side showing the flight of steps to the Vestry room

Stowford, Launceston. Their house is shown on Speed's 1610 map of Devon and stood until the present building replaced it in 1810. Tradition has it that William Harris, a relative well-known for his staunch loyalty to the Stuart dynasty, hid the fleeing King Charles II in a room in the middle of his house in Plymstock until arrangement could be made for his escape to France. Charles II subsequently struck a medal to commemorate his escape and presented it to William who was also created a Baronet.[2]

John Harris however was not a Cavalier and was more interested in Parliamentarian politics, becoming a Member of Parliament for Launceston in 1640, and entering the Long Parliament as a burgess in 1641. He led a privileged life and had been sent abroad for three years as a young man to broaden his horizons, travelling through France and Spain, but he had showed little interest in an active career in the military and preferred to spend time in Cornwall and Devon.[3] He was in his fifties when he decided to build Church House on an awkward plot of land in the village of Cheriton. It was a sprawling building backing on to the churchyard and with a small strip of land running along the front. He also owned the triangular plot of land which stood on the northern side of the churchyard that was called Church Hay. Whilst Church House was in construction Harris must have met with parish officials to discuss the future use of the building and the land, and the result was in some ways ahead of its time. The plan they came up with was an innovative one and in some ways we are still living with its legacy today, almost five hundred years later. The building was to be used by the local court, the Vestry, for schooling and for the poor, and the land behind it, now known as The Hayes, was to be a meeting place for the youth of the village. In 1648 he drew up the necessary documentation and Church House and the Hayes were given to the parish in perpetuity:

> By indenture bearing the date 27th April 1648 between John Harris of the one part and John Moore and others of the other part, a moiety of Church House was granted in consideration of the love and affection which he bore to the parishioners of Cheriton Fitzpaine and for the better maintenance of the poor of the parish. Together with Church House he gifted a moiety of Church Hay, being half an acre of land north of the churchyard. It was to be 'used heretofore as a place of recreation and sporting for the youth of the parish.' Harris made provisions for a chamber in the newly-built Church House, also called the' school house', to be always available for courts and vestry meetings @ the yearly rent of 2s.6d.[4] With this great act of generosity in the seventeenth century John Harris ensured that the parishioners had a meeting place, the poor had shelter and income, and the youngsters of the village had a safe place to play.

Patron of the church, John Harris 1649[5]

Harris died in 1657 but the second phase of his plan had already started and within a few years, a number of leasehold cottages had been built along the southern and western edges of The Hayes, offering accommodation to a variety of villagers and generating an assured income for the maintenance of the poor in the parish. These cottages ranged from simple, two roomed dwellings to larger houses with their own gardens, allowing the tenants to have a vegetable patch, chickens and perhaps a pig. As such, they were an early form of social housing and still stand as a monument to John Harris' benevolence. He did not live in the parish but must have spent considerable time in Cheriton, for he developed a fondness for its people and showed great generosity to the community.

An angel in the porch at Cheriton Fitzpaine – can you see any likeness?

The present day Church Cottage is an amalgam of three cottages, with the one at the western end having a fireplace dated 1659; The Cottage in The Hayes (formerly Belmont) has the date 1674 on the outside wall; three two-roomed cottages are now single storey kitchens at The Ring of Bells and the lower part of the kitchen belonging to The Cottage in the Hayes; a two storey house and garden are now the upper dining room of the pub together with the plot where a barn now stands; the original garden of The Cottage in The Hayes now has a Victorian cottage built on it called Cary Cottage. Later buildings were added in the south-eastern corner of the plot with 'Hayes' (formerly Hazledene, alias The Boot Inn, now occupied by the Avery family), and Scut's Almshouses (formerly two cottages) dated 1717.

There are stories that The Ring of Bells Inn was a fourteenth century building that once housed the monks who built the church, but standing as it does on the half acre plot that is Church Hay, it actually started life as a leasehold dwelling built on The Hayes after Harris' 1648 Indenture. There are bee skep holes in the back wall redolent of an established farmstead but the interior has been much altered and is difficult to read. Rental on the house was paid to The Overseer of the Poor for many years. Certainly by 1830 it was operating as a licensed house called The Ring of Bells when the lease on it was bequeathed to John and Ann Oliver by their father Richard Oliver.

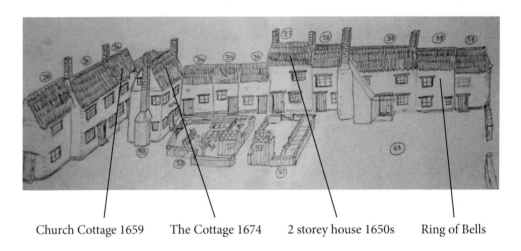

Church Cottage 1659   The Cottage 1674   2 storey house 1650s   Ring of Bells

The rector of Cheriton in John Harris' time was Nathanial Durant 1639–1662, a graduate of Exeter College, Oxford and a man fiercely loyal to the Crown. The English Civil war commenced in August 1643 and Nathanial Durant was to become a casualty of it because of his publically held beliefs.[6] Co-incidentally, John Harris, M P for Launceston and owner of the manor of Cheriton had entered the Long Parliament in 1641 as a Puritan, despite his own family's strong Royalist sympathies. To begin with, he was party to reporting and removing rectors with Royalist sympathies from their parishes and he sat on the 'Committee for Plundered Ministers' which had been set up with the sole purpose of replacing and effectively silencing those clergy who were loyal to King Charles I.[7] In

September 1645, Nathanial Durant the traditional and very public Royalist rector of Cheriton Fitzpaine became one of the Plundered Ministers and he was removed from the parish and his property sequestered, meaning that he could only retrieve it by buying it back from the Government. He was the placed in the rectory of Abinger in Surrey where officials kept a very close watch on him. As John Harris knew him well and attended his church services on occasions, Durant's treatment would have had an effect upon him.

Abinger had itself been deprived of its rector, Anthony Smith who had been reported for speaking out against the Parliamentarians in church.[8] Whilst there, Nathanial was coached to preach appropriately to the congregation and obviously played the game, for the following year officials felt that he was a reformed character and he was allowed back to practise in Cheriton Fitzpaine.

By 1648, the year of Harris Gift, John Harris' experiences had led to changes. He decided to take up the Royalist cause again and follow his family in supporting the Crown. Falling out with the Commonwealth regime, it was only a matter of time before he came under suspicion himself. He joined together with others who sought to disband the New Model Army and was one of 180 MPs who were barred from entering Parliament by Colonel Thomas Pride on December 6th 1648.[9] This event came to be known as Pride's Purge. MPs who were considered to be a greater threat than John were arrested and imprisoned. John was put under constant surveillance and in 1649 he was followed to Cornwall when visiting a friend who was a known Royalist and his swords

Pride's Purge, an engraving c1652

were seized from him. In 1651 he was reported for abetting plans for a Royalist landing in the region.

John died in 1657 leaving a young son called Arthur to inherit, amongst other things, his 'moiety of the manor of Cheriton Fitzpaine.'[10]

Tucked away in deepest Devon far away from prying eyes, Nathanial Durant would have been supported by his loyal parishioners in continuing to hold church services the way he had done before his removal. Everyone would have been very wary of strangers in the village and church-life seems to have continued unchallenged for many years. In 1662 however Rev Durant's luck ran out and once again he was reported for his services and unceremoniously ejected from Cheriton for his 'non-conformity'.[11] The term non-conformist today holds very different connotations, but in 1662 it referred to those ministers who fell foul of The Act of Uniformity. Durant was one of nearly 2,000 clergymen who were *ejected* from the established church for refusing to follow a prescribed format for public prayer and for refusing to administer the rites and sacraments as found in the *Book of Common Prayer*. Possibly one of his last actions was to

The Coat of Arms hanging above the door at Cheriton Fitzpaine church

commission the Royal Coat of Arms of King Charles II that hangs above the main doorway, inside the church. Anglican churches were obliged to put up the Coat of Arms of each new monarch, reminding the congregation of the link between church and state, and this practise had been interrupted by Cromwell's reign. Only about 15% of churches now has an example of such a painting and because each one was removed when the next monarch was crowned, many are of a later date.

In Cheriton the example for Charles II was never replaced, but it bears the date not of 1660 when Charles came to the throne, but of 1665. It is perhaps significant that rectors and parishioners left it on display to mark the restoration of the monarchy and did not commission any later Coats of Arms. It was naively overpainted by an amateur restorer in the 20th century.

After 1648 the middle section of Church House was used to care for poor men, women and children who had nowhere else to go. Over the years general maintenance was carried out, but things came to a head when in 1737 the building was said to be in a very poor state of repair and major renovations were carried out.

Further major maintenance was carried out on the one hundred year old property in June 1753 when the sum of £16.0s.0d. was collected from parishioners towards the bill, but it was recognised that something more needed to be done to make the building fit for purpose. In August 1753 a newly formed committee agreed to 'erecting and preparing a workhouse' on the site. This involved altering and improving it to meet the needs of the poor pensioners who lived there. Those who already lived in Church House were to be lodged temporarily elsewhere in the parish until 'the following Christmas'. The three cottages known as Tower Hill Tenement, bordered on the east by Tower Hill and on the south by the road to Stockleigh English called Chugbear Lane (a site occupied now by Grey Gables) belonged to the parish, and it was here that most of the paupers were housed. Others were boarded out with villagers in return for costs incurred.

Paid for glazing the Parish House at Tower Hill 9/6d

It may be significant that the cobbled Trim Tram path leads from Church House down to the crossroads at the foot of Tower Hill, indicating perhaps that this was a well-trodden path for the poor and needy who would be regularly escorted to and from work and church.

Once completed, Cheriton folk sometimes called their refurbished building a 'Workhouse', but often continued to refer to it either as 'the Poor House' or as 'Church House'.

As a result of the committee meeting a mason called John Rowe and a carpenter called Joseph Pope were appointed to undertake the work: two men who would benefit hugely from such a lucrative contract. Builders as such are

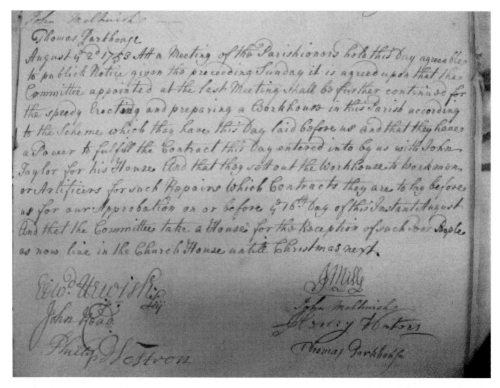

Minutes of August 1753 showing that the committee had agreed to erect
a workhouse fit for purpose and invited tenders for the work

never mentioned as a trade so one has to assume that it was the norm for general labourers to be employed to dig and prepare the cob and to construct walls. Everyone in a village could turn their hand to cobbing and lyme-washing and these were not considered to be the specialist professions they are today. One entry in the accounts records that a man and horse were employed 'to draw water to make cobb'.

Accounts show that copious amounts of material, labour and portage were needed for the project, each item meticulously recorded in the ledger. It was a costly business and parishioner were obliged to give their contributions:

> John Manley for sawing; three days and half labour for Davy about the Church House; lyme supplied by me – William Moxey; Edmund Sharland for carrying etc. William Moxey was the Governor.

pd for a man rope _____ 0 – 0

pd John Manley more for sawing _____ 0 – 2

It for three days & half Labour for Davy about y Churchhouse – 0 – 4

pd John Pope for one days work _____ 0 – 0

It for one days work for my self _____ 0 – 1

pd for h{s} Busholls of hair at 8 pr Bushall _____ p – 1{4}

Allowed my self for providing Materials for y Churchhouse as by agreem{t} 1 – 1

pd Mlere for Lyme as by y whole bill Appeares _____ 0 – 1{4}

pd more to Edm: Sharland for Carryage as by his bill Appeares ___ 1 – 6

It for my Expences on y Labourers at severall times when in their Labour – 0 – 5

    Receipts _____ 119 = 18 = 02   12 – 8

    Disbursm{ts} _____ 118 = 03 = 08   Disbursm{ts}   118 = 0

    Due to y p{ish} 001 = 14 = 06

Recd of James Philips y above s{um} by me Wm Moxey

To y{ears} after in D{o} _____

To Will: London in D{o} _____

To the Way Wardens Instructions _____

To Thos Moxey more in Necessity _____

To 90 Nutches of Reed for the Lower Church House ____

To Spears for laying the same _____

To Jno Drake for thetching _____

To Roger Horland as by Note Appeares _____

To Wm Wotton ab{t} that House as by Note Appea[r]

To the Expence ab{t} taking John Papis _____

To making a Change for Wm London & Joan Row ____

To Mr Garnica{s} by bill _____

To Cloth & mending John Manley's Coat _____

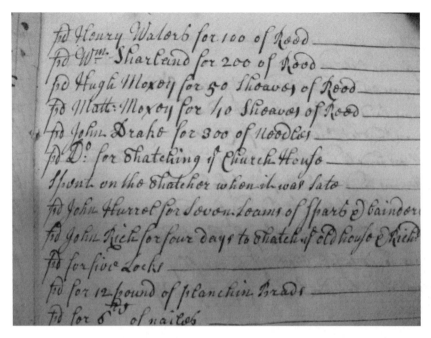

John Drake for thatching; 90 hutches of reed for the lower Church House; William Wootton about the House etc.

Spent on the thatcher when it was late (overtime rates!)

Thatching the Church House when it was a school in the 20th century –
techniques would not have changed over the centuries

For carriage of deal boards; for fetching seams of sand by 2 men and 3 horses; 4 horses to fetch stones from Dolbury and 2 from Thorveton; 5 hogsheads of lyme and three quarters; 12 seames of stones etc. N.B. Dolbury is the site of the Iron Age fort on the Killerton estate.

But a pile of building materials was not always safe from the youth of the village, looking for mischief, and in 1754 it was found necessary to mount a guard overnight on a stock of elm to stop it being thrown into the Pump Pit in The Hayes by 'the designing ones'. Some have felt that this might be because villagers resented the improvements at the Poor House and wanted to stop progress, but there is no other evidence to support this and villagers seemed enthusiastic about the project.

Reasons for being admitted to the Poor House 1753

Because nationally workhouses were being brought into line, new demands were made upon those elected and employed to run them and one stipulation was that new pensioners were to be listed not just by name and date of admission and discharge. Cheriton had been very good at doing this and the only new demand for them was to list the reason for a person being admitted. There is a list dated 1753 that records the names of twenty four pensioners considered worthy of a place in the workhouse:

Blindness: William Gibbons, Sarah Hill, Prudence Butt

Cripple: Widow White, Christian Back, Elizabeth Back

Inability: Grace Jestin

Large family: Lewis Gifford and children

Orphan: Mary Glanville

Old age: Walter Labdon and his wife. John Manley, Robert Maunder, Rose Peasler, Grace Moxey, Widow Glanville, Olive Boutson, George Peasler, Henry Ward and his wife, Widow Kempt, Anne Back, Elizabeth Taylor, Widow Elsworthy and George Camp.

New rules drawn up meant that pensioners had to be clean and well-dressed; rise at 6 am (7 am in the winter) and go to bed at 9 pm (8 pm in the winter); work for twelve hours a day from 7 am to 7 pm, and to refrain from smoking at work or in bed. All were to sit at the table to eat their meals in a decent manner and to stand reverently before and afterwards for Grace, said by the Master. Children were from time to time to be taught to read and write and to repeat the catechism either by the Master or Mistress, or by any pensioner qualified to do so.

The rules adopted by Cheriton Fitzpaine were available in published form and certainly the nearby parishes of Sandford and Cruwys Morchard adopted them too.

The Village Green alias The Hayes

This drawing of the southern and western sides of The Hayes clearly shows that The Ring of Bells is comprised of several dwellings with different roof-levels numbered 33 to 38. Church Cottage was an original row of three cottages numbered 30-32. Cary Cottage was not yet built and The Cottage in The Hayes was a cottage and garden numbered 33.

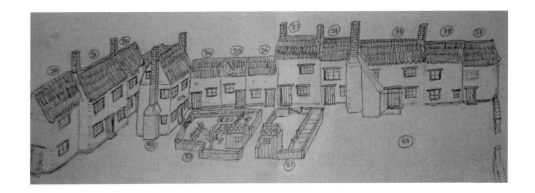

The barn now part of the pub was built on the garden of number 37. Cottage number 34 has been given a second storey and been added to house 33.

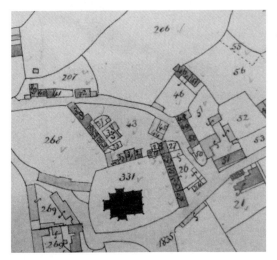

The village green at the centre of the community, number 43 on the 1840 Tythe map

The Charity Commissioner surveying the village in 1823 wrote that 'Church Hay consists of a green containing about half an acre of land, upon which eight houses are built.' These houses were paying annual rents to the Trustees of the Charity and bringing in revenue for the parish poor. For their part the Trustees maintained the fabric of these properties together with the village green itself which would have been a regular meeting place for sport and recreation. John Harris, a benefactor of the church in the 1630s was so fond of the village and its people that in 1648 he had gifted The Hayes as a green for the youth of the village to enjoy forever. It would be a place of summer fairs, markets, maypole dancing, carnivals, hunt meetings, ball games and seasonal celebrations. Sadly, the area has long since been cobbled and gritted and is increasingly used as a car park, preventing young people from playing any type of sports there. For several years in recent times however the village hosted the Crediton Folk Festival and Morris dancers, Mummers and musicians brought the area back to life for a couple of days each year. Open air activities now take part of the forecourt of The Ring of Bells which is a small triangle of land that was purchased for the pub from The Trustees in the twentieth century. A skittle alley was built along the north-eastern boundary of The Hayes in 1903 and the owners of The Ring of Bells are still liable for a small yearly rent on the ground beneath it, payable to the Trustees.

> Monday morning brought forth thunder, lightning and rain, with heavy fog, which made everything bad for holiday keeping. Later in the morning fairing stalls were soon fixed in the Hayse, and swingboats and shooting galleries were in action. At 4.30 the new town brass band formed up, and played some choice music in different parts of the town in a very excellent style. At 8 p.m. a dance was held in the schoolroom, when about 40 were present, and dancing was kept up until 2 a.m. At the Half Moon a dance was held in the barn, when a large number gathered until 11 p.m., and again on Tuesday night until 10. On the whole a good number of people were present, considering there was no harvest dinner or tea, as in previous years.

In September 1902 for Revels Sunday, 'fairing stalls were soon fixed in the Hayse, and swingboats and shooting galleries were in action'. This was an annual event and one can imagine the whole village in party mode with a band playing' in different parts of the town', a dance in the school room until 2 am and a dance in the Half Moon barn. There is a tinge of disappointment in the Western Times' report over the fact that there was 'no harvest dinner or tea as in previous years'. Three church services had been held on the Sunday to give thanks for the harvest. Mrs Pridham was the organist, the church had been decorated with flowers,

Photograph of Cheriton Band from Phyllis Trott's estate

vegetables and fruit and the bells were' freely rung' by teams from Chawleigh, Cadbury and Poughill. The tradition of Harvest Revels in the Hayes continued into the 1930s when stories have been told of dancing under The Folly and along the Trim Tram path to the churchyard, and then into The Hayes. The Folly was the name given to the jettied walkway at the end of the Old School.

The Cheriton brass band formed in 1902 with a membership fee of 2s.6d. and a weekly sub of 1/. There were twelve men and boys who performed in the band and they were much in demand in the village, often playing in neighbouring parishes too. An earlier band had been formed in 1885.

It is believed that this photograph came into the Trott family of Stockleigh Pomeroy via Phyllis Trott's who was descended from George Way carpenter who lived at Hayes Cottage in Backhayes Lane. This picture was taken in the gateway of The Rectory looking towards the church.

In addition to The Ring of Bells in the Hayes there was a second public house, The Boot Inn (numbered 44), wrapping itself around part of what is now Scut's Almshouse and making this village green the hub of village life. A deep well stood on the forecourt of Scut's almshouse for neighbours to use and there were pumps standing to the left of cottage 48, now Rose Cottage, and in the garden marked 33, now Cary Cottage from which inhabitants also drew their water. In later years a row of four outdoor privies was built for inhabitants to make use of but these

The Hayes shown as a village green as it was intended when gifted to the youth of the village for their sport and enjoyment in 1648

have long since disappeared. A tethering post for horses allowed drinkers at the pubs to bring their transport with them. The Hayes is a notoriously dark area and you certainly need your wits about you when negotiating the narrow exit which has been much widened now but still poses problems for some vehicles. In 1890 Mr Conibear, a wheelwright drove Mr Thorne out of The Hayes in his cart, did not keep sufficiently to the right, had a problem avoiding a low wall in the dark and pitched Mr Thorne out, dislocating his shoulder in the process. The accident was reported in The Western Times that December and was said to be the second reported accident in the Hayes.

As the little house 37 and the cottages 36, 35 and 34 fell empty, they were all made part of the Ring of Bells Public House and now form the upper dining area, the kitchen and the store room. When Sheila Benson the landlady of the pub

At the entrance to The Hayes, left to right, Rose Cottage, April Cottage
and Bawn Cottage (Bawn is an Irish word celebrating the present
owner Molly Cotter's Irish ancestry)

retired in 1972 she retained cottage 34 for herself, giving it a second storey and merging it with house number 33 to form an L-shaped dwelling. At that time it was called 'Belmont Cottage' and then, the rather confusing 'The Cottage'. The present owner re-named it 'The Cottage in The Hayes' to avoid being mixed up with nearby houses called 'Hayes' and 'Hayes Cottage'.

For many years number 30 on the plan was a one up and one down cottage, but 30, 31 and 32 were later brought together as one long property called Church Cottage.

The separate cottage numbered 29 in the Tythe is not as old as the other properties and it is now a garage block belonging to Church Cottage.

Cary Cottage built in the garden of 33 after the 1840 Tythe, was occupied for many years by the Manning family. A stable door once opened into The Hayes at the eastern end of the cottage and Miss Manning sold little bags of

Scut's Almshouse built 1717 at the entrance to The Hayes had a
deep well on the forecourt, now capped.

sweets from behind the door to the children as they came out from the nearby school.

In 1880 the lease on Backhayes meadow was put up for auction together with Backhayes garden and the outhouse built on it. The former was owned by Mr Prior and the latter rented by Mr Willis.

Hayes Cottage and Katherine Cottage in Back Hayes Lane

George Way lived at Hayes Cottage, the left-hand side of the building shown in the pictures. He was a joiner and wheelwright who had been apprenticed to Samuel Langworthy at Bowdell and he ran his business out of the shed next door to the electricity generator. George and Sarah had two daughters, Ellen Maud known as Nellie who became a much-loved village school mistress having started as a trainee teacher when only fifteen years old, and Ethel Mary, just a year younger. Ethel was sent to Stockleigh Pomeroy where she worked as a housemaid for farmer William Tuckett and his wife Susan. She met William Westcott who had taken over the village smithy on the Green from his ailing father Robert Westcott, and the couple married in Crediton in late 1918. Their daughter Phyllis M Westcott was born in 1919 and died at the age of ninety four in 2014. Phyllis was married to Arthur G Trott in 1940.

The Westcotts lived at The Green in Stockleigh Pomeroy for many years with Robert Westcott operating as a wheelwright, undertaker and blacksmith. He was born c1847 in Thorverton and his wife Elizabeth in Shobrooke c1848. For a few years after their marriage the couple lived at Thorveton, and had their children Sarah Ann 1874 and Emily 1877 there. Their three sons Henry 1879, James Robert 1886 and William 1888 were all born in Stockleigh Pomeroy. Since childhood, little James Robert had been sickly and was variously described as being 'feeble minded' and 'partially blind and paralysed' so he was not able to follow in his father's footsteps but Henry and William both became wheelwrights. Henry set himself up in business at Washford near Tiverton, living in Nibb's Cottage with his wife Maria and several children. Sarah Ann stayed in Stockleigh Pomeroy and worked for some years as a school assistant, before her mother died. Like so many daughters at that time, she then gave up paid work and became housekeeper for her ailing father. William Westcott was left to inherit the business.

Facts about properties in and around The Hayes, using the identification numbers from the Tythe	
1840 Tythe Map and Apportionment	Deeds in the Devon Record Office 1823 Report of The Charity Commissioners 1876 charity Commissioners report
24 Cottage, outhouse and court Humphrey Berry	Humphrey Berry used the large bread oven that juts out into the churchyard to bake for the village. His daughter married into the Wotton family and lived at Moxeys, using her baking skills in the cottage at the rear, formerly The Angel Inn
43 The Hayes 44 The Boot Inn owner William Pitt snr occupier John Pike 45 Almshouse, owned Trustees of Scutts Charity, occupier Susannah Ellis	
25 Upstairs Vestry room/School room Owned and occupied by the Trustees of C F	
26 Cottage and yard Owned and occupied by the Trustees of C F	The Poor House and then the village school (each end was generally rented out to householders)

27 Cottage Owned by William Pitt snr Occupied by John Pike	1754 House conveyed from John Harris of Haynes esq sine deceased to Thomas Taylor, thatcher. Thomas Taylor married Elizabeth Maunder 1750 and they had Betty 1752, Richard 1754-8, Mary 1757, Ann 1759, George 1761, Ann 1764, William 1766, Rebecca 1770. 1795 Rev William Harris to John Drake, lately in the possession of Thomas Taylor with a garden and passage at the north end of the court of the workhouse. 1833 House with rooms, chambers and buildings lately erected and added thereto with the court, and a passage at the north end of the workhouse with stabling and outhouses. Robert Maunder, now deceased to John Drake, for the use of John Tuckett Will of John Drake, thatcher 1818
29 Cottage and outhouse Owned by Thomas Squire Occupied by Samuel Cockram	Jim Butt 20th lived in this cottage in the 20th century. It is now the garage block for Church Cottage
30 Cottage John Prior 31 Cottage John Prior 32 Cottage and outhouse John Prior All three now comprise Church Cottage block	1659 fireplace in 32 (west end of row) 2614A/PF13 1764 Trustees to William Maunder, cordwainer, a house on the north of the churchyard John and Richard Oliver. John aged 5, son of John and William 2, son of Richard, a messuage that was in the possession of William Maunder containing 3 ground rooms and 3 chambers and a wood house or stable at the north end of the said houses or ground rooms and a garden at the door. 1801 2614A/P F 16 1819 Trustees to John Stabback, yeoman, three tenements part of Haysland 1819 as above to Thomas Stabback on the lives of John Manley 10, Thomas Manley 7 and Abraham Hewish 6, 3 tenements with curtilages, gardens and appurtenances which are part of Hays land. And now in the possession of John Edworthy, Richard Mare and John Challis.

Three cottages let by the Trustees to Thomas Stabback for 99 years in 1819 for £70 determinable on three lives at a rent of 4/6d pa tenanted out to
John Elsworthy
William Stevens
John Challlis

2614A/P F 17
1837 Thomas Stabback, miller of Sandford to William Wotton of C F woolcomber
3 tenements with gardens in Haysland the Elsworthy, Mare and Challis and now in the possession of
William Elsworthy
William Stephen
Samuel Davie.

2614A/P F 18
1843 Trustees to John Wotton, three spots of ground adjoining the churchyard
lease on the lives of Edwin Wotton 13, Emma Wotton 11, Ellen Wotton 9. 3 spots or parcels of ground adjacent to the churchyard at the north from north to south 14 ft with a small parcel of ground joining towards the north 7 ft wide and 22 ft from east to west and a parcel on the east side 10 ft long and 8 ft wide now in the possession of John Wotton as tenant.

2614A/P F 18 P F 19
1880 surrender of leases to the Trustees from beneficiaries of William Wotton's will
3 tenements then in the possession of
John Edworthy
Richard Mare
John Challis, part of Haysland
demised to Thomas Stabback.

1876 C Greenslade paying £3 for Church cottage

33 Cottage and Garden 1 ¼ owned by William Wootton occupied by William Wotton and others	1674 inscribed on building 33 George Wootton paying £5.8s.0d 1925 the Trustees sold it for the first time to William Avery, tailor for the sum of £30
34 Cottage William Wotton (since made into a two storey extension to The Cottage in the Hayes) 35 Cottage William Wotton (now single storey store-room of the pub, widow but doorway blocked) 36 Cottage William Wotton (now single storey kitchen of the pub, window and doorway)	
37 Cottage, outhouse and garden John Bradford (This is the two storey house adjoining the pub on the southern side, now in the middle of the range of building and has a barn in its original garden opposite)	A house with small garden leased to John and Richard Oliver for 99 years in 1800 in consideration of £9 determinable on three lives (2 still living) for 1/- rent pa to Trustees
38 The Ring of Bells Owned by John and Mary Oliver Occupied by John Berry	1831 will of Richard Oliver left The Ring of Bells pub to his children John and Ann Oliver. It was built as a house in the 17th century when the Hayes was developed.
43 The Hayes lease held by Richard Hewish, John Hewish jnr and William Oliver from the Trustees.	The Hayes is still owned by the Trustees.
44 The Boot Inn owned by William Pitt snr, Occupied John Pike (now part Scut's almshouse and part, 'Hayes')	
45 Almshouse owned by Trustees of Scut's Charity, occupied by Susannah Ellis	Still owned by the Trustees.

46 Cottage and garden owned by Andrew Hewish and tenanted (modern day Hayes Cottage) 47 Cottage and garden owned and occupied by Grace Ridge (modern day Katharine Cottage)	Formerly three cottages with large garden in front sold by Andrew Hewish 1880 in occupation of James Prior, builder William Willis, police constable Susannah Snell Now called Hayes Cottage and Katherine Cottage
48 Cottage and garden Owned by Andrew Hewish and tenanted (modern day Rose Cottage) 49 Cottage and garden Owned by Andrew Hewish and tenanted (modern day April Cottage) 50 Cottage and garden Owned by Andrew Hewish and tenanted (modern day Bawn Cottage)	Cottage and garden occupied by Thomas Manley Cottage occupied by Samuel Oaten Cottage occupied by Mrs Sarah Snell All Sold by Andrew Hewish 1880 Jack Griffiths family bought April Cottage 1950s Fairchilds sold Rose Cottage to Griffiths 1958 and the garden was divided between the two May Frost lived in the cottage in 1950s that was later called Bawn Cottage by Molly Cotter, headmistress
206 Back Hayes Meadow owned and occupied by Andrew Hewish (a small part built on by Bluehayes bungalow) 207 Back Hayes garden owned and occupied by Andrew Hewish	Backhayes meadow – meadow used by James Prior 1880 Backhayes garden and outbuildings used by William Willis 1880

Other documents describe properties in the vicinity of The Hayes that are more difficult to identify:
Cottage in Churchtown leased for 99 years in 1794 (1) from William Harris of Keneggie, Cornwall to John Moxey in consideration of £7 determinable on three lives John b 1761, wife Ann and son John b 1785 (2 still living) for a rent of 1/- pa to Trustees
1764 House lying on the west side now converted into a stable and loft and garden behind the same, the whole being 23 foot long and 32 foot wide lying on the north side of the churchyard
1723 House John Cruwys lease and his wife Joan, Part of Church Hayes now in the ownership of John Rich and lately of John Taylor under a lease to John Crewis. He should repair it if waste, spoil or destruction …
1784 to Hockaday, a house many years since erected in a plot of ground south to north 15 feet with a small parcel of ground adjacent towards the north of 7 feet in depth and another parcel of ground on the east of the said house containing 10 feet long and 8 feet wide now in the possessions of the trustees

Leased for 99 years in 1784 to Richard Hockaday for 99 years in consideration of £10 determinable on three lives (one still living) at rent of 1/- pa to Trustees. In the occupation of Thomas Hockaday

An agreement for 99 years in 1806 to Thomas Tucker in consideration of £15.15s.0d. determinable on three lives at a rent of 1/- pa to the Trustees but no lease was executed in consequence of the tenant declining to bear the expense

Leased for 99 years in 1802 to Samuel Pridham and John Hewish in consideration of £96 determinable on three lives at a rent of 5/- pa to Trustees. In the occupation of Thomas Hosegood

References

1.   White's Devonshire Directory 1850 and STAC2/26/304 1509–1547
2.   Granville, Roger. History of the families of Radford and Hayne of Plymstock 1900
3.   History of Parliament online
4.   Report of the Commissioners concerning Charities…vol 3 1830
5.   Portrait held by the family of Vivien Allen
6.   A Chronological history of Abinger St James list of rectors
7.   Information from Wikipedia and other online sources
8.   A Chronological history of Abinger St James
9.   Colonel Pride refusing admission to the Presbyterian MPs – unknown engraving
10.   Will of John Harris of Hayne, Stowford 1656 2527M/W17

In the Poor House at Cheriton

Henry VIII's dissolution of the Monasteries 1538 to 1541 removed the main source of support for the poor and needy across the country, but with no religious houses in mid-Devon, Cheriton support would have been parochial from very early on with the Rector and his Churchwardens taking responsibility for parishioners who were unable to support themselves and required indoor or outdoor relief. Outdoor relief included rent, clothing, shoe-repairs and money for food and fuel, whilst indoor relief might involve paying for a child or invalid to be boarded out with a villager, or to be admitted to the Poor House itself.

An Act passed in 1601 formalised each parish's obligation to relieve its aged and infirm together with any un-protected children and adults who could not find employment. Parish Overseers of the Poor and Churchwardens were required to collect poor rates and allocate them fairly to the deserving poor. They also had to provide the raw materials for work e.g. wool, flax, cloth and gardening equipment and had to ensure that able-bodied people completed the tasks they were given.

Collection of the poor rates was done by the parish Overseers who were unpaid and elected annually by the parish vestry. In Cheriton there was a rotation from farm to farm in an attempt to make this fair to all. It was never a popular job as it was time consuming and carried a lot of responsibility and Overseer who did not carry out their duties effectively could be liable for a fine. In Cheriton it became the norm for landholders to pay one or two of their fellows who were good at the job to take their place for the year.

The Settlement Act of 1662 also known as the Poor Relief Act 1662 allowed for

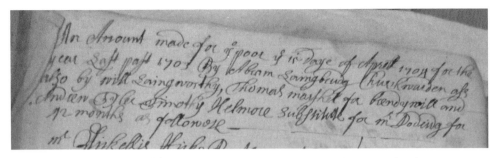

Andrew Tyler and Timothy Helmore were substitutes for Mr Doderidge
for a period of twelve months for the year 1703–4

relief to be tailored to those who had a right to live in the parish through birth, marriage and apprenticeship. If a pauper could not prove their right to settlement they were removed under supervision to the parish of their birth, or the place where they had a valid connection. Being off the beaten track, Cheriton had few itinerant beggars to contend with but with limited funds, the officials still sought to help only those with a rightful settlement in the parish. To make it easier to identify those who were entitled an Act was passed in 1697 requiring a "badge" of red or blue cloth to be worn on the right shoulder with an embroidered letter "P" and the initial of their parish. This certainly happened in the Cheriton Fitzpaine Poor House for a time:

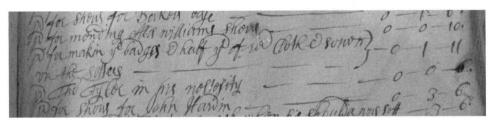

Paid for makin the badges and half yard of red cloth and sewen on the letters ...... 1/11d.

Between 20 and 35 pensioners lived in Cheriton's Poor House at any one time, housed in four dormitories on the upper level allowing for men, women, children and the sick to be separated at night. The day-time workrooms below were generally occupied by the women although a few children and frail older men would join them there for the work schedule whilst more able men and boys were taken out to work the land. Women in Cheriton were put to work knitting, sewing, spinning and brewing. An entry in the Cruwys Morchard

Overseers Accounts refers to purchasing 'six pounds of white wool of George Trull of Crediton at 4d. per pound' for spinning.

The Accounts for 1809–10 show that a 'spinning turn' required mending.

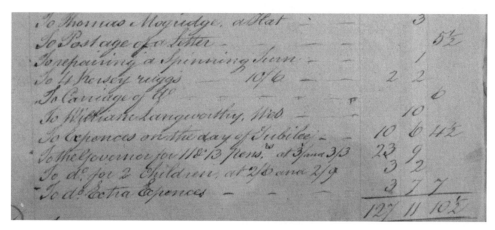

To repairing a spinning turn 1/-

Those who were too ill to work would be tended to in their dormitory with meagre food rations brought to them by other pensioners.

Men laboured mending bridges and filling in pot holes on the highway; preparing wattles and cob for building; ploughing, pruning, digging, sowing and harvesting in the fields.

Tower Hill Tenement

The Tower Hill Tenement was a parish holding with its own orchard and garden plot where fruit and vegetables could be grown to sell or be consumed in the Poor House. Whatever skills the male pensioners could be taught they would carry out either as external work to bring in a small wage for their keep in the House, or to maintain the fabric of the Poor House or other parish-held properties. Their lives revolved around long hours of physical work, eating, sleeping and attending church.

The outside courtyard together with the building labelled 26 formed the Poor House. In an attempt to show that the vestry room/school room was separate, it has been labelled 25, but in fact it only took up the space in an upper room in the central part of the Poor House and the Poor House operated beneath

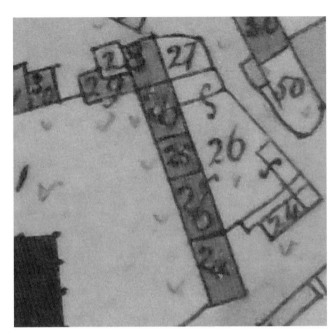

on the ground floor. An inventory made in the building listed a brewhouse, kitchen, dining room, work room, pantry, cellar and four wards as well as the council chamber, accompting house and store room. At either end the properties labelled 24 and 27 were dwellings let out by the parish to bring in an income, and sometimes pensioners were boarded out there with the lease-holders. There was at that time a very narrow entrance to The Hayes where there were two or three pumps and a set of four privies. A well has been capped under the forecourt of Scut's Almshouse, and the northern end of the long thatched Church House building has been demolished to widen the entrance to The Hayes and to form a little garden for Scut's.

The rules of the House were taken from a standard set adopted by both Sandford and Cruwys Morchard and included a system of punishment for those who told lies; those who failed to finish their tasks by supper time; those who feigned sickness or inability to work; those who made a disturbance; those who were insubordinate; those who were absent from church etc. In contrast there were obligations to provide inmates with two shirts or shifts – a clean one each week, tools for work and a small wage. Children in the house were to be taught civil behaviour and honest labour.

In Cheriton there was never a mention of punishments in the Accounts Books

12: Inmates to attend church with the Governor on every occasion if able.
13: Absence from church, or unsuitable behaviour on Sunday, to forfeit Monday's dinner; expulsion if incorrigible.
14: Inmates to have 1d in the shilling of the profits of their work 'as an encouragement of industry, provided it be not laid out on strong liquors'.
15: The Poor in Parish Pay to be given notice to bring themselves and their goods into the Workhouse; outdoor relief to be stopped except for cases mentioned above, or when Vestry allows this 'on very extraordinary occasions'.
16: Inmates to be able on request to make complaints privately to Inspector or Overseer.
17: Child inmates 'shall from time to time be taught to read and to repeat the Church Catechism by the Master and Mistress (i.e. the Governor or his wife) or by such of the Pensioners as are qualified thereto'.
18: Inmates to have 2 shirts or shifts each, and to have a clean one each week.
19: Tools etc. to be provided for employment of such Inmates as are able.
20: No alehouse to be kept near the Workhouse.
21: The Governor to enforce personal cleanliness and tidiness, and to see the children taught civil behavious and 'knitting, spinning, or other kinds of good and honest labour'.
22: No outsider 'except gentlemen and ladies' to enter the premises beyond the dining-room, or call to speak to the inmates, without leave.
23: No strong liquors to be brought in, or goods smuggled out.
24: Inmates making a disturbance to be 'sent to the Dark House' or lose meals.
25: Inmates 'forging or telling lies' to be set on a stool in the most public place in the dining-room whilst at dinner, and a paper fixed 'to his or her breast with these words wrote: Infamous Lyar, and likewise to lose that meal'.
26: Inmates not finishing their task by supper time to continue till finished.
27: Inmates feigning sickness or other inability to work to be taken before a magistrate for committment to Bridewell.
28: Insubordination to be reported to an Inspector, and magistrates asked to punish the incorrigible.

This extract has been written up by R R Sellman.[1] The Sandford version can be compared by looking in A Parish Patchwork by Daphne Munday.[2]

which shows that each parish could choose how they enforced the rules and ran their Workhouse.

Cruwys Morchard

Despite the rules and national guidance Workhouses in some parishes did suffer from a lack of good supervision. In nearby Cruwys Morchard for example the Governor of the Workhouse had to be dismissed for his unsavoury practises. These were brought to the attention by pensioners who at first complained about the Governor's dishonesty when buying and selling goods, and then about something far more bizarre. A letter dated December 1741 survives in the estate papers for the Cruwys family explaining that the parishioners had been uneasy about the management of the Workhouse for some time and had held a meeting to hear complaints. Most of the parishioners attended and emotions were running high. Amongst his many financial faults there was an accusation that the Governor had charged for five bushels of malt but only brewed four bushels. But far more bizarrely, it was also reported that he had kept a horse in the long room of the Workhouse building and when it grew sick, it made terrible groaning sounds which could be heard in the entire neighbourhood. The horse then died in the room and was left there to putrefy with the smell being so nauseous as to cause some of the paupers to be taken ill. The letter was written to Mr Samuel Cruwys esq, Lord of the Manor. The author of the letter, Richard Avery then tried to be helpful by suggesting that some of the parishioners were willing to have paupers boarded out with them, and because there were only fourteen pensioners, boarding them out at £4 per head would work out cheaper than the cost of buying provisions and employing a new Governor in the Workhouse. He listed the provisions as wheat, butter, cheese, peas and malt. Avery tried very diplomatically to offer his much respected Lord a reasonable resolution and this may well have softened the blow of the news and made sure that the villagers were taken seriously.[3]

In the previous year, 1740 the Overseers Accounts indicate that the Governor at the time was called Richard Manly. The Governor was, quite rightly, dismissed for embezzlement and neglect in 1741.

When things got back to some normality at Cruwys Morchard Workhouse Mr Cruwys made amends by gifting an orchard plot to the pensioners so that they could grow produce for themselves, provided that they did not damage the apple and fruit trees growing there.

Cadbury

In contrast, at Cadbury where there was a small, well-run Workhouse, the Governors went to great lengths to care for their poor. The winter weather in 1775–6 was particularly harsh and an entry shows that extra cloaks and blankets were made for the inmates and a substantial sum of £1.19s.4d, was given away to the poor to help them out. In January and February the River Thames was frozen over and people wrote about 'The Great Frost' and the prolonged severe cold. In Devon there were deep snow drifts, farm land was hidden for weeks and many

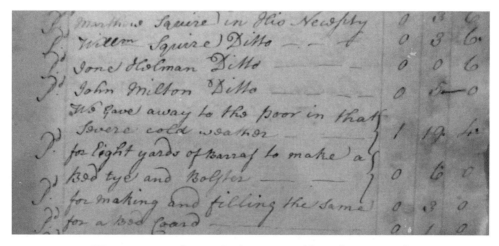

We gave away to the poor in that severe cold weather £1.19s.4d.
Cadbury Overseers Accounts 1775–6[4]

animals suffered. Parishioners would have needed copious amounts of firewood
to keep themselves warm.

As well as collecting rates from those who owned property and rents from those
living in parish-held cottages, Overseers looked for additional ways to defray their
costs. Produce and hand-made goods were of course sold to the public but when
a person was admitted as a pensioner, their household goods were confiscated
and either auctioned off or used within the House. When a pensioner died, their
clothing could also be sold off. Such sales or auctions were called 'surveys' and
there is a good example of one in the Cadbury Accounts when shirts, breeches, a
pair of buckles, a silk napting, a frockcoat and waistcoat, a coat, a hat and lengths
of cloth and fustian belonging to Absalom Escott were auctioned off in 1765.

Absalom was buried at Cadbury in August 1765. He had been lodged by John
Sharland at a cost of 4/- and tended to in his sickness by John Thomas at a cost
of 3/. Mary Ears and Grace Bass had laid him forth and money was spent on his
coffin, grave and shroud and for ringing the bells at his funeral. Roger Matthew
mended his coat for 6d. so that it could be sold off. Altogether the Overseers
costs for Absalom came to £1.5s.6d. and their income from his sale of clothing
amounted to £1.14s.1d. It was a good effort to balance the books.

Generally household effects were 'taken' by Officials when a pauper was
admitted to the Workhouse and their existing clothing was put into the general
stock. If anything of value was left at the time of their death, it was auctioned off

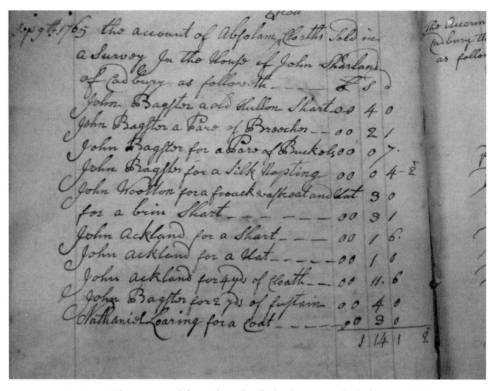

£1.14s.1½d. was raised from the sale of Absalom Escott's clothing in 1765

in the village, and because Absalom's clothing appears to be of a higher quality than normal, the sale took place soon after his death.

At Cruwys Morchard a 1756 entry records that 'John Weeks and his wife shall be admitted in the workhouse on Wednesday next provided he shall deliver up to the Overseers what goods and chattles he hath a right to.'

The Cheriton Accounts for 1725 reveal that Richard Manley had just died and his clothes were washed with soap so that they could be re-distributed.

Paid to John Manley for bringing home the widow Miller's goods and putting them up 2s.6d.

There was also a responsibility to educate children who came into the Poor House. It was usual for any pensioner who had a little reading and writing themselves to school the children but this was very sporadic and of poor quality. There was a bequest that enabled one child to be properly educated and this was used to pay for someone to run small classes, but in the case of William Maunder in the extract below, he had multiple jobs including delivering fish and was not qualified. Many years later a qualified teacher was employed. The vestry room and the room above the Parvis in the church were used for this purpose. There is to this day a copious amount of graffiti on the walls of the Parvis where young men have written their names and added dates.

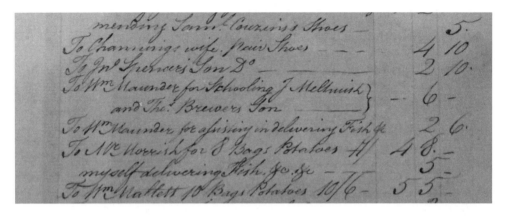

To William Maunder for schooling J Melhuish and Thomas Brewer's son 6/-

To William Maunder for assisting in delivering fish etc 2s.6d.

To Mr Morrish for 8 bags potatoes £4.8s.0d

Myself for delivering fish etc 5/-…

The 'quart of yeast' would have been used for brewing beer and the 'pound of treacle' and 'quarter brimstone' were a purgative mixture to avoid constipation. The Governess (wife of the Governor, not teacher) was supplied with tea, possibly as part of her wages.

The menu for a week was laid out in the Cheriton Accounts and looks sparse for someone working all day in the fields, but in reality it was at least a guaranteed regular ration of food and drink.

Monday breakfast: broth, 4oz bread, 1 oz cheese

Monday lunch: 1 oz suet, 12oz pudding, 1 pint beer

Monday supper: 1 pint milk, 4oz bread, 1½oz butter

Tuesday breakfast: 1 pint milk, 4oz bread, ½oz butter

Tuesday lunch: a sheep's head and hange between five, 4 oz bread, 1 pint beer

Tuesday supper: broth, 4oz bread, ½oz cheese

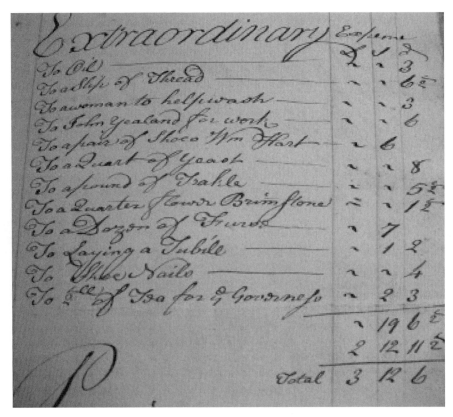

Provisions in the Poor House.

Wednesday breakfast: broth, 4 z bread, ½ butter

Wednesday lunch: 1 pint flour milk, 4oz bread

Wednesday supper: 4 oz bread, 2 oz cheese, 1 pint beer

Thursday breakfast: 1 pint milk, 4 oz bread, ½oz butter

Thursday lunch: 8oz beef or mutton, 4 oz bread, 1 pint beer, garden stuff

Thursday supper: broth, 4oz bread, 1oz cheese

Friday breakfast: broth, 4oz bread, 1oz cheese

Friday lunch: 1 pint flour milk, 4oz bread

Friday supper: 4oz bread, 2oz cheese, 1 pint milk

Saturday breakfast: 1 pint milk, 4 oz bread, ½oz butter

Saturday lunch: 1oz butter, 4 oz bread, 1 pint pease, 1 pint beer

Saturday supper: 4oz bread, 2oz cheese, 1 pint beer

Sunday breakfast: 4oz bread, 2oz cheese, 1 pint beer

Sunday lunch: 8oz beef or mutton, 4oz bread, 1 pint beer, garden stuff

Sunday supper: broth, 4oz bread, 1oz cheese.

The flour and milk mixture was obviously supposed to line the stomach and make the milk go further, and the distinct lack of vegetables would have led to problems long term if the Governor had followed the rules by the letter of the law. In a country parish however there were opportunities to eat fallen fruit and glean discarded vegetables in the fields during the course of the working day and pick blackberries from the hedgerows on the journey there and back. The regime in Cheriton was certainly not a punitive one.

On their limited diet in 1720 pensioners were sent out to help Aaron Phillips who had been employed to pave 175 yards of 'parsonage causeway', shifting sixteen seams of stones for the outside of the causeway and ninety six seams of stones to pave the causeway itself. A seam was generally a cart-load. Phillips was paid 14s.10d. to cover his own cost and to pay for the materials and their portage.

By 1784 the inmates' diet had improved a little and included bacon, turnips, carrots, potatoes and cabbage; and by 1800 there was veal, currants, lump-sugar, rice and beans. In 1801–2 Mr Anstey was paid £3.10s.0d. for seven bushels of barley and £2.14s.0d. for three barrels of 'sardinia fish'.

At Christmas time each year a swine hog was killed and roasted for the pensioners to enjoy and the church bells were rung to celebrate. It appears that the pensioners kept and fattened their own pig in later years because there is an entry in the Accounts explaining that James Pridham, mason was employed at a cost of £1.4s.3d. to make a hog sty in 1808.

The Overseers showed a real entrepreneurial spirit at one stage by becoming middle-men, buying in sacks of potatoes from local farmers and taking them to market to sell for a profit. They did the same with fresh fish from the local river and ponds, paying locals a small sum for their catch and taking the fish to markets in Crediton, Exeter and Tiverton. By doing this they were able to bring in a considerable income for the Poor House, after being paid their own expenses:

8 bags of potatoes @ 10-6d per bag £4.4s.0d.

20 bags of potatoes @11d per bag £11

To Rev Mr Arundell 33 bags @ 10/6d per bag £17.6s.6d.

Mr Morrish for 8 bags of potatoes £4.8s.0d.

William Mallett for 10 bags of potatoes £5.5s.0d.

Myself for delivering fish etc. 5/-.

Numerous entries in the Overseers' Accounts record payments to the cobbler for shoes and boots and for tapping and mending the same. There are also many entries for bolsters and blankets and for bed-tyes, which were the ropes strung back and forth across a wooden bed frame to create a sprung surface upon which to place a mattress. These often needed tightening as they sagged with use (hence the expression 'sleep tight') but when they eventually frayed and gave way the whole frame would need re-stringing.

Other less frequent entries show what special care was taken over some pensioners in the parish.

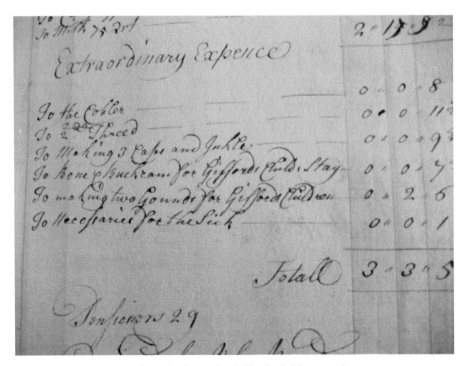

To bone buckram for Gifford's child's stay 7d.

121

One of Gifford's children required some sort of stay, possibly a leg or back calliper made from buckram which was a stiff cotton or linen fabric. There are several mentions of this stay which might have needed adjustments to allow for growth or just because it wore out quickly. The mention of 3 capes and 'inkle' refer to a linen tape used for lacing clothing together. On occasion baby clothes were made for a new baby in the Poor House and described as 'little clothes' for an infant. Other interesting entries list expenses for:

6 handkerchiefs for the poor of the House 8/-

90 ells of ticklenburgh @18¾d and 36 yards of seal canvas @14d. per yard £8.18s.0d. Both of these were course, hard-wearing types of cloth.

The case of the Labdon family in Cheriton Fitzpaine Poor House

In the summer of 1773 John Labdon fell ill and being no longer able to work he was admitted as a pensioner. In December his two youngest daughters had to join him because the extended family was no longer able to look after them. Parish registers show that their mother Mary Labdon (nee Crook) had died in February that same year having been married to John for fifteen years and given birth to William 1759, Hannah 1761, Joseph 1764, Mary 1767, John 1769 and Sarah 1772 and it seems possible that she died as a result of complications after Sarah's delivery. With their father failing, one imagines that the older children in the family did their best to care for six year old Mary and baby Sarah but were left with no alternative but to approach the Overseers of the Poor for support. Almost as soon as she was admitted little Mary was bound out in a parish apprenticeship which was far younger than was the custom in the village. Brother Joseph was nine years old when he lost both parents, but against the odds he did well for himself, staying out of the Poor House by working for his board and lodgings in the parish; completing an apprenticeship on the land; meeting and marrying Elizabeth Comins in 1788, and producing and bringing up a family of his own. His poor start in life had not damaged either his ambition or his health and in the 1841 census he is listed at the age of seventy seven, living with his son George Labdon who was a foreman tanner for Mr Sharland at Upham – a prestigious job. After such a difficult early life it is surprising that Joseph Labdon lived until his eighty second year.

Historically the Labdons came from poor stock and can often be found receiving parish relief in Cheriton although there were one of two members of the family who held small parcels of land in the 17th century.

The fate of Cheriton Poor House

After 1834 Great Reform Act there was no longer any need for the Poor House at Cheriton and all those requiring support were taken the five miles to Crediton to be admitted to the new Union Workhouse at the western end of the town. Crediton Poor Law Union formally came into existence on 19th April 1836. Its operation was overseen by an elected Board of Guardians, 34 in number, representing its 29 constituent parishes as listed below:

Bow or Nymnet Tracey, Brushford, Chawleigh, Coldridge, Cheriton Bishop, Clanaborough, Cheriton Fitzpaine, Colebrooke, Crediton, Down St Mary, Eggesford, Hittisleigh, Kennerleigh, Lapford, Morchard Bishop, Newton St Cyres, Nymet Rawland, Poughill, Puddington, Sandford, Stockleigh Pomeroy, Stockleigh English, Shobrooke, Thelbridge, Upton Hellions, Wembworthy, Washford Pine, Woolfardisworthy, Zeal Monachorum.

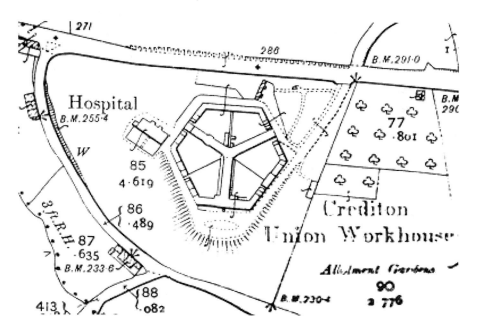

Because of their size some parishes were entitled to more than one Guardian to represent them on the board so Crediton had four and Morchard Bishop and Sandford, two.

Designed by Sampson Kempthorne who was also the architect for other Devon workhouses the Union Workhouse was intended to accommodate 300 inmates. The Poor Law Commissioners authorised the sum of £6,500 on its construction.

The existence of the new Crediton Union Workhouse meant that after 1837 the poorhouse in the village was redundant and it was let for 14 years to Thomas Sharland for the sum of £6.15s.0d. per anum. The goods in the workhouse were sold for £8 and the workhouse section itself was put up for sale. The buyer had instructions to wall up the doorway leading to the churchyard with stone and other such materials as the wall was built of, indicating that there was an original ground floor door to the churchyard, and to stop the two doorways leading to the Vestry room. This upper room was be retained for Vestry meetings, accessed via the external stone stairway. Church Path was then altered 'leading through the folly' and the new tenant was instructed to 'repair and plaster the whole of the wall adjacent to the churchyard on the churchyard side with good lime and hair mortar and white wash.' He was to do the same 'in a good workmanlike manner'. The Folly is the name given to the jettied walkway at the southern end of the The Old School.

It seems that the leases on the two cottages at either end of the building were left to run their course and villagers lived in them for some years afterwards. The one to the north was partially demolished later on in order to allow easier vehicular access to The Hayes and the remaining portion was subsumed into Church House. Its courtyard and garden also disappeared, but a small portion of the plot was given as a garden for the tenants of Scutt's almshouse, directly opposite its front door. An alleyway into the churchyard was walled up and this can still be seen between the Old School and the garage to Church Cottage.

After a School Board was set up in 1875 the whole building was used as the village school until the new building near White's Cross opened its doors in November 2010.

Strangers in the village

Strangers were warned off officially in 1731, 1738, 1741, 1745 although one off payments for maintenance were given to passing soldier and to sailors.

1737 for a warrant to warn out the strangers 6d.

For a warrant for Pinhoe and carrying him there 2s.6d.

A journey and expenses for carrying James Morrish and family to Pinhoe 3s.9d.

1749 to several passengers 3/6d, paid when the official pleased ignorance to a resolution passed that money would not be handed out in such circumstances

1753 a traveller with a lawful pass 1/-

1765 to 3 sailors not agreeable to the resolution of 1749 1s.6d. which is passed without apparent objection.

Maintenance of buildings in the parish

The parish certainly owned other properties in the village that were used as affordable homes for the poor and there are references to rental collected from them and repairs carried out upon them.

1692 John Moxey for 70 knitches of reeds for Roger Mandly's house 12/-

1711 plastering Thomas Fursdon's chimney 2/6d

1717 For a hatch for widow Mares house 1/-

Glazier for 9 foot of glass for the houses where John Taylor and the widow Mare now live 4s.1d.

128 kneeches of reed 18/- 6 bundles of spars 3/- to Francis Kerslake for laying the reed 8s.10d.

6 foot of board and keels and nails about John Taylors chamber 2s.6d.

1719 Robert Brewer for 6 days work about widow Mare's chimney and plastering in William Taylor's house 8/-

3 men to attend Robert Brewer 4 days 12/-

A horse to carry water 3 days 2/-

For tables to put on the chimney 6d.

For straw for the chimney 2/-

1729 for a lock and key for James Roberts chamber 1/-

For a plate and nails to keep in the shutter 2d.

For board staples and nails and for setting the same and for mending the planching 2/-

1737 for righting the lock and staple on the door where John Hart lives 5d.

1733 300 of reed to lie on the almshouses 14/- 100 reeds for the almshouses 14/- etc.

5 days labour about the almshouses 6s.8d.

7 days labour about the almshouses 10/-

1739 John Manley and Roger Hoxland's man for 6 days work in erecting a pair of stairs and other work about late Manley's house 6s.8d.

For board about the same 2s.3½d.

1740 'that posts be placed at each end and at the middle of the causeway before the house to keep off horses and carriages, as formerly' most likely this is outside the row of 6 almshouses in the east of the village opposite the current village hall.

1741 Thomas Taylor for 2 days work on Smiths House 2s.8d.

80 sheaves of reed 5/- 3 bundles of spars 1s.6d.

John Manley for work and nails about Mary Mare's house 7d.

1744 to John Manly for righting Joan Davey's hatch 1/-

John Drake for thatching on Smith's house 6s.6d.

1752 Thomas Mogridge for 60 sheaves of reed for Smith's House 8/6d.

John Drake for thatching 6/- and spars 2/-

1753 Thomas Glanvill for making the hooks and twists and staple and righting the lock and hatch and nails for Andrew Manley's door 2s.3d.

John Brewer for 7 days work about Andrew Manleys house and a labour for one day 30s.4d.

Mr Hewish for stone and other things used about Andrew Manley's house and by his bill appears 5s.6d.

John Gervice for work done 16s.4d.

Roger Hoxland for timber and for work done about Andrew Manley's house 33s.8½d

1801 James Pridham jnr. For repairing the house at Tower Hill 3s.8d.

For glazing the parish house at Tower Hill 9s.6d.

William Pope for new window for the parish house

John Manley for putting a rafter to his house 6d.

Highways and bridges in the village needed maintenance:

1693/4 for repairing Coddiford Bridge £1.13s.6d.

Mending the parish tools concerning the highways 4s.8d.

1710 for timber and putting up the bridge at the lower end of Perry Green 5/-

1716 stakes for Philip Whidons bridge 1s.6d.

But by far the most expenditure however was for the upkeep and alteration of Church house itself, including the school chamber.

In 1753 a meeting agreed that Joseph Pope would be the principal carpenter for the project and John Rowe the principal mason. Local Raddon stone was used and large quantities of oak, and elm, and thatching materials were needed.

1711 for reed to lay on the church house 3/- 6 bundles of spars 3/- to the thatcher to lay the reed 5s.4d. his tender 4 days 4/-

1716 290 kneeches of reed £2.3s.6d. 16 bundles of spars 8/- laying the reeds 31.0s.4d.

1717 60 kneeches of reeds for the church house 9s.7d. 4 bundles of spars and nails and binders 2/6d/ thatcher and his tender 2 days 4s.8d.

Glazier for mending the school chamber windows and the little chamber window adjoining 4/-

15 ft of plank for the school chamber 5/-

Timber and labour about the school chamber stairs 2s.6d. for the school chamber stairs …

For mending the church house windows and threshold 3/-

80 ft of board to lay the chamber over the house the widow Mare now lives in

Carpenter for 2 days work and for nails to lay the board 3/0½d.

1719 40 kneeches of reeds 5/8d. 3 bundles of spars 1s.6d. laying reed 3/-

For leent of a ladder 4d.

For carriage and recaring the ladder 3d.

2 stocks of oak timber for the church house chamber 15/-

1 stock of ash timber 5/-

For drawing aforesaid timber 5/-

For spars and nails 2/3d.

1729 For a lock and key for the school chamber door 1s.1d.

1737 Mr Collins for 'coullering' the windows of the church house and chambers 12/-

Samuel Phillips for breasting it up against the church house wall and paving and guttering 5s.8d.

For carrying lime from one church ouse to another 3/-

1742 John Manley for digging the pit in the Hayes 3/-

John Manley for digging in the Hayes 1/-

1743 for glazing the parish house 6s.6d.

1753 3 yds of sail cloth for the furnace 2/7d. halfpenny

George Wootton for cleaning the Pump Pit 2 days 3/-

For outscales? And posts about the pump pit

To helping up the beams in the brewhouse 1/-

For sawing timber for the linhay 15s.3d.

A lock for the cupboard over the desk 1/-

John Manley for making a new form and other work in the school house chamber

1754 removing a coffer into the store room and the pump trough in its place 1/-

1801 James Pridham snr for making the oven and other work £2.7s.10d.

1804 John Hodgeland for labour about the poor house 4/-

For timber used about the poor house 12s.6d.

References

1. Sellman, R R. Cheriton Fitzpaine: Notes from the parish records and other sources 1978
2. Munday, D. A Parish Patchwork – Sandford and Upton Hellions 1985
3. Cruwys Morchard parish records
4. Cadbury Overseers of the Poor Accounts

Apprenticeship and Humphrey Winter

U nder the Settlement Act of 1662 an apprentice took settlement from his place of apprenticeship. It was therefore attractive for officials to place an apprentice in a different parish which would then have to take responsibility should he or she later become a charge on the poor rate.[1] Pauper apprentices did not usually learn highly skilled trades, instead, the boys would be taught "husbandry" and the girls "housewifery" so in effect labourers and household servants.

This drawing on the edge of a map of Fords Farm, Twyford in Shropshire dates from 1797. It depicts the harvest being gathered, cart-horses watered, pigs fed, and a cow milked. Apprentices would have been taught many skills on the farm.

The Parish Apprentices Act of 1698 reduced the allowable age of entry to seven years.[2] An apprenticeship normally lasted until the apprentice was twenty four if male and if female, twenty one or until married. Apprenticeship was the subject of a legal agreement or indenture and usually involved the paying of a premium to the master who would also provide the apprentice with board and lodging for the period of the apprenticeship. The apprenticeship system could be used by parishes to remove poor children from the Workhouse in order to unburden the rate-payers from supporting them, both in the short and long-term.

Some parishes prevailed upon their own rate-payers to take a pauper child for at least a year, or else face a £10 penalty. Sometimes, children were assigned by a lottery and such impositions were often extremely unpopular, with many householders who preferred to pay the fine rather than having to take in a poor and possibly weakly child. When a child was received reluctantly, the chances were that he or she risked being overworked and poorly treated.

A more common approach was to offer a premium of up to £10 to anyone willing to take on a pauper child for a set period, typically seven years, giving him or her the skills needed to find work in later life. In Cheriton the vast majority of apprenticeships were for husbandry on the farm. Boys would learn every aspect of agriculture and animal management, much of it hard, physical labour. Girls in the countryside would not just be taught cleaning, cooking and washing, for a farm-woman's work also involved raising chickens, geese and ducks; milking cows and goats; cheese-making; tending pigs and horses; curing meat; tending the kitchen garden; running errands and a host of other duties. At busy times they were also deployed in the fields, sowing seeds, harvesting, gathering fruit crops and gleaning cut corn.

Apprentices were generally bound out for their entire youth and if they absconded there were harsh punishments, not least being brought back to work for the same master from whom they had escaped, who no doubt treated them with less respect than before. There were few prospects for a young person at the end of an apprenticeship, and if paid labour was not needed, many would end up begging for their food or stealing. One example close to home was Robert Currell who had completed his time with William Upham in Cadbury and travelled to Exeter to look for employment. He ended up wandering the streets of Exeter, where he was picked up as a vagrant and examined by officials who decided upon his fate:

'… let him be whipped and sent by pass to Cadbury.' Midsummer 1774.[3]

When he got to Cadbury however he was removed to Cruwys Morchard being the place where he was last settled. Cadbury officials were so anxious to get rid of him that they gave half a guinea for his maintenance.

In Cheriton there are many instances of apprentices continuing to live and work in the parish as paid adults. With so many successful farms in the area it appears that there was a constant demand for labour. In 1773 Daniel Tremlett of Upcott Barton took on a poor child called William Lamacroft 'with him to dwell and serve from the day of the date of these presents, until the said Apprentice shall accomplish his full age of twenty four years … during which term he his said Master shall serve in all lawful business, according to his power, wit and ability. That the said Daniel Tremlett the said apprentice in husbandry shall teach and instruct during the said term, and shall and will, during the term aforesaid, find, provide and allow unto the said apprentice, meet and competent and sufficient meat and drink and apparel, lodging, washing and all other things necessary and fit for an apprentice.' (Apprenticeship indenture in private hands)

Lamacroft did serve out his allotted time with Tremlett but there was no paid work for him after that and he spent the next few years hiring himself out to farmers in Thorveton, Kenn, Kenton and Alphington.

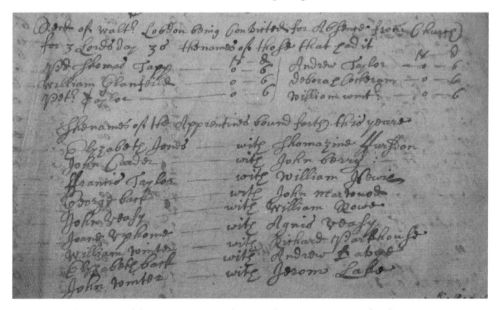

Overseers of the Poor Accounts for 1678 listing apprentices for that year

A list of apprentices bound out in Cheriton in 1678 shows three girls and six boys with two of the farmers listed being widows, Thomasin Fursdon and Agnes Veasy. The youngest child to be found in the apprenticeship records for the parish was only six years old and the oldest, twelve.

Included in this list are two children from the Winter family, William who was to work for Richard Parkhouse on northside and John who went to live and work for Jerome Lake.[4]

But there is was one member of the Winter family who was taken into the Poor House when orphaned but never bound out to be an apprentice. Curiously, he lived for the rest of his life in the Poor House, dying at the age of fifty eight.

The case of Humphrey Winter

Humphrey Winter was baptised in the village in February 1687 just 2 days after his father Thomas Winter married Mary Lee, ensuring that the boy would not be labelled a 'base child' in the registers. When Humphrey was five years old his father was buried in woollen at the expense of the parish and his widowed mother Mary struggled to keep her two sons fed and clothed. She died in 1700, leaving Humphrey, aged thirteen and William aged ten. Traditionally, the boys would have become the responsibility of other family members, but their Uncle Stephen Winter was not a healthy man and was by then in the Poor House having first received charity money in 1680 and then, when sick, in 1681. He too passed away in 1700 and was buried in woollen at parish expense. His widow Mable Winter pre-deceased him in 1699. Humphrey and William had no family left to care for them and parish officials met to discuss their future. Entries in the Accounts that year show that William was bound out in a parish apprenticeship but that Humphrey was boarded out in the village with a William Smith. There are expenses in 1702 for 'Winter's boy' and in 1703 for 'a shirt for Humphrey Winter and 13 months 3 weeks of care, costing £3.15s.7½d'. At the age of thirteen for some reason Humphrey was not considered to be a suitable candidate for apprenticeship. This was extremely unusual because his on-going presence as a non-earning pensioner in the poorhouse would demand a huge financial investment. There was no explanation given for the fact that, given his age, he was not bound out in an apprenticeship.

Humphrey Winter lived in the Poor House, receiving parish relief from the age of thirteen until the very end of his life. He died aged 58 in 1745 having lived there for almost 45 years. He must have been quite seriously incapacitated.

An entry in the Accounts for 1707 indicates that the twenty year old was being boarded out in a dwelling next door to the Poor House, and was not able to look after his personal needs:

'1707 to Elizabeth Glandfill for washing and lodging Humphrey Winter 3 months @ 6d. per week.'

Later he was transferred into the Poor House and entries in the Accounts over many years record that he was provided with shoes, stockings, bedding, clothing, a coat with buttons, a suit, a hat and other necessary things e.g.

1728 For a pair of shoes 3s.10d. for tapping and mending shoes twice, 1s.4d. for a pair of stockings 1s.1d.

for 7½ yards of cloth to make Humphrey Winter a suit of clothes @ 1s.8d. per yard, making buttons, tape and lining 18/-

for mending Humphrey Winter's clothes 1/-.

In fact, Humphrey's need for shoes and repairs to his shoes (tapping), far outstrips that of any other pensioner over the years. This offers a clue as to his condition for he must have been physically active – perhaps pacing to and fro or scuffing his feet repeatedly. The amount of wear and tear on his shoes and boots bears no relationship to the nature of work he would have undertaken as an inmate either in the workroom or out in the fields. One wonders whether he was on the autistic spectrum, repeating movements over and over again. He certainly posed no threats to other pensioners and was never reported as a violent person needing restraint. The parish took great care of him for most of his life, feeding, clothing and keeping him safe. The fact that he lived to the age of fifty eight is testament to the care he must have been given. As a well-known resident it is a little sad that no extra effort was taken over his funeral however: no bells, no pall bearers, no refreshments, no footnote in the accounts.

Humphrey's younger brother William Winter 1690 completed his apprenticeship, survived poverty, married Jane and had six children baptised in nearby Cruwys Morchard. Three of these children died young – John at six days in 1724, Elizabeth at one month in 1732 and Mary at fourteen years in 1739. There were other premature deaths in the family for Humphrey's cousin Elizabeth 1697 died aged two years, another cousins Joane 1690 died aged one, and another, Abigail Winter 1673 died aged one year. This family was poor but this represents an unusually high instance of infant mortality in the parish and seems to have been confined to the Winter family. Tracing back through their shared ancestors, four of the children were descended from Thomas Winter 1663 and two from Stephen Winter his brother. Taking Humphrey's incapacity into account as part of this unusual pattern, there may well have been a genetic factor playing its part in the fate of the family.

What happened to William and John Winter who were bound out as apprentices in 1678?

It is not certain who young William Winter was but John was the son of Stephen Winter, Humphrey's uncle. Stephen and a William Winter snr received 1/- each in 1680 as part of 'Mrs Murgings money', designed to help out the secondary poor in the parish. On Mrs Mary Murging's death her relatives had refused, or omitted to bury her in woollen. This practice was introduced in order to bolster up the woollen industry in 1666 with an Act passed, 'for the lessening the importation of linen from beyond the seas, and the encouragement of the woollen and paper manufacturer of the kingdom.' (18 & 19 Cha.II c.4 1666). An additional Act was passed in 1678 (30 Car.II cap.3). The Act required that when a corpse was buried it should only be dressed in a shroud or garments made of wool:

> "No corpse of any person (except those who shall die of the plague) shall be buried in any shift, sheet, or shroud, or anything whatsoever made or mingled with flax, hemp, silk, hair, gold, or silver, or in any stuff, or thing, other than what is made of sheep's wool only."[5]

A sworn affidavit was presented to officials to show that a body had been wrapped in woollen before burial and in Cheriton these are copied into the Overseers of the Poor Account books. This has been a godsend to researchers, being a duplicate recording of the deaths of those people whose names were entered into a burial register that has since been lost. In some parishes the affidavits, written on pieces of paper and stored in the parish chest were not copied into the Accounts and information has therefore not survived.

A fine of £5 was levied on those who failed to comply with the Act, and to ensure that cases were reported, one half of the money was given to the informant whilst the other half was distributed to the poor of the parish. Technically the affidavit had to be presented within eight days of the burial but there are a few examples in Cheriton of 'late' affidavits that were never-the-less accepted. Some people wanted to be buried in their best clothes rather than a woollen shroud and they opted for the £5 fine. This may be true of Mary Murging in 1680. Her money went a long way towards helping the poor in the parish when it was distributed to forty four people that year.

References

1. Poor Relief Act 1662 (14Car2c12) also known as the Settlement Act or the Settlement and Removal Act
2. Overseers of the Poor Accounts for Cheriton Fitzpaine 1698
3. Quarter Sessions records for Cadbury 1774
4. Overseers of the Poor Accounts for Cheriton Fitzpaine 1678
5. Burial in woollen commenced as a result of the Act 18 and 19 Cha.IIc.4 1666 and additional Act 30 Car.II cap3 1678

Illegitimacy and Life Chances in Cheriton Fitzpaine

'Between 1500 and 1700 it was the community of neighbours who's influence on and control over family life had been of the greatest importance,' but there was 'a growing interference by Church authorities, supported by neighbours and parish officials ...' 'Domestic life in the village was conducted in a blaze of publicity.' Lawrence Stone.[1]

It would be interesting to see how the Cheriton Fitzpaine church and community responded to illegitimacy in the past, and to follow both mothers and babies throughout their lives to discover how they were affected by their status. Were girls able to find husbands in the future? Did they continue to be dependent upon parish relief? Were the children accepted in the community? Did they have the same chances as their legitimate peers? Did they grow up to marry or did they continue the cycle of illegitimacy?

In some rural areas it was a common practice to test out the fertility of a girl prior to marriage in order to ensure that she was capable of producing children, specifically males, who could undertake agricultural work and help to secure a fair standard of living in the future. Routinely, very young children were able to supplement their parents' income by labouring for others or undertaking a range of husbandry and cottage industry tasks at home. Parents, who themselves supported grandparents and other elderly relatives when they were too infirm to bring in a wage of their own, expected the same in their own old age. It was imperative therefore to produce a brood of children to ensure a reasonable level of subsistence in future years. Parish relief was always available for the deserving poor, but generally, extended families did their utmost to be self-sufficient. In close communities like Cheriton neighbours shared with each other when they could spare food and manpower, knowing that any one of them could fall upon hard times through accident, illness, the death of a provider, failure of a crop, or disease amongst their stock. Cheriton had developed a strong sense of community over time and villagers were used to pulling together to survive. All children, legitimate or not, were seen as essential for continuing the cycle of life in this rural area.

Because it was a close-knit parish with the church at its core, all young people would have been well known to the vicar and all families would have attended church regularly, standing together for Sunday worship and listening to the rector's sermons. Cheriton was unusual in the region for holding twelve communion services a year rather than four, and two services on Sundays each with a sermon.[2] Addresses to the congregation would have promoted morality and honesty, but they would also have carried the message of love, tolerance and forgiveness. Any rural cleric living amongst his farming flock would have recognised the tight support networks already in existence and the strong spirit of co-operation that existed during times of famine and plenty. Within the farming community, even now, there are unwritten rules about helping out a neighbour come what may, pulling together, lending man-power and equipment, looking out for each other, and laying personal opinions to one side. The vagaries of the weather and the threats to stock were enemy enough for most men labouring on the land. Of course there would be whispers about Walter being a poor husbandman and letting his pigs wander along the lanes; about Richard failing to maintain his fencing; Thomas not trimming hedges on the bridleway and William refusing to fill in the pot-holes on the highway, but there was a deeply ingrained loyalty between the men that was not easily challenged. Because agricultural families in the 18th and 19th centuries needed man-power to bring in the crops, plough and harrow the fields and tend the stock, children were vital for survival. The poor provided an effective workforce. Procreation was more important to most than questions of legitimacy. With few personal possessions and little or no land or property to pass on, there was no importance attached to being a legitimate son and heir and the relatively small numbers of children who were born out of wedlock were comfortably absorbed into the community.

There are several instances of Cheriton girls marrying less than nine months before the birth of a child, but the majority of them were no younger than twenty years old, indicating that they were probably entering into a consensual relationship with the father rather than being taken advantage of. The tradition of testing out fertility may hold true for Cheriton but it might also point towards sexual ignorance once couples were courting.

Illegitimate births were not formally recorded in England prior to civil registration in 1837, leaving rectors free to use their own wording in baptismal registers. Some employed the term 'bastard child of …' whilst others adopted the words 'base child of …' To our sensibilities the former sounds far more pejorative and the latter less judgemental, but whatever the case at the time, unmarried mothers presenting their children for baptism were not turned away. Having an illegitimate child baptised at the local church was not a legal requirement, so there were children who never had their names recorded until their marriage or death, but many mothers did choose to take their babies to be baptised. It might have been because their child was sickly and they wanted to secure a Christian burial in the event of a premature death; or because they held traditional views about being 'churched'; or there was pressure from their immediate families to conform; or because future employers preferred apprentices who were baptised. In Cheriton there appears to have been little or no stigma attached to presenting

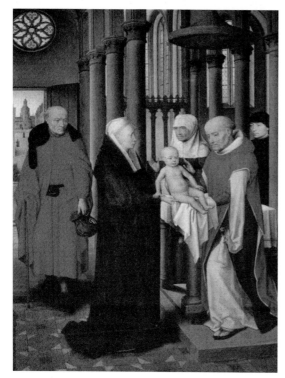

Churching a mother and child, Hans Memling (circa 1433–1494)[3]

a base child for baptism, and each one was welcomed into the congregation as readily as its peers.

Churching was a ceremony that took place when the woman was fit enough to leave home and go to the church to offer thanks for survival and to receive a blessing. After churching a mother was expected to re-join weekly worship with the rest of the congregation.

Couples who married whilst pregnant in Cheriton stayed together and produced more children until one or other of them died. Surviving widowers, especially if they had a small-holding were very likely to marry for a second or even third time, fulfilling the need for a wife not only to care for the house and children, but also to manage poultry, gardening and dairy production. Surviving widows sometimes married older widowed men to assure their future security, but on many occasions they continued to live with the eldest son and his family providing for them until their death. Richer widows in Cheriton rarely re-married, and showing considerable intelligence and strength of character they continued to run their husband's businesses, sometimes with the help of a son or a son-in-law. The children of the yeoman classes in Cheriton had a lot to lose if another man married into the family and they may have actively opposed their widowed mothers entering into a marriage contract. When marriages in such circumstances did happen, the woman would first ensure that all property was held in trust for her children, thus preventing a new husband from claiming it as his own. It was not until the Married Women's Property Act of 1870 that a woman could retain her rights over the property that she brought to a marriage.[4]

Because most mothers in the parish married a partner before the birth of their child, there are questions around the handful of women who did not. Were they in a relationship with a married man, were they fooled by a man with no intentions to stay with them, or were they raped?

Surviving records identify only one or two examples of reported rape over three centuries and none resulting in a pregnancy. There is one example of a girl getting pregnant by a visiting soldier, several by single men who did not want commitment and quite a few by men who were already married.

There was a responsibility on the parish to support pregnant unmarried mothers and in Cheriton they were usually delivered in the Poor House by a local woman who acted as midwife. If there were complications the doctor would attend, paid for from the Overseers' funds, and if the child and/or mother did not survive, a shroud, coffin and funeral were provided, all at parish expense:

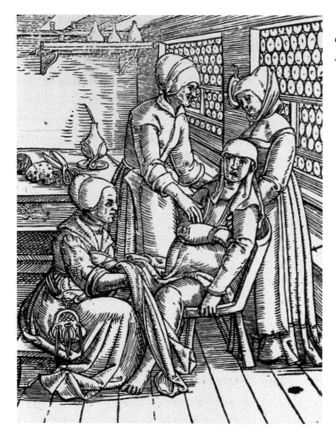

Woodcut of three midwives attending to a pregnant woman. Jakob Rueff, ca.1500–1558.[4]

Swaddling clothes for Mary Back's base child

for keeping the child for 6 months and 2 weeks.

William Back for laying forth Mary Back's base child

Christopher Butt for making the coffin

John Pope for making the grave (1728 Overseers of the Poor Accounts)

Officials in Cheriton's Poor House took as much care as they could over women in childbirth and nursed them until well enough to leave and find work. It was in everyone's best interests for the woman to survive so she could re-join the work-force and help pay for her child. The baby could be wet-nursed out in the community or kept in the Poor House and looked after by the pensioners themselves, with the mother visiting regularly to breast-feed. It was common for the child to remain in the house until old enough to be bound out as a parish apprentice, whilst the mother lived and worked in the community, contributing

141

what small sums of money she could towards the upkeep of the child. If the father could be traced and held to account, he had to bear the cost of the woman's lying-in and the child's maintenance.[5]

In Cheriton Fitzpaine the paternity of illegitimate male children was generally acknowledged at the point of baptism and no secret was made of a boy's identity. In some parish registers the father is named outright, but in Cheriton a more subtle approach was adopted with a boy baby being given the same baptismal name as his father:

Thomas Downing Pope bap 21.4.1745, a base child of Mary Pope

John Gill Discombe bap 10.12.1749, a base child of Mary Discombe

William Cruwys Taylor bap 19.3.1766, a base child of Betty Talyor

John Kimins Sharland bap 13.1.1771, a base child of Hannah Sharland

Thomas Melhuish Holland bap 29.5.1774, a base child of Mary Holland

Richard Chamberlain Coombe bap 26.1.1783, a base child of Thomasin Coombe

John Hewish Mogridge bap 29.6.1785, a base child of Grace Mogridge

Robert Harding Davie bap 3.8.1788, a base child of Hannah Davie

William Purchase Cruys bap 2.11.1794, a base child of Sarah Cruys

William Russell Elston bap 13.3.1796, a base child of Mary Elston

Thomas Sharland Chamberlain bap 16.11.1800, a base child of Mary Chamberlain

Samuel Wootton Bradford bap 6.4.1806, a base child of Mary Bradford (Samuel Wootton brought back from Salisbury to be accountable)

William Dummet Hitchcock bap 1.10.1809, a base child of Faith Hitchcock

James Kerswell Tincombe bap 7.10.1810, a base child of Mary Tincombe

Thomas Bulliford Ford bap 28.11.1813, a base child of Grace Ford

John Pratt Currell bap 15.10.1815, a base child of Mary Currell

William Marcus Shearman bap 19.10.1800, a base child of Faith Pope Shearman

One mother claiming parish support, told officials that she could only identify the father of her child as 'a soldier called John', but by the time the boy came to baptism Mary Chamberlain's son was given a middle name which looked very like a man's surname. Persuasion may have helped her to regain her memory just in time:

Samuel Dedham Chamberlain bap 29.9.1783, a base child of Mary Chamberlain.

Whilst growing up, the identity of these children would have been entirely transparent: 'I am the illegitimate son of x because I proudly carry his entire name before my mother's, telling the whole story of my parentage.'

The above named baby William Marcus Shearman was taken to Portsmouth after a Removal Order was issued on December 14th 1801. The records show that his mother Faith Pope had died in the Poor House within a year of his birth (burial expenses of 7/-). She referred to herself as Faith Pope *Shearman* whilst alive, so tragically, she must have considered herself to be betrothed to the father although there had been no public marriage. The sum of £1.10s. had already been received from the father for maintenance, showing his willingness to acknowledge his son, but now the parish considered that the boy was no longer their responsibility as he was not the child of a local man. It cost them the princely sum of £16.7s.2d. to travel with the toddler to hand him over to his father, but this was a considerable saving when compared to the cost of having to board him in the Poor House until he was eight or nine years old, and then to apprentice him out. There was a William M Shearman who was a 'mate' working at the Royal Naval Hospital at East Stonehouse in Plymouth in 1801 (survey 1801).[6] Shearman was not a Cheriton surname nor was it common in Devon as a whole at that date and the middle initial of 'M' seems too much of a co-incidence for this not to be the father. In addition, Plymouth and Portsmouth were both naval bases and itinerant sailors and soldiers were often responsible for transitory relationships with young women that resulted in a pregnancy. Commanding officers in Plymouth would have readily directed the Overseers of the Poor from Cheriton to William M Shearman in Portsmouth.

With the Removal, Faith's illegitimate son William Marcus Shearman jnr was given fresh start in life and managed to change his fortunes. When he was about fifteen years old he signed up for the Navy in Plymouth (May 4th 1815). Like many boys who looked upon the services as their adopted family he did very well for himself, passing his exams in June 1822 and receiving a commission as lieutenant in 1841.[7] He died in Yarmouth at the age of sixty four, married, and with a family and a dynasty of his own.

One of the two parish chests or coffers in Cheriton church. This one has many initials scraped on to the lid with the main ones being R M 1611

Bastardy Bonds and Orders directing putative fathers to pay for their children were kept safe in the parish chest together with accounts and registers, but over time some incumbents and churchwardens have not realised the worth of these paper sheets, and many have not survived long enough to be deposited safely in the County Archives.

In the absence of extant Bastardy Bonds and Orders, evidence can be found in the Overseers of the Poor Accounts where money needed to be laid out in order to

- interview the mother in front of a Justice of the Peace
- apply for a legal Bond or Order tying the father into a financial commitment
- apply for an arrest warrant for the father

In the Cheriton Accounts however there are very few entries for these expenses, indicating that it was not the norm for men to deny their financial responsibility when a woman became pregnant by them, even if they were already married and living nearby. On the contrary, there were some families who took the trouble to make private arrangements with a woman in order to support the child born out of wedlock.

Holding the putative father to account seems to have been straightforward enough and some men stepped forwards voluntarily to pay regularly for their base child. After being prompted with a Bastardy Order dated October 17ᵗʰ 1804, John Oliver paid on the nail over a period of several years for the child he had with Mary Adams. When the boy, John Adams was almost eight years old, the payments stopped:

1805 £2.10s.d.

1896 £3.11s.d.

1809 £2.12s.0d. etc.

1812 £1.9s.0d.

One would think that this was because John jnr was apprenticed out, but there was another reason. The boy was not actually apprenticed until 1814 but when he was, he was listed as being the son of 'John Oliver and Mary Holsgrove' rather than John Oliver and Mary Adams.[8] Against all the odds Mary had found herself a husband, even though she already had an illegitimate child. Not only was she supported by the natural father John Oliver, but in 1810 she found herself a husband in Thomas Holsgrove, a man seven years her junior, who was prepared to take on the boy. The couple then had six children of their own between 1812 and 1825. Oliver and Holsgrove were close neighbours and would have worked and socialised together. Thomas Hosegood alias Holsgrove had leased a cottage in The Hayes since 1802 and Oliver, a butcher and yeoman had held the lease on another property in The Hayes since 1800. Hosegood, an agricultural labourer brought up his new family in the cottage whilst John Oliver, who had married Susannah Lake in 1808 lived nearby with his legitimate sons William 1808 and John 1810 with later children Mary Ann 1818 and Edward 1822. The Oliver, Adams and Holsgrove families must have co-existed and co-operated openly over little John Adams.

Others couples entered into a partnership to support their illegitimate son or daughter e.g.

1702 recd. Mary Chowne towards the maintenance of her child 6/-

recd. William Taylor towards the same child 6s.6d.

1703 recd. Mary Chowne and William Taylor £1.17s.0d. for maintaining their base child

Significantly, a property called Taylors and Chownes on northside appears in the poor rate lists for many years. Later on it was just called Chownes, but Taylors Hill still exists close by. For years the two families owned and farmed the property jointly and whilst there are several branches of the Taylor family there is only one Chowne family in the parish. It may well be that Mary and William lived at the property but were unable to marry for some reason.

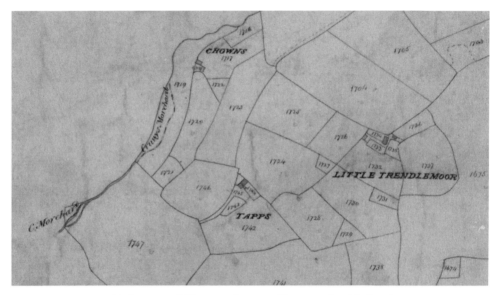

Tythe map of Cheriton showing Chownes alias Taylors

Another case of bastardy involving the Chownes is dated 1744 when Thomas Chowne, husbandman was bound to appear at the next Quarter Sessions to answer a case of bastardy involving Mary Rowe. Thomas was the son of John and Amy Chowne and was born in 1724. He, like most putative fathers was in his early twenties. Years later when the child of this liason, Thomas started producing children of his own, the curate repeatedly entered the surname 'Rowe alias Chowne' as there was another Thomas Chowne producing children at the same time.

Between 1732 and 1744 a number of changes took place in how the law dealt with responsibility for illegitimate children:

- In 1732–3 a pregnant woman had to name the father of her child.

- In 1733 the putative father was deemed responsible for maintaining his child, and although officials would still support the mother and baby, the father was required to reimburse the parish and pay regularly.
- In 1743–4 a vagrant mother could be publicly whipped and then sent back to her place of settlement with the child.

Overseers of the Poor were obliged to bring up these 'unprotected children' after the 1601 Poor Relief Act (43 Eliz.1.c.2.) by offering financial support from the poor rate levied from tenants of land and property in the parish. It was imperative therefore to use this limited pot of money wisely, and the 1662 Settlement Act (13 and 14 Car.11.c.12) allowed for the Removal of 'strangers' back to their place of settlement if they were 'likely to be chargeable' and did not belong in the area.

When a legitimate child was born it was generally understood that the child's settlement was taken to be the same as that of his or her father, but if born out of wedlock, the place of settlement was taken to be the place where he or she was *born*. Overseers would therefore do their best to move a single pregnant woman out of the area before she gave birth so that the child did not become a drain upon their relief system. This avoided the necessary cost of the woman's delivery and lying-in and the future costs of supporting the child and finding a parish apprenticeship for it when it reached a suitable age.

If Examination (by interview) of the woman could ascertain the name of the father and his place of settlement, officials could apply to the court for a Bastardy Order for maintenance from him and if that failed, a Warrant for his arrest could be issued, at some cost, to locate him and bring him to court to stand accountable for future costs. Even when a father left the area and travelled some distance parish officials would consider it worth their while going to some lengths to locate and bring him to justice. The important aim was to ensure that he contributed financially to his child's upbringing. The Overseers Accounts are sprinkled with various expenses concerning illegitimacy:

1710 for a Warrant for Priscilla Back, Mary Taylor and Mary Marting 1/-

Mary Taylor to ride to Exon 1/-

to enquire out Thomas Middleton 2/-

2 days at Exon (Exeter) to take Thomas Middleton 4/-

For an Order against Thomas Middleton to pay 1/- per week

Efforts on Mary's behalf were successful to begin with because Thomas Middleton paid up:

1710 received from Thomas Middleton towards his base child £1.8s.0d.

He did not however commit himself readily to his new financial burden and the Overseers had to pursue him again in order to extract further maintenance in 1713:

To the bailiff to arrest Middleton £1.1s.6d.
1713 concerning Thomas Middleton £3.4s.0d.

As the father of Mary Taylor's child he must have been relieved when the child died in 1714 but he was still expected to help pay for the child's funeral:

'stretching out' 6d.
her shroud ½d.
her coffin 4/- and
the making of her grave 1/-.

Another reluctant father was Matthew Langham who ran off to West Leigh:

1711 to a Summons and fetching Ann Lee to Crediton concerning Matthew Langham
A Summons to West Leigh, an order to send Matthew Langham to West Leigh.

The un-named father of Rebecca Hawkings' base child was also pursued for money:

1719 warrant and summons concerning Rebecca Hawkings 3/-
Richard Smart 2 days at Crediton and Exon concerning Rebecca Hawkins 6/-
Expenses at Exon and Crediton 2/-
To William Hill for keeping Rebecca Hawkins 5/-
For Rebecca Hawkins examination 2s.6d.

148

Henry Bagtor to ride to Justice Quicke's for a warrant from thence to Exon concerning Rebecca Hawkings 2/-

For the warrant 1/-

Henry Bagtor for riding to Exon castle 2/-

Thomas Gibbs for riding to Tiverton by the parish consent 2/-

One father had fled as far as Brandninch:

1715 Summons for Elizabeth Channon when examined concerning her base child 6d. (Jane Channon bap 21.11.1714 a base child of Elizabeth Channon) One Overseer at Crediton the same day 2/-

A Warrant to take the father of Elizabeth Channon's base child 1/-

To the mayor of Bradninch to sign the warrant 1/-

Warden and Overseer to Bradninch one day to take the father of Channon's base child 4/-

To send Briefs 11/-

Although Cheriton Overseers actively sought out putative fathers, there was never a witch hunt either for the men or for the unmarried women and their children. The stigma of illegitimacy was not pronounced in this rural parish.

Matched partners of illegitimate children appear in the Bonds and Orders issued by the parish:

Thomas Melhuish and Mary Holland for *Thomas Melhuish* Holland bap 29.5.1774

William Salter jnr of Broadclyst and Jane Davy 1822

Edward Boyce, carpenter of Tiverton and Ann Bright 1777

Moses Conybear and Martha Gifford 1779

James Chamberlain of Shobrooke and Grace Badcock 1781

John Hewish labourer and Sarah Williams 1783

Richard Chamberlain of Sandford and Thomasine Coombe for *Richard Chamberlain* Coombe bap 26.1.1783

John Stabbick yeoman and Sarah Sharland 1784

John Mitton of Cadbury and Joan Bulliford 1786

Joseph Pine and Ann Taylor 1786

Thomas Powe labourer and Mary Jerwood 1788

John Turner and Thomasine Channing 1790

Silas Richards of Upton Pyne and Ann Davy 1792

William Russell of Shobrooke and Mary Elston 1796

George Waybourne and Hannah Woodyetts 1796

William Taylor and Mary Bulliford 1797

Abraham Powe labourer and Mary Williams 1800

Thomas Sharland and Mary Chamberlain for *Thomas Sharland* Chamberlain bap 16.11.1800

James Davy of Burlescombe and Elizabeth Dunn 1804

John Oliver and Mary Adams 1804

John Noble labour of Tiverton and Mary Tolly 1808

James Rendell labourer of Upton Hellions and Mary Tolly 1808

Samuel Wootton labourer and Mary Bradford 1812

William Norrish of Sandford and Mary Hookway 1819

John Mortimore and Thomasine Langworthy 1821

William Moxey of Shobrooke and Mary Hart 1822

John Gill and Mary Discome 1749

Joseph Brewer tailor and Mary Baker 1765

Richard Bright the younger, husbandman and Alice Combes 1765

Mary Chamberlain, the daughter of James Chamberlain had already given birth to two base children in the parish: Mary jnr bap 20.3.1776 when her mother was twenty five years old, and Samuel Dedham Chamberlain, the soldier's child bap 29.9.1783 when she was in her thirties, and it is just possible that she also gave birth to a child in Sandford called Mary Newton Chamberlain who was baptised there 30.3.1782. It seems that Mary had settled into a particular way of life but was quite open about naming the fathers. Her younger brother Richard Chamberlain was being pursued for maintenance for Thomasin Coombe's illegitimate son in 1783, the same year that his sister delivered the soldier's son. Another relative, James Chamberlain who had moved to Shobrooke was being pursued for maintenance for James Chamberlain Badcock, base child of Grace Badcock born 26.11.1780.

This family did not appear to have a problem with illegitimacy. As for future life chances and marriage, none of the girls concerned found a husband to support them, even Thomasin Coomb who was only 20 when her son was born. For the men however it was a different story and Richard Chamberlain married Margaret and lived in Sandford with his legitimate children William 1788 and Betty 1791. James Chamberlain married Ann Gill in Cheriton in 1792 and went on to have legitimate children.

Mary Chamberlain's illegitimate daughter Mary carried on as her mother had done and had three illegitimate children of her own: Thomas Sharland Chamberlain 1800, John Chamberlain 1806 and James Chamberlain, not baptised, but born 1811 and later apprenticed by consent in 1821 to John Luxton, yeoman, to learn a trade.

Carrying the same surname of Chamberlain, but hailing from Stoodleigh, north of Tiverton, Jane Chamberlain gave birth to an illegitimate daughter in Cheriton, baptised Cecilia Morrish Chamberlain 25.8.1833.

When there was little hope of finding a way to support an illegitimate child, the parish did adopt a creative approach and on a couple of occasions they paid for a wedding. Whether the man involved was actually the father of the child is not clear, but in offering this package, it could be seen to be a win-win situation for the new husband would be financially responsible for both woman and baby, and the woman could look forward to a measure of security.

Take the example of Robert Blackmore in 1770:

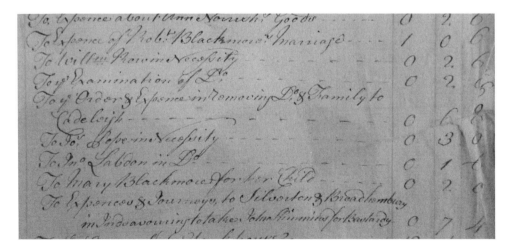

To expense of Robert Blackmore's marriage £1.0s.6d.

To Mary Blackmore for her child 2/-[9]

Another example can be found in the 1791–2 Accounts when 'William Gosland's bill of 19/5d' was paid. William had married Mary Ellis on February 1st 1791 just two days after her illegitimate daughter Ann Ellis was baptised. The couple then moved to Cruwys Morchard parish where they had further children together: Mary 1793, Sarah 1796 and John Davey Gosland 1800. By marrying Mary and moving out of the parish, William released the Overseers from their responsibilities for Mary and her daughter. Gosland was definitely *not* the father of the baby. (see The Case of Daniel Tremlett in the next chapter.)

The parish was willing to pay for another arranged marriage in September 1739 but this time there was no pregnancy involved. Instead, they settled a bill for £3.15s.8d to cover the cost of marrying Grace Jestin to John Bradford. Grace had been receiving poor relief for some time, living in one of the supported parish houses. In 1731–2 there were expenses of 3d. for mending Grace Jestin's chamber and 6d. for making a gutter at Grace Jestin's house. It could be that Grace was incapacitated in some way and an arranged marriage was a good way to ensure that she had a wage-earner to support her. There are no records for children from the newly married couple until Mary in 1746 and Sarah in 1758, both baptised at Cruwys Morchard.

Many putative fathers made dutiful payments to the Overseers over several years for an illegitimate son or daughter, living as their close neighbours and inevitably seeing them on a daily basis. As it was the tradition in the village to give illegitimate boys the same name as their fathers at baptism, and the fathers of illegitimate girls were generally known these children would grow up with everyone accepting their paternity.

The handful of mothers who were not able to marry went on to have further children, usually by different men. One would hope that they did not see this as a career choice with money changing hands, but rather a by-product of innocently hoping that that they might reel in a husband in the end. Realistically, if they did not have the support of a family to look after their baby during the day, an unmarried mother would have no way of finding work and earning the money to climb out of poverty. Because there was always parish relief available in Cheriton it is surprising that they did not take the option of leaving their child in the Poor House and hiring themselves out as domestic or agricultural workers. If an illegitimate child *was* left it would be looked after for at least seven years before being bound out in a parish apprenticeship but perhaps for some, the bond with their child was too strong and they preferred to take their chances in the community, bringing up their son or daughter?

Although after 1700 church authorities across England were interfering more and more with the fabric of family life, relationships and morals, it would appear that in Cheriton it was still the community of neighbours who exerted most influence. The church did not seem to show or encourage any prejudices towards unmarried mothers and children in the village and indeed, there is evidence of husbands, wives and children living in close proximity to illegitimate children and no evidence of pump-gossip or disagreements.

1600 and 1840 baptismal records for base children in Cheriton Fitzpaine:

Cheriton Fitzpaine	1600–1650	1651–1700	1701–1750	1751–1800	1801–1840
Total Illegitimate baptisms	4	19	34	58	36
Illegitimate boys	1	14	16	29	24
Illegitimate girls	3	5	14	22	12
Unspecified boy or girl			4	7	
Mothers returning with another illegitimate child for baptism	0	Carder 3x Lock 2x	Davey 2x Back 2x Back 2x Pope 2x	Davey 2x Taylor 3x Thrasher 2x Chamberlain2x Hex/Herles twins	Dunn 2x Chamberlain 3x Cuddiford twins + 1 other
Mothers from the same family baptising an illegitimate child	0	2 x Back	3x Davey 3x Back 2x Taylor 2x Marting	2 Davey 2x Brewer 2 x Coombe 3x Taylor 2x Gifford	3x Dunn
illegitimate baptisms	4	19	34	58	36
Total children baptised, Including legitimate	c110	c750	c850	c990	

A true picture cannot be gained because there were some babies who were not presented for baptism at all, but the available data shows only between 2% and 5% of births being illegitimate in Cheriton.

Percentages in cities were higher but data for three similar country parishes in England show that although Cheriton rates were higher up to 1750, they were considerably lower after that:

Baptismal years	% of illegitimate baptisms for Similar parishes	% of illegitimate baptisms for Cheriton Fitzpaine
1601–1650	0.69%	3.6%
1651–1700	1.35%	2.5%
1701–1750	1.96%	4%
1751–1800	9.97%	5.8%
1801–1835	6.18%	

Some women fell pregnant outside marriage twice: Lock, Davy, Back, Pope, Thrasher, Cuddiford, and Dunn whilst some presented three children for baptism: Jenny Carder, Taylor and Mary Chamberlain. Most of these girls were from families who had lived in the community for generations and their married siblings were producing legitimate children for baptism at the same time as them. In a city one might expect to find many unattached girls arriving to give birth with no extended family around them, but the girls in Cheriton's static community had genuine support.

Sometimes sisters or cousins fell pregnant at the same time and bore illegitimate children together, these included the Backs, Taylors, Daveys, Dunns, Martings, Giffords, Combes and Brewers.

Of all the unmarried mothers in Cheriton, Elizabeth Dunn was the most notable. Unusually she was an in-comer from Burlescombe north-east of Tiverton but she started a chain of illegitimacy in her family that was to affect four generations with two daughters each having their own illegitimate child, and a grandchild having an illegitimate daughter of her own.

Mary Chamberlain, born in the village had three illegitimate children by different fathers, and her brother Richard Chamberlain fathered an illegitimate son of his own. Perhaps for them it had become acceptable to throw caution to

The Cheriton font dates from 1874 and is dedicated to Maria Rashleigh, nee Arundell bap 1797 who married Rev George Rashleigh. An earlier font was set up in 1776

the wind and get pregnant because there was sufficient support available in their extended family and from parish officials. There is no evidence to indicate that such families suffered religious or neighbourly persecution or prejudice, so there was little moral deterrent.

In Cheriton a woman called Catherine Upham acted regularly as a midwife and was paid well for her troubles. In 1710 she received 2s.6d. for attending Priscilla Back and Mary Taylor when they gave birth in the Poor House but as early as the 1680s she was being contracted to look after babies and young children in her own house whilst their mothers went out to work. When Mary West (nee Hoxland) died, Catherine was paid 2/- a week by the Overseer to care for the motherless three year old Mary jnr. Mary was not actually an unmarried mother and her husband Nicholas West did his best to work in the community whilst the parish helped him out with the toddler. There was no Removal Order issued but Nicholas was not a local man and he was persuaded to return to London with his daughter in 1684 and the pair were escorted there at parish expense. After they left, Catherine Upham was accused of receiving money from the officials for the child but refusing to look after the child. The Overseer that year was Andrew Taylor and he was faced with the problem of trying to recoup the 2/- per week that he had paid out to Catherine.

John Kimins Sharland bap in January 1771, was the base child of Hannah Sharland and he was looked after by his grandmother who was awarded parish relief for so doing.

Unmarried mothers who had to stay in the Poor House earned their keep by spinning, sewing or knitting in the work-room on the ground floor, or baking bread and preparing vegetables in the kitchen, brewing beer in the on-site brew-house or dealing with the laundry.

References

1. Stone, L., The Family, Sex and Marriage in England, 1500–1800 (1977)
2. The Bishop's Visitation of 1744 mentions four communions p.a. but in 1764 there were twelve communions p.a. with sixty communicants at festival times and thirty at other times. There were two services a week, each with a sermon
3. The Churching of Women by German-born painter Hans Memling 1490 working in Flanders. Held by the Museo del Prado, Madrid
4. Pregnant woman sitting in a birthing chair with three midwives in attendance, painted 1580 by Swiss physician Jakob Reuff
5. Lying-inis an old childbirth practice involving a woman resting in bed for a period of time after giving birth, even if there were no complications
6. 1801 survey East Stonehouse, Plymouth
7. O'Byne, W.R., Naval Biographical Dictionary, (1849)
8. Cheriton Fitzpaine Apprenticeship Register covering 1812
9. Cheriton Overseers Accounts

Case Studies in Illegitimacy in Cheriton Fitzpaine

In large towns such as Exeter and Tiverton heavy demands were often made upon parish funds to support unmarried women and their illegitimate children. With a growing population and significant numbers of itinerant women looking for work and relationships, the incidence of pregnancy outside marriage was high, and church and parish officials needed to weed out those who were not properly deserving of their limited support funds. This they did by examining paperwork proving place of settlement and by face to face interviews. Because of the large number of applicants it is probable that parish officials in cities and towns followed the letter of the law using all their legal powers to make bastardy an unattractive prospect, thus exerting a strong influence on their local community.

In Cheriton however, the population was not a fluctuating one and it was only at harvest time that a handful of itinerant workers arrived from outside the parish. The village was not on the road to anywhere in particular and it was rare for travellers to pass through. Before the advent of steam-driven machinery, farm labourers were always needed and villagers had little reason to venture as far afield as Tiverton or Exeter to find employment and it was only in the second quarter of the 19th century when Sharland's Tannery at Upham expanded that a significant number of new, semi-skilled labourers were attracted to the area. Cheriton folk knew each other well and their internal support networks were strong enough to remain non-judgemental when their own fell pregnant outside marriage.

One woman who did travel to Exeter was returned in 1792 with a Removal Order issued on January 31st by the Overseers of St John's parish. They sent her back to her place of legal settlement after she had been apprehended in St John's parish as:

> 'a rogue and a vagabond, wandering abroad in the open air and not giving a good account of herself.'

The interview with her revealed that she had been a covenant servant with John Reed, a yeoman in Cheriton Fitzpaine and that was reason enough to settle her back in the parish. Their paperwork omitted to mention the fact that Ann Davey was eight months pregnant at the time. Officials in Exeter thus relieved themselves of the financial burden of her confinement and future care.[1] Priscilla Davey, her daughter, was baptised in the village on February 26th 1792 and grew up 'on the parish'. When old enough Priscilla was bound out as an apprentice to John Jackman at East Ford in May 1799. Her mother remained in the village but did not manage to make a fresh start for herself by finding a husband or employment and went on to have another illegitimate child the following year. She was interviewed by Cheriton officials and this time she named Silas Richards a carpenter from Upton Pine as the father of her female child born on February 9th 1793 so Ann must have conceived her second daughter when Priscilla was only three months old. The parish funds supported this child too but some maintenance was extracted from Silas to help defray costs. With two illegitimate children, Ann Davy's life chances had no way of improving but with support from the community she lived on in the village for many years.

Between 1727 and 1807, a period of eighty years there are sixteen surviving Removal Orders returning paupers back to Cheriton Fitzpaine and seventeen removing paupers from Cheriton back to their own parishes. The status quo seems to have been maintained.

The case of Elizabeth Dunn

By far the most protracted case of illegitimacy centres on Elizabeth Dunn. It has already been mentioned that she was the first of four generations to give birth out of wedlock and her story is an interesting one. Her first child was Sarah Dunn 1801, and because the father had been named in a Bastardy Order as James Davy a wheelwright of Burlescombe, parish officials eventually managed to retrieve some payments for the mother and child:

158

1803 received from James Davy of Burlescombe for Elizabeth Dunn's lying in £1.1s.[2]

Between 1804 to 1809 varying sums of money (£2.1s.0d., £2.12s.0d., £3.18s.0d. etc.) were sent from Burlescombe to support the base child – quite an undertaking for a man with a family of his own.

Elizabeth Dunn herself hailed from Burlescombe and it is not clear why she chose to travel from her home to Cheriton Fitzpaine in order to have her baby, for there were certainly no Dunns living in the parish at the time. The fact that James Davey had refused to marry her might have been a reason for Elizabeth to leave. He chose to marry Amelia Wall in 1803 and went on to have eleven children, but for a number of years James sent money to Cheriton for his illegitimate daughter.[3]

If Elizabeth had wanted to make a fresh start and build a new life for herself as a single mother in a new parish, she did not succeed. Once again she returned to Burlescombe and either fell pregnant whilst there, or travelled there in order to give birth with her family around her. Whichever the case, a Removal Order issued by the Overseers of Burlescombe in December 1811 succeeded in sending her back to Cheriton just four months before the birth of Elizabeth Dunn jnr.[4] Once again Cheriton Fitzpaine took on financial responsibility for mother and new baby, and ensured that Elizabeth jnr, baptised in the village in April 1812 was kept at the parish expense. Overseers accounts in 1812 mention 'small clothes for Elizabeth Dunn's infant 8s.6d.'

Because no maintenance payments were received for this second child she was a good candidate to be apprenticed out when old enough, and indeed when nine years old she was bound to serve Richard Strong, yeoman at Higher Chilton in 1821. Unfortunately for young Elizabeth Dunn, it was to be an ominous contract.

What did the future hold for the two illegitimate Dunn sisters?

The elder of the two, Sarah Dunn grew up and gave birth to her own illegitimate daughter in May 1834, naming her Elizabeth after her mother and sister. She was one of the few fortunate women who married the father of her child *after* it was born. John Packer became her husband just five months later in October 1834. In the 1841 census this child had adopted the surname Packer and was listed as the eldest child in the family with John Packer as her father. Other children born into this marriage were John 1837, James 1839, Agnes 1842, and Ambrose William in 1845. Sarah's husband was a few years younger than her and her final pregnancy occurred when she was over 40 years old. Her last child may well have died in infancy because it has not been possible to trace him later than 1851 when he was 6 years old. Often called Sally rather than Sarah, she and John lodged at Balle near Peach Hayne farm with another family, until they both died. Still young, the children were taken care of with the eldest boy John lodging with the Mogridge family in the village, and Agnes employed as a house servant at East Ford farm. Agnes Packer did well for herself, eventually marrying a shoe-maker called William Hopper in Crediton. Elizabeth the eldest however, born out of wedlock ended up in The Crediton Union Workhouse aged 26 with an illegitimate daughter of her own – two year old Mary Ann, a third generation of illegitimate children born to this family. Ten years later Elizabeth had managed to leave the workhouse, finding employment as a servant at Stockleigh Pomeroy Mill with the Prior family. She remained there for many years but it is not known what happened to her daughter.

The younger of the two Dunn sisters, Elizabeth was apprenticed out as a nine year old but just before the end of her contract to Richard Strong at Higher Chilton she gave birth to an illegitimate son. John Dunn was baptism on September 1st 1833 with no public mention of the father. Later records however reveal a story typical for its day, for when John Dunn jnr was himself bound out as a parish apprentice at the age of eleven his name was given as John *Strong* Dunn. As the master Richard Strong had a twenty year old son John Strong whilst Elizabeth worked for him, there is little doubt that he was the father. A private maintenance arrangement must have been set up to support the boy during his childhood for there are no records him falling upon parish funds. Two years later his mother Elizabeth Dunn managed to find herself a husband who would give shelter to the child, but he was not the father and did not give him his name. This man was the James Packer, brother to her sister's husband, John Packer. Two brothers James and John had therefore married two sisters. Each sister had an illegitimate child but both marriages were long and fruitful.

After getting married in 1835 James and Elizabeth Packer had their own children: Mary 1836, Robert 1839, Ann 1841, Richard 1843, Emma 1846, Susan 1848 and Ellen 1853. John (Strong) Dunn became the eldest child in the new family, but the entry in the 1841 census returns lists him last of all, even after grandmother Agnes Packer who lived with them. He was still named John Dunn and one wonders what his status was in the family. As a 17 year old he worked as a live-in servant at Cotton farm next to Colman Cottages where the family was, and alongside him at the farm were 12 year old half-brother Robert and another close relative, Thomas Packer, aged 40.

The Packers held a good set of values and were known in the parish to be hardworking and honest. Agnes (nee Whey) was the matriarch of the family and she and Robert produced children who were easily placed in apprenticeships when they reached a suitable age. The records show Elizabeth placed out in 1807, Robert in 1810 to Robert Manley, yeoman for Cheriton Mill, Mary in 1816, John in 1819, James in 1821 and Charles in 1826. For a family to have a string of healthy willing children with a strong work ethic was something to be applauded. Agnes herself lived until she was almost ninety years old having given birth to at least 10 children. One would like to think that she was an amenable soul with a strong family values. She lived with her daughter-in-law Elizabeth who was left a widow when James died in 1856.

In the 1861 census the Packer family had moved from Coleman Cottages at Upham to Cheriton village. Ellen and Emma the two youngest children were still living at home. Emma was described as a scholar like any other 13 year old, but by the age of 23 she was labelled 'an imbecile'. After matriarch Agnes' death Elizabeth, aged about 57 by then married a widowed shoemaker called Robert Maunder who was obviously willing to take on the challenge of Emma's

Workshop attached to the later building, Hedgehog cottage

161

disability. At their home in Wells Terrace, Churchtown the three of them lived for many years. The house has since been replaced by two cottages (3 Wells Terrace and Hedgehog Cottage), but the outhouses where Robert carried out his shoemaking business still remain, attached to the right hand side of Hedgehog Cottage.

The furthermost door in the photograph was once a south-facing window and one can imagine Robert working at his bench where the light streamed in. Being opposite The Ring of Bells and right at the heart of Church Town his premises were perfectly placed for trade.

Elizabeth Maunder died in 1891 aged 79, Robert in 1892 and Emma in 1896 when she was 51 years old. Elizabeth Dunn had many difficulties in her life but she worked hard and never fell upon parish funds after her childhood.

Other connections with the Dunns of Burlescombe occur with a Mary Dunn aged 12, daughter of James and Thomasin Dunn of Burlescombe who was apprenticed out to James Stabbick at West Burrow farm in Cheriton Fitzpaine in 1816. In the 1841 and 1851 census returns there is a Sarah Dunn, a single pauper from Burlescombe lodging in Cheriton with John Greenslade, a wheelwright and his family. Remembering back to James Davey, was there a connection through the trade of wheelwright?

There is also a cottage at the western end of the village called Dunn's.

The case of Cecilia Chamberlain

Cecilia Morrish Chamberlain was an illegitimate child presented for baptism on August 25th 1833 by Jane Chamberlain of Stoodleigh. Although she did not marry until the child was thirteen months old the fact that her husband was John Morrish indicates that he was the father. They married not in the village but at St Mary Arches Church in Exeter. The three of them came back to Cheriton and in the 1841 census were living 1, Leys Cottages, Cruwys Morchard with two other children: Mary born 1836 and Richard 1839. All the children carried the surname Morrish and were given equal status in the family. By 1851 however Jane was widowed but still living in the cottage with Richard aged 12 and a younger child Elizabeth, born 1842. John Morrish had worked as an agricultural labourer in several neighbouring farms but Jane had had an education and when widowed, she managed to secure herself a job as a 'school mistress'. Cecilia her eldest child went on to marry well – John Griffin, a farmer at Bear Forge Farm,

Cruwys Morchard. She called herself Cecilia *Chamberlain* Morrish, having kept her mother's family name as a middle name. This was a family that remained close and when Richard Morrish was old enough he was employed as a bailiff on the Griffin's farm. From a shaky start this family had certainly improved their futures.

The case of Mary Rowe

Mary Rowe was born in the village and apprenticed out to John Melhuish in Cruwys Morchard. When she was twenty she returned to her mother, pregnant, and with her help supported the child for the next eight years. She managed to hire herself out to William Badcock, then to Peter Snow in Sandford and then to Mrs Alice Stabback at Bickleigh Court where she was a yearly servant for three years. During her time in Bickleigh she fell pregnant again and officials there removed her to Tiverton, most probably because the father lived there. After only two months Mary returned to her mother in Cheriton in 1762 and presented herself and the child to the parish, asking for support. Her story was typical of a single woman unable to rise above the problems accompanying illegitimacy.[5]

The class divide and illegitimacy

Documentation survives for four cases of the putative father being of higher status than the mother. Each was a yeoman farmer holding considerable property and commanding respect in the neighbourhood. Two of these men responded to a Bastardy Order that was served upon them but one needed an arrest warrant to be issued before he could be challenged to pay for his child and one went to extraordinary lengths to protect his reputation, inciting the mother to abort their unborn child.

The case of George Waybourn

Parish officials had an arrest warrant issued against George Waybourn, yeoman of Hannabeth farm in regard of a male child born to Hannah Woodyetts on December 8th 1796. The boy was baptised John Woodyetts (later this name appears as Woodgates) a month later on January 1st 1797. According to the

Apprenticeship register, Hannah Woodyates was baptised in January 1778 but it is not known where. At the time there were branches of the family living in Cheriton, Crediton, Cadeleigh and Tiverton. Hannah was apprenticed at the age of ten to Philip Badcock at East Ford, a farm adjacent to Hannabeth. George would have seen young Hannah working in the fields but it is not known whether they developed a relationship over time or whether as an older man, he took advantage of her.

East Ford Farm

George does not appear often in the records but it is known that he had arrived from Uffculme in 1794 when it was arranged for John Gillard to stand as a substitute for him there in the Militia. The names of eligible men were drawn in a ballot for each parish and those selected then had to leave to serve for a term of three years.[6] It was acceptable to find a substitute provided that the sum of £10 was paid, but in George's case the Overseers of Cheriton paid only £6.3s.0d. in Militia money to the Overseers of Uffculme for John Gillard and family to release George Waybourne from his duties. This may represent a private agreement between the two parishes but may also indicate that George had already served part of the three year period.

In June 1794 Waybourne took on a parish apprentice called Mary Pope at Hannabeth and the following March the Overseers allowed him 3/- to provide a pair of shoes for Mary Pope. But then there is an unusual entry in the records:

'Mary Pope rebound to Richard Elston of Morchard Bishop 10.6.1796.' [7]

At this time Hannah Woodyeates would have been three or four months pregnant. Had it come out that George had attacked the girl? Did he suddenly give up the farm and move away from the village? No other mention of him has yet been discovered in the area and his sudden disappearance has no explanation. Perhaps he left the area in a vain attempt to rescue his reputation, but this is pure conjecture.

Hannah entered the Poor House and gave birth to a son but died in 1804 and was buried at the parish expense. Officials had supported her since the birth of her child and sought to bind out the 8 year old John Woodyeates in apprenticeship as soon as they could. There is an unmarried John Woodgates of the right age living in Crediton High Street at the time of the 1851 census. He was a mason by trade and he gave his place of birth as Cheriton Fitzpaine. He may well have been Hannah and George's illegitimate son.

Waybourne is a very unusual name in the area and searches have only uncovered one: George Waybourn the 'bastard child' of one Elizabeth Waybourn who was removed to St Lawrence, Exeter from Stoodleigh parish by their Overseers of the Poor in 1747. The young George seems to have been removed without his mother to the place of settlement of his father (under the terms of The Act of Settlement and Removal 1662). His mother Elizabeth is most likely to have been the daughter of Robert Waybourn of Oakford, near Tiverton, a man with a large and flourishing family.[8]

To rise from illegitimacy in Stoodleigh to the status of 'yeoman farmer' in Cheriton would have been impossible unless the family stepped in and gifted money or land, so this may not be the same George Waybourne of the arrest warrant. Whatever the case, George Waybourne was something of an itinerant soul and more remains to be discovered about him.

The case of John Stabbick

John Stabbick, yeoman farmer, received a Bastardy Order for his male child born to Sarah Sharland dated January 28th 1784. He was ordered to pay £1.13s.0d. for the child's delivery together with 1s.6d. per week for maintenance.

John Stabbick's father, also John was married to Margaret and had at least seven children: John 1757, James 1759, Betty 1760, Robert 1762, Sarah 1766, William 1768 and Thomas 1771. He was widowed in 1782 and then married Mrs Elizabeth Beedle in 1790. She brought with her considerable wealth. The Stabbicks held leases on property in Cheriton that included West Burrow, and in Bradninch and Rose Ash. John snr can be traced in the list of freeholders in the parish from 1759 onwards. He was a man of good standing in the community, listed at different times as a leaseholder, a copyholder and a freeholder, and in the 1760s he examined the accounts of the local Poor House and even acted as a Hundred Constable from 1780. As one of the two elected Constables he held a prestigious office and was responsible for conserving law and order amongst parishioners.[9]

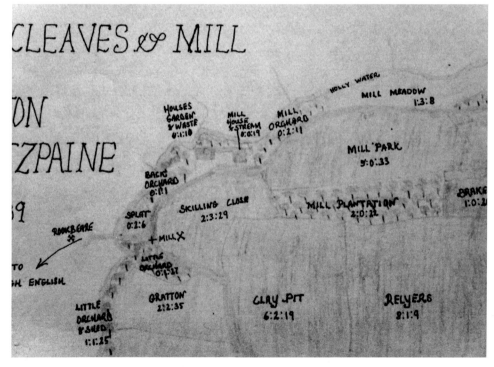

Hedgecleave and Cheriton Mill shown on Manley's estate map

His grandfather a third John Stabbick was born in the year 1696 at Plymtree and married Mary Hutchings at Silverton in 1727. The following year he was recorded in Huxham, and by 1730-2 at Silverton before moving to Bickleigh by 1735. He and Mary had five children: John (1728–1807), Mary (1730) who possibly died in infancy, Sarah who married Andrew Hewish (1732–1805), Elizabeth (1735) and Mary (1738). Stabbick also farmed a piece of ground called Taylors in north Cheriton, but in 1765 he bought West Burrow Farm, Cheriton Fitzpaine and remained there until his death in July 1776. His widow died in 1782 aged 77 years.[10]

John 1757, the youngest generation was in his twenties at the time of the Bastardy case and for him and his family, exposure would have been significantly damaging and inconvenient.

Stabbick died in 1809 but in his will he made no mention of Sarah's illegitimate child and named only his two sons, Thomas and William.[11] He made reference to his property 'Hedge Cleave' in Cheriton Fitzpaine, owned by Robert Manley of Venn who held a 'reversion in fee expectant' in the property. Betty Stabbick his sister had married into the Manley family – Richard Manley of Lower Claw in Cruwys Morchard, and Robert Manley had married into the Beedle family, namely Sarah the daughter of Elizabeth Beedle. The families of Beedle, Stabbick and Manley were thus closely inter-linked.

Thomas Stabbick 1771 the legitimate son tenanted the mill from c1803 to the 1820s and his older brother John lived at Rose Ash.

Sarah Sharland was not apprenticed at the mill or indeed on any of the farms in the area and was fairly well connected and she may have got to know John Stabbick jnr through the Beedle family. Sarah Sharland was baptised in 1786 in Washfield by John and his wife Joan (nee Beedle) and moved to Cheriton soon afterwards where her brother William Sharland was baptised in 1770.

When Sarah gave birth to John, the family had connections they could use to ensure his future, but probably also called in favours from the Stabbicks. When John was old enough he was set up as an apprentice grocer in Alphington, St Thomas, Exeter. In 1815 he married Elizabeth Mary Wippell, the daughter of a wealthy Alphington merchant and soon became a successful tea dealer and grocer.[12] One branch of the Wippell family were tanners in Alphington with business ties to the Sharland tanners of Cheriton Fitzpaine, but Elizabeth Mary's branch were successful traders and sea-farers operating out of Plymouth docks, importing tea and other commodities. John would have been active in marketing their imported goods and he certainly made a very good life for himself and his own children Peter, William, Jane and Caroline Sharland. Significantly, other Sharlands married into the tanning branch of the Wippell family out of Alphington.

Rather than holding him back in life, John Sharland's unfortunate start in life served to be the making of him.

The case of Thomas Melhuish

An intriguing piece of paper survives upon which one young mother, examined under oath, told Officials what happened to her. Dated August 6th 1774 it is the Examination of twenty four year old Mary Holland of Cheriton Fitzpaine.[13] Mary was born in Poughill to John and Elizabeth Holland and moved to Cheriton shortly afterwards where her siblings John 1755, Elizabeth 1758, Sarah 1760 and Faith 1765 were born. In a sworn examination Thomas Carrington scribed for her:

> Mary Holland 'saith that on 11th April last she was delivered of a male bastard child in the said parish of Cheriton Fitzpaine which Bastard is likely to be chargeable to the said parish and that Thomas Melhuish of the said parish, yeoman did get her with child of the said Bastard of which she was delivered. He the said Thomas Melhuish having had carnal knowledge of her body some time in the beginning (of July) of May 1773 and twice after that time and that no person other was cons … With her with respect to the begetting of said Bastard child except the said Thomas Melhuish only.'

The story then took a sinister turn:

> 'And the said Mary Holland further on her oath said that upon her informing the said Thomas Melhuish that she was with child by him that he the said Thomas Melhuish did give her an herb which he advised her to take in order to procure an abortion and at the same time gave her a guinea directing her if the herb should not have the effect to procure some mercury and take it in her tea which would answer the purpose, charging her to conceal the thing from her mother who would take the mercury for sugar or salt. However she immediately carried the said herb to her mother and told her what had

168

happened who thereupon charged her not to take the said herb or anything else.'

After the Examination a Bastardy Order was issued to Thomas Melhuish dated October 7th 1774. He received it and signed to the terms using his personal seal (showing his elevated status). His bondsman was Robert Kerslake the younger of Cheriton Fitzpaine, thatcher.

Who was Thomas Melhuish? Most likely a man of some standing with a reputation to uphold, judging by the extraordinary lengths to which he went to try and protect himself from future troubles. Although there are several Melhuish men of that name who were property owners or tenant farmers, it is difficult to identify which one this Thomas was. Searches have turned up

Thomas son of John and Susannah Melhuish baptised at Cruwys Morchard in 1740 and Thomas son of Christopher and Sarah Melhuish baptised Stockleigh Pomeroy in 1742.

There is a possibility that because the Holland family started off in Cruwys Morchard in 1750 that the first Thomas might have been known to Mary.

Another Thomas Melhuish living at Woolfardisworthy is known to have been a man who liked to protect his honour, going to considerable lengths to pursue an apprentice called Elisha Mills who ran away from his service and took refuge at his uncle's house in South Molton. Elisha told his story when he was claiming settlement in 1792, adding that Melhuish had demanded a release fee of £2.2s.0d. from his uncle.[14]

This Thomas may be the same man who took on an apprentice called Robert Packer in Cruwys Morchard, the same Robert Packer who married Agnes Whey in 1799 and was the father of James and John who were mentioned in the Elizabeth Dunn's story above.

The Melhuish family was an illustrious one, able to trace its roots back to Edward the first. Devon wills reveal a Thomas Melhuish of Cruwys Morchard leaving property to his children in 1726, and a John Melhuish of Hill, Cruwys Morchard leaving a part share of property his son Thomas Abraham Melhuish and to a nephew Thomas Melhuish of Poughill, gent in 1830.

Mary Holland presented her illegitimate son *Thomas Melhuish* Holland for baptism on May 29th 1774 but the boy was encouraged to drop the Holland surname as he grew up, being known in later life as Thomas Melhuish. He did not marry but in 1815 the forty one year old had an illegitimate son himself by Joan

Yendel. The couple presented their child for baptism and named him *Thomas Melhuish* Yendel. Joan was an in-comer, probably from Rose Ash. Although they were unmarried the boy remained close to both parents and he is found in the census looking after his elderly father until he died at the age of eighty eight. Each of the Thomas Melhuish Yendel's children was given the middle name of 'Melhuish' and there was even a grandson christened Thomas Melhuish Yendel. The family made no secret of their infamous beginnings and took advantage of the cache that the Melhuish name afforded them.

The Case of Daniel Tremlett

Daniel Tremlett of Upcott Barton had a little indiscretion in 1791 when he impregnated a local girl called Mary. Mary could well have been one of the farm servants on this rather remote property in the north of the parish. Mr Tremlett had been married for over thirty years at the time and was a very successful farmer so this was definitely something he wanted to avoid dealing with. He came up with a devious plan to wriggle out of his commitments by marrying Mary off to a man called Gosling who was settled in nearby Cruwys Morchard. Rumour had it that Gosling was something of an imbecile and the offer of a marriage would have been very attractive to him. Mary too may have been easily persuaded to take a husband of any kind, knowing that her alternative would be a life of struggle and poverty. It was said that because Gosling was of Cruwys Morchard, Tremlett hoped that the Overseers of that parish would then have to take responsibility for a child born to the marriage, thus releasing him and Cheriton from future expenditure. The following entries in the Cruwys Morchard Overseers' Accounts show that the marriage did take place and that Gosling was even kitted out with a coat, vest and breeches for the ceremony and for his future life:

3ʳᵈ month 1791

To the constable of Cheriton touching Mr Gosling 1s.6d.

for Mary Gosling's examination 2/-

for the Order touching her child 2/-

my journey and expenses 3s.6d.

Journey to Exeter to take opinion and counsel touching Mary Gosling 3s.6d.

for a copy of the register touching her marriage 1/-

my trouble and expense about Gosling 5/-

6th month 1791

expenses touching Gosling at the Assize £12.8s.8d.

11th month 1791

4 yards 'carsey dragett' for a coat for Mary Gosling 5s.4d.

extra expenses last year

Mary Gosling 3s.3d.

9th March coat, vest and breeches for Gosling.[15]

Cheriton Overseers also made a payment in respect of William Gosling in the year 1791–2:

To William Gosling's bill 19s.5d.

But the cover up was not as successful as Tremlett would have wanted. Daniel was not popular with everyone and there were complaints made against him in this matter. An Assize action was brought against him on behalf of the Cruwys Overseers by a William Thorne of neighbouring Lower Yeadbury Farm and this resulted in Tremlett being given a six month prison sentence.[16] By some means or other Daniel managed to get his sentence reduced to three months, but begrudgingly had to pay the £50 costs incurred.

Forced to do his dirty washing in public and to have his authority challenged, Tremlett was incensed, and immediately launched a personal and somewhat self-righteous counter-attack on Thorne who was known to have married his deceased wife's sister. Although Thorne had been a widow at the time of the second marriage, such a union was still against the law, and Tremlett was keen to 'out' him and the children of this union who were technically therefore illegitimate. He prosecuted Thorne for incest. The action against Thorne commenced in the Exeter Consistory Court in September 1793 but Tremlett wanted to broadcast the fact and publicly stated that if Thorne cared to pay him back the £50 expenses, he would drop the prosecution. One can deduce a lot about a man who would go to these lengths to get revenge and score a moral victory. After a protracted ten month hearing the case ended in 1794 with each party having to pay their own costs. Thorne's marriage was *not* declared illegal.

In Cheriton Fitzpaine there is sufficient evidence to suggest that neither the church nor the community appear to have held derogatory views about illegitimacy. On the contrary they often took great care of unmarried mothers and their babies, and families supported the putative fathers to step up and offer support to the mothers. The base children do not seem to have been ostracised by the parish and in fact some did very well for themselves, raising themselves out of poverty and back into the mainstream. This was not the case in some neighbouring parishes where there was distinct prejudice and social labelling which children could not easily shed. A very few mothers in Cheriton Fitzpaine did find themselves unmarriageable and they went on the have further children, thus perpetuating the cycle of illegitimacy and dependency, but there were other women who must have had the strength of character, neighbourly support and probably the attractiveness to marry later on, and to create families that flourished, unhindered by the events of the past. There is no evidence of negative interference from Church or parish in this place.

References

1. Removal Order Ann Davey St John's Exeter via St Thomas the Apostle1792 1633A PO530/20
2. Cheriton Fitzpaine Overseers of the Poor Accounts
3. Burlescombe parish registers
4. Removal Order Elizabeth Dunn Burlescombe 1633S PO531/18
5. Settlement papers Mary Rowe, 1762 1633A PO 528/7
6. www.**devonfhs**.org.uk/forewords/D105
7. as 2
8. Removal order George Waybourne Stoodleigh 1747 2985A/PO11/1
9. Devon Quarter Sessions West Budleigh Hundred
10. Research completed by C H B Cole
11. Will of John Stabbick 1807 IR26/335 abstract
12. Whipple family research compiled from Census returns and marriages, births and deaths records
13. Examination Mary Holland 1774 pariah records
14. Settlement papers Elisha Mills 1792 1633A PO528/22
15. Cruwys Morchard Overseers of the Poor Accounts
16. Gray, Todd (ed) Devon Documents 1996 Smith, Mike. A Family at Risk; The Thornes of Cruwys Morchard in 1793.

Health Matters

In 1732 the parish made an attempt to rid the farm lands of vermin, enlisting the help of boys and young men to kill hedgehogs, badgers and fitches (polecats) in exchange for money. John Hewish awarded the princely sum of 1s.8d. for killing five hedgehogs, whereas John Labdon killed four for 1s.4d. No doubt it had been a sort of competition between the young men but the champion by far was Thomas Gibbs who managed to kill two badgers and one hedgehog for 2s.4d. Several boys killed fitches (polecats) and John Taylor managed to kill one fitch at Pool. In later Accounts even sparrows were killed for pocket money to

Rewards for killing vermin

help protect the farmer's crops. In 1736 Mr Bodley of Cruwys Morchard was rewarded with 6/- for killing three foxes.

The importance of keeping stock healthy was of vital importance and county parsons would see the need for prayers to support a farming congregation. In 1758 thanksgiving prayers were offered in Cheriton

'for the distemper of the cattle being ceased.'

Of equal importance however was the good health of the workforce in the village. There were certainly a few epidemics throughout the centuries but generally speaking families kept themselves free of disease by using the herbal remedies passed down from generation to generation. Even if a family only had a small patch of ground to call their own, there would be a herb-bed of sorts, and any additional plants could be gathered from the hedgerows. There are still many different species growing along the lanes that wind in and around the parish that could be used in the home: tansy for worms, ragwort to ease swellings, scabious for coughs, saxifrage for stomach ailments, loosestrife to stem the flow of blood etc.

But in 1681 an unusual number of parishioners fell sick and were supported from the parish funds, being unable to work:

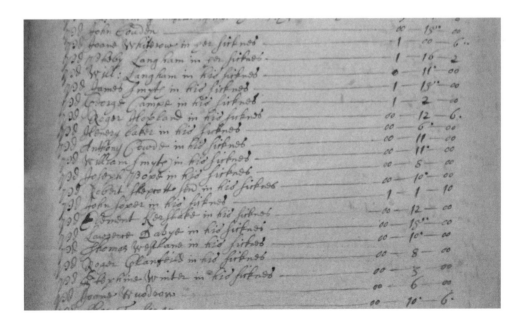

Thankfully many of these folk recovered and did not end up as entries in the burial register that year.

As time went by modern medicines became available and there were even mass vaccinations in the area. In 1808 seventeen poor children in the village were inoculated at a cost to the Overseers of £1.14s.0d. This was in response to a resolution passed by the House of Commons (60 votes to 5) concerning small pox inoculation. Its members had considered the Report of the Royal College of Physicians in London, of April 10th 1807 and decided that such vaccinations should be carried out around the country. Cheriton parish officials were therefore obliged to administer vaccine to those children in their care. Given the cost of 2/- per vaccine, these children were indeed fortunate, as their parents did not have to find the money needed for such preventative treatment. One assumes that other children in the parish were brought to the doctor for their inoculations but there may have been some who slipped the net and were not therefore protected against the disease. In this instance, pauper children were the fortunate ones. Another entry states that fifty two others in the village received vaccine at a cost of 2s.6d per person. The higher price may indicate an adult rather than superior dose:

For inoculating 52 people £6.6s.0d.

Water quality

By far the greatest threat to health in the parish was the polluted water supply in the village itself where a growing population was drawing water from the many wells along the main road but also disposing of sewage and detritus. Ignorance about how to keep sewage well away from drinking water meant that the centre of Cheriton became a breeding ground for germs. And with poor personal hygiene habits as well, there was a disaster waiting to happen.

Severe cases of fever were reported in 1846 because of the state of the drains and the want of a proper sewerage system, and in 1865 there was an attempt to remedy the unsanitary conditions by installing a nine inch sewer pipe with stench traps down the main road, using the natural fall of the land to direct waste away to the western end of Church Town where it emptied into a stream on a piece of land next to the old smithy.

Black Measles

In 1886 the daughter of Sarah Wotton the well-loved school teacher died from 'black measles'. Edith Ann Wotton was just six years old when she died in Church Cottage, having contracted the disease from her classmates. She was not the only one to die and one labourer was reported as having lost six of his children to fever and measles. Officials concluded then that the village had issues of water quality that needed addressing urgently. The epidemic certainly attacked the weakest first and the first quarter of 1885 saw these tragic deaths:

Eliza Davey aged 8, January 28th

Florey Davey aged 12, January 31st

Lucy Ellen Davey aged 3, February 7th

Edith Agnes Davey aged 15 months, February 7th

These four little girls were all the children of Richard Davey and his wife Eliza Stoneman who lived at Upham – for some time at Higher Harsh and later at Barton Cottages near Waterhouse. Their remaining children were Bertha aged five and their illegitimate daughter Elizabeth Stoneman Davey aged fourteen. They did go on to have further children after the tragedy – Aleena Dora and Ellen, but one cannot imagine the trauma of having so many deaths to deal with in the space of only two weeks that winter. Richard's brother Walter lost his only son the following January:

Walter John Davey aged 3¾, February 21st

An itinerant family living at Foxes Cross lost three of their children in the first quarter of 1886:

Tilly Manning aged 1, January 30th

Frederick Manning aged 11, February 1oth

Laura Manning aged 8 months, April 30th

It is worth noting that these fatalities were not from children living in the village itself and the outbreak seems to have been confined to particular families, suggesting that they may have taken the trouble to isolate themselves from others once the illness had taken hold. This seems to be at odds with theories that either shared facilities were responsible for the spread of the bug or that attendance at the school and church were a means of spreading disease.

In Uffculme, where there was also an outbreak of measles in the summer of 1885, officials debated the matter in the press, and put forward their theory that sharing a closet between four families was responsible for spreading the disease. Doctors in that town reported that some children actually appeared to recover from the measles attack, but then succumbed to a bad throat and died. Some held parents accountable because they did not take enough care over keeping their homes clean. Bad throat was a symptom of mumps rather than measles but it was also a symptom of diphtheria. The fact is that the causes and spread of disease were still something of a mystery to the medical profession, and remained so well into the 20th century. An effective measles vaccine was not available until as late as 1963, whilst a diphtheria vaccine was only introduced in the 1920s.

In 1907-8 there was another measles and diphtheria epidemic which affected many children in Cheriton. There was still a confusion as to how illness spread in the community and some felt that this was due to unsanitary conditions in the main road of the village where sewage pipes laid in the 1860s were now cracked and leaking. Cheriton however was not the only village affected that year, so although not the primary cause of the underlying illness, its spread was probably aided by poor water quality. The Education Board decided to publish statistics in local newspapers to show how many children were affected in each school. Newton St Cyres School had to be shut completely due to illness, whilst East village had only fifty five children attending and Cheriton only sixty six.

1907 Charles Sidney Melhuish aged 2, buried March 24th

He was the son of William and Ellen Melhuish of Buddle whose older children were unaffected: Alfred 1896. Albert 1898. Walter 1900, Ethel 1903 (and Edith 1910.)

1908 Annie Raymont aged 3, buried February 2nd
1908 Frederick John Raymont aged 9, buried February 9th

Frederick lived with his parents Thomas and Mary Raymont (nee Butt) at Whites Cross Cottages with siblings Thomas, Lily, Emily, May and William. His case certainly did not lead to siblings being affected and indeed his parents continued to expand their family with Amy and Samuel being born after Frederick passed away. The family also adopted one year old Myrtle Ada in 1910. She was born in the village to a single mother and housemaid called Ada Green. This large and welcoming family seems to have flourished against all odds and the children were said to be very happy. When Thomas died in 1939, Myrtle his adopted daughter was just about to marry Granville Thorne, the eldest son of the baker, draper and grocer Edwin Thorne of Victoria House. Granville was a lot older than Myrtle being forty six. Mr Raymont had suffered 'a lingering illness' and had not been able to work for about ten years and his final employer had been Rev Arundell. His parents John and Fanny lived at Orchard Cottage, next to Moxeys, (now demolished) after moving into the village from Kenn in the 1850s.

The three year old Annie Raymont who died was not a member of this family but may have been related in some way.

1908 Daisy Frances Melhuish aged 2, buried February 11th

At the time of her death Daisy Melhuish's family lived at the buildings, Upham and her father James was working as a road contractor. Born in Cullompton and married to Bessie, James also had Edith, Florence, Elsie, Ernest and Ivy.

1908 Edith Sharland aged 14 months, buried March 8th

Emma was the daughter of waggoner Francis Sharland and his wife Hannah from Foxes Cross. Older children were Rose 1898, Jessie 1901, Maude 1903, Walter 1905, (Emma 1909 and William 1911.)

Because the affected children came from different parts of the parish many rumours flew around as to how the disease was spread, ranging from not isolating children from their unaffected siblings, to misguidedly self-medicating them, not disinfecting furniture in the house and sharing books with the sick without fumigating them afterwards. Some children it seems were not allowed to attend Sunday school as a precaution but did attend chapel etc. This 'Indignant' letter writer to The Western Times airs his views on the matter

In 1906 a survey in the village had found that the main drain, of stone construction was in a most unsatisfactory condition – one of the worst in the district. Sewer gas was escaping through openings in the soil, even a few feet

HEALTH OF CHERITON FITZPAINE.

To the Editor of the " Western Times."

Sir,—Week after week, in this parish, we hear of fresh cases of diphtheria. They occur in places remote from each other, and, according to all accounts, present a very difficult puzzle to the medical men of the neighbourhood. The question is asked, "However is the infection carried?" Independent inquiry supplies information which suggests the following as possible reasons :—

(1) Cases of bad throat occur and, in consequence of the co-existence of mumps, are described as "mumps" and treated by the parents. In more than one case the parents state that they are sure their children have suffered from the same complaint as other children who have been under treatment for diphtheria. The treatment has been "sulphur, etc." Of course, these cases not having come under the observation of a doctor, and so not being reported to the Medical Officer of Health, proper isolation has not taken place. The brothers or sisters of the victim have slept with him or her, and, in the end, there has been no disinfection of the house, furniture, etc.

(2) Failure to properly isolate the patient in known cases. The sister of one patient actually slept with her at night, and played with the children of the village by day.

(3) The children of the family affected, though not allowed to attend day or Sunday school, yet attend church or chapel without restriction.

(4) The interchange of books takes place, the friends of the family, wishing to make the sufferers as comfortable as possible, lending books for the patients to read, which books quite probably are returned to their owners without disinfection, and, also quite probably, lent to the little neighbour who is suffering from measles, with which disease we are now surfeited.

from dwelling houses, and it was felt that an effectively ventilated drain should be laid, and all private drains connected to it. It also highlighted the fact that the main drain ran down Back Hayes Lane to the west end of Church Town and eventually discharged into an open ditch at Tower Hill crossroads. The contents of the ditch ran into the orchard near the blacksmiths shop with the sewage being used for irrigating and fertilising the meadow belonging to Mr Pridham of Pool Barton. This orchard ran behind Cheriton Barton down to Tower Hill cross roads where The Old Smithy bungalow now stands and behind the present day doctor's surgery. Presumably the pipe entered the open ditch between the Smithy bungalow and the small triangle of land opposite the gate to Morles Farm. It was proposed that a covered concrete tank holding 4,500 gallons be constructed in the orchard with both inlet and outlet chambers to enable it to be pumped regularly.

There is mention of this set up in an 1835 sale of part of Gidshay or Pynes including Lot 7: 'An extraordinarily rich watered meadow of 4½ acres fertilised by the drose within the village, now in the possession of Mrs Oliver.'

At the east end of the village the alms-houses and some nearby cottages drained into a pond 'below', which meant that the surrounding wells were in danger of being contaminated. Businesses on the north of the main street drained into a six inch socket pipe with clay joints that had been laid some twenty years before. This then discharged into a meadow.

Plans were drawn up for improvements to the sewerage system in the village and parish council met two or three times to discuss the most economical way forward, debating whether an extra tanks should be laid and whether the section from the smithy to Cheriton Barton should be included when pipes were renewed. One hundred and fifty ratepayers were consulted about the sewage scheme and in the end most just wanted the best outcome for the village. Many felt that this procrastination was adding to the suffering but money was also an issue when funds were limited.

The Education Board also appeared to have been biding their time and the school still opened every day even though children were succumbing to the disease by mixing with others. The incubation period was short and an unlucky child could develop the disease as soon as two days after being exposed to it. This newspaper article in May 1907 pointed out that before Board Officials decided to formally close the school it had opened one day with five teachers and only twelve children. The remaining one hundred and thirty had been kept away either because they were ill or because their parents did not want them to catch the bug, but also because rumours had been circulating that the school had already been closed officially when this was not yet the case.

Great satisfaction is felt by the parishioners at the recommendations of Mr. Siddalls, jun Tiverton, as to the drainage of this village. It is felt that the matter is in competent hands, and that the suggested scheme is a vindication of the resolution passed at a parish meeting last Christmas, but not accepted by the Authority. The feeling becomes unanimous that this, or any other means of restoring the village to a proper state of health should be speedily effected. The diphtheria epidemic has become alarming, and great indignation is expressed at the School having been opened before the disease was stamped out, some parents feeling confident that their children contracted it there. It is felt that the Sanitary Authority might be more energetic, and adopt different methods in this respect. For instance, last Monday the school was opened, and, it is understood, at 9.30 a.m., there were present five teachers and a dozen children, the numerous absences (about 130) being caused by various rumours that had gone the rounds, e.g., that the Authority had ordered the closure of the school for a week; that the school was not to be opened for a month; and that it would not be open again till further notice. Of course, nervous parents welcome the rumours, and act upon them. In this instance, the managers closed the school until Monday next, 13th inst.

The officials of the Bible Christian Sunday School have, in consequence of the epidemic, postponed the anniversary sine die.

Western Times May 10th 1907

In early July 1912 there was a Medical Officer at the school following up reports of a very prevalent complaint amongst the children, affecting the kidneys. It was said to be due to the dirt, and witnesses had reported that the school was only cleaned three times per year and only one bowl of water and one towel were left out for the one hundred children to wash in. With no water supply, staff fetched water from a well that was condemned as being situated too near the churchyard. This was the deep well, since capped, outside Scut's Almshouse at the entrance to The Hayes

A week later a newspaper article refuted some of the published findings saying that contrary to the report, a fresh bowl of water and towel were put out in each play shelters (boys' and girls') every morning and that the well had served the school and three cottages for sixty years without being condemned. It was 48' from the nearest grave that had last received a burial forty five years ago and 60' from the grave of two young children who died twenty four years ago (the Roskilly toddlers). Until the County Council had disturbed the well there had been no problems and because children who attended the school lived within a two mile radius it was said to be up to their parents to make sure that they came to school clean.

The following month officials decided to erect a pump over the existing well, but it was recognised that the water supply was insufficient for the village.

Mental Health

The case of Hermon Taylor in the 1720s stands as testament to the forward-looking attitudes held in the parish towards mental health. And the lack of discrimination towards the Hewish family after the case of William Hewish in 1753 is further evidence of a non-judgemental community. But what of treatment and neighbourly attitudes to those with mental health problems in later years, when officials had had to relinquish their parochial responsibilities and to rely instead upon local and national government facilities? In many ways, this enforced conformity of new Poor Laws meant that a parish like Cheriton Fitzpaine could no longer make its own decisions about individuals in the community, and had little to offer except access to the provisions available to all communities.

In 1886 Thomas Cole, farming at Barnshill wanted something different for his beloved wife, Emma when she started to struggle with her behaviour and her health. He specifically did not want her taken to the Exeter Lunatic Asylum although she had become too difficult to keep safe in the dangerous environment of a busy farm. So it was that a private arrangement was made and she was sent to stay with a Mrs Bradford at Shobrooke who undertook to keep her safe and watch her day and night. But the newspapers reported that whilst there she tried to cut her throat with a table knife that she had sharpened and secreted about her body. Fifty year old Mrs Cole was being well cared, for but a search of the property revealed that her state of mind had led her to hide several sharp implements around the house. Her family had a diagnosis that Emma was suffering with a brain tumour which explained her head-aches and erratic behaviour. Today her state of mind and actions would have been sympathetically received, but in 1886 suicide was still considered to be a criminal act, hence its newsworthiness at the time. Emma had one surviving daughter, Winifred Hewish Cole 1876.

Emma died a painful and troubled death, but she was still considered to be the love of Thomas Cole's life and he ensured that she was not committed to the Asylum.

Just ten years earlier in 1875 Emma's father John Hewish, farmer of Holes Farm had been committed to the Exeter Lunatic Asylum so the family would have had first-hand knowledge of the treatment on offer. Aged about eighty, John died there a few months later. In 1890 Emma's nephew Ben Hewish, the son of her elder sister Maria, was committed as a lunatic. He was aged only 29 when he died. One is reminded of William Hewish who in the 1750s who was tried for the murder of both his parents, then hung in 1753.

Herman Taylor was offered extraordinary care when he suffered 'a period of lunacy' and members of his family were not stigmatised during or after his demise.

There is no evidence that the village treated these people with any less care and understanding that those who were taken ill with physical symptoms.

Accidents

Most accidents in the parish were caused by horse-drawn vehicles or other live-stock, although a few involved drowning.

A Mr Cole of Higher Waterhouse was travelling home in his trap in the summer of 1886 when he turned back to talk with a neighbouring farmer. The step of the trap caught on a gate that was open into the lane and he was thrown out and pinned under his vehicle. He broke several ribs and suffered other internal injuries and was then treated by Dr Champney.

John Greenslade came to some considerable harm negotiating the notoriously steep Dover's Hill in 1891, when his horse slipped and the shafts of his cart broke. After being seen by the doctor the following day he was transferred by the local vicar to the Exeter hospital for further treatment.

SERIOUS ACCIDENT NEAR CHERITON FITZPAINE

A serious accident occurred about half a mile from Cheriton Fitzpaine to John Greenslade, general haulier. He was returning from Crediton with a heavy load of coal, and in descending the steep incline known as Dover's Hill, either owing to the road being slippery or being overloaded the horse appears to have slipped and broke the harness, with the result that the trap came over on the horse, breaking the shafts. The animal falling knocked the man over, and the wheel grazing his head inflicted some deep cuts and bruises. The Rev. W. H. Arundell fortunately was returning from Crediton, and hearing the man's cry for help he rendered every assistance and got him conveyed to his home. Dr. Thorne attended to his injuries, and the next morning Greenslade was removed in the Rev. W. H. Arundell's carriage to the Devon and Exeter Hospital. The full extent of the injuries received cannot as yet be ascertained. The horse escaped without injury.

November 1891 Exeter and Plymouth Gazette

In 1906 William Taverner the seventeen year old son of Mr and Mrs Taverner of Welcombe Farm died when a horse bolted and knocked him down whilst he was moving manure. The boy appeared to have no broken bones and was carried home by his brother George where he was put to bed but later died.

1864 Isaac Lee a carpenter had gone to Exeter to buy and pony and trap but when he did not return his family assumed that he had stayed the night. On the

Saturday morning his body was found near Cadbury with his horse nearby. It was assumed that it had stumbled and thrown him from the vehicle.

The road from Tower Hill to Stockleigh English meant that the traveller had to negotiate crossing Hollywater. When it was raining the water flowed dangerously fast and a Mr David Retter, farmer of Stockleigh Court almost became a fatality of it in October 1886. His horse lost its footing in the swirling water and he was wrenched from the saddle and washed downstream. Luckily he managed to cling to a tree, but it took a considerable time for help to arrive after his horse returned home without him. It highlighted the fact that a horse bridge was badly needed at that point in the river. Squire Moore's Bridge now enables vehicles to travel safely to Stockleigh English.

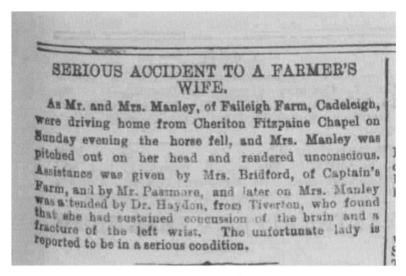

SERIOUS ACCIDENT TO A FARMER'S WIFE.

As Mr. and Mrs. Manley, of Faileigh Farm, Cadeleigh, were driving home from Cheriton Fitzpaine Chapel on Sunday evening the horse fell, and Mrs. Manley was pitched out on her head and rendered unconscious. Assistance was given by Mrs. Bridford, of Captain's Farm, and by Mr. Passmore, and later on Mrs. Manley was attended by Dr. Haydon, from Tiverton, who found that she had sustained concussion of the brain and a fracture of the left wrist. The unfortunate lady is reported to be in a serious condition.

Western Times December 1890

Mrs Manley suffered serious head injuries on her way home from Chapel when the horse pulling the cart that she and her farmer husband were travelling in, fell, pitching her out on to the road.

The Exeter and Plymouth Gazette dated May 8th 1841 had a very sad tale to tell about one of the Oliver brothers, who were much respected in the parish. Mr William Oliver was found dead on his horse in the road leading towards his home from Tiverton Market. The horse was standing still and his hands were grasping the reins, so it was supposed that he was seized with a sudden apoplectic fit. He had previously taken tea with his brother Mr Thomas Oliver who was schoolmaster at the Tiverton Union Workhouse and Thomas witnessed that his brother had left him in apparent perfect health.

Mr William Ridge drowned in the river at Cowley Bridge when his blind horse pitched him over the rails on his way home from Exeter in 1825.

1910 Farmer Paddon was thrown from his horse near Bickleigh and suffered fatal injuries. His wife sent out a search party for him when his horse returned home of its own accord to Court Place Farm at Upham.

Other accidents involved day-to-day hazards included the following:

> 1902 saw a shooting accident when T Mehuish aged 21 was shot in the wrist and shoulder when he got in the way of his master Mr John Greenslade's gun when they were out rabbiting. The wording of the report makes very little of this, and appears to blame the youth for his inattentiveness!

In 1932 Mrs Rose Stone was found dead in bed at Higher Holne six weeks after her husband had died. She was seventy four years old.

In 1886 Mary Sharland aged seventy three was walking into the village when she slipped and fell, breaking her thigh, whilst Thomas Jeffery fell as he got out of his cart and broke his leg, having to be taken to the Devon and Exeter hospital for treatment.

It was a miracle that no-one was hurt at Perry Farm in August 1933 when a spark from an oil-fired threshing machine set fire to a barn. Such was the strength of the wind that the thatched roof of the farmhouse caught light and the entire building was gutted. It was a beautiful old Devon long house complete with oak beams and screens. As well as losing their home, James and Charlotte Yendall also lost their corn and two years' worth of wool that was being stored in the farmhouse itself. The Crediton fire brigade attended quickly but soon ran out of water, using up the contents of the pond and then pumping the stream dry.

Life in an agricultural community is probably just as hazardous today as it always was, with more danger now from machines and vehicles than from livestock and guns. The medical care is vastly different of course but the tragedies remain as vivid.

References

1. All facts have been taken from local newspapers, too numerous to mention

Crime in the Parish

A set of village stocks in the porch of Rose Ash Church

The earliest evidence of crime in the Cheriton Fitzpaine can be found in the Manorial Court Rolls and the Quarter Sessions Records. Generally speaking the village was a peaceful one and inhabitants resolved their differences without matters having to be referred to higher authorities. The Manor Court was presided over by twelve sworn jurors chosen from the locality: men who had a good reputation and standing amongst the population; men who could be trusted to reach a fair verdict on the evidence presented to them, and men who were themselves aware of good moral behaviour. Meetings would have been held with due ceremony in the Vestry of Church House after 1648 and in the church itself before that. Unfortunately there are very few extant documents for the Hundred of West Budleigh to which Cheriton Fitzpaine belonged and therefore very few details of court cases for the village survive. The Hundred was

186

comprised of the parishes Cheriton, Poughill, Shobrooke, Stockleigh English, Stockleigh Pomeroy, Upton Hellions and Washfield. Within Cheriton itself there were six manors: Upcott-Stockley, Coddiford, Coombe, Chilton, Dunscombe and Cheriton itself. Each manor was then subdivided into tenths or tythings originally containing ten households. These separate tithings were Cheriton, Sutton Satchvill (or East Stockleigh/Estocheleia, which was Upcott), Stockleigh Luccombe (Little Stockleigh or South Stockleigh which covered much of Upham) and Lower Dunscombe.

Confusingly the name 'Stockleigh' was used for several of the hamlets within Cheriton parish and it is important to recognise that Stockleigh English and Stockleigh Pomeroy were separate from Cheriton Fitzpaine and its manors.

Cases were heard at the Manor Court and recorded on rolls of vellum by a scribe. Witnesses could stand forward and give their version of events and the plaintiff and the defendant were then at the mercy of decisions made by the twelve jurors presided over by a steward. Punishment was usually a fine but there could a penalty imposed such as repairing a wall or cleaning out a water-course, very like community service today. The Normans had altered the English feudal court system by adding a jury of twelve local freemen who were to hear evidence and come to an agreed verdict. The lord of the manor or his steward would chair the hearing and the parish clerk would record the facts on a roll of parchment.

In the Manorial Court Rolls for Cheriton, part of the Hundred of West Budleigh, Richard Reynold acted as a tithingman for Stockleigh Luccombe (Upham area) in 1591 and again in 1595. Andrew Reynold held the same office. A tithingman was responsible for ensuring that anyone in the neighourhood accused of a crime appeared at the court to answer for it, and if they ran away, it was their responsibility to bring them back to face the court's judgement or to raise a 'hue and cry'. Tithingmen also acted as the eyes and ears of the court by informing on any criminal activity in the area in the form of a sworn Presentment to the court. On many occasions the Cheriton tithingmen presented that there was absolutely nothing to report to the court, which is significant given the size of the parish.

In 1454 William Scutt was a juror followed by John Scutt in 1515 and Thomas Scutt in 1548, showing that as a family they had settled early in the village and were considered to be free-men of good character.

In 1599 Richard Reynold, who had been a tithingman was one of the twelve jurors at the court, but the following year, 1600, a case was brought to the court stating that he had been attacked by John Bartlett. One wonders if this had anything to do with a verdict Reynold had been responsible for making against him, and it showed that when the court was not sitting, the jurors were just ordinary men capable of falling out with their neighbours. Unfortunately the West Budleigh rolls do not go into any detail and the scribe at the time was both factual and succinct.

In 1591–2 and again in 1595 Agnes Scutt, widow, presented herself at court, complaining against her brother Andrew Reynold, but again there are no details given. The matter may have been her ongoing dispute over a dowry of money and property, promised by her late father William Reynold, which was taken to the higher Court of Chancery.

In the 1596 Court roll there is a report that a stray animal was found on Richard Reynold's land. Generally an animal would have been kept in a pound until the owner came forward and paid a fine for its release. If it was not claimed, the court would make a decision to sell it or sometimes to gift it to a deserving villager. An entry in 1599 records that Walter Thomas by the pledge of Hugh Thomas came to the court to prove a stray found on land of Richard Reynold to be his. One hopes that this was not the same animal as reported three years earlier!

Milling in Cheriton Fitzpaine

A common complaint in the period was against a succession of millers in Cheriton Fitzpaine, said to be taking excessive tolls: 1454 William Batyn/Baten, 1549 John Lovell, 1535 Robert Whyterowe, and 1631 Martin Wescombe. An ancient Law stated that:

> 'The toll of a mill shall be according to the custom of the land and the strength of the water course, either to the twentieth, or the four and twentieth corn … whereby the toll shall be taken shall be agreeable to the King's measure, and toll shall be taken by the rase and not by the heap or cantel,' (the words rase and cantel both mean a portion or a cut of bread.)

The watercourse at Hedgecleave was never a torrent and there were other mills in the area where a farmer could take his grain, and although there were

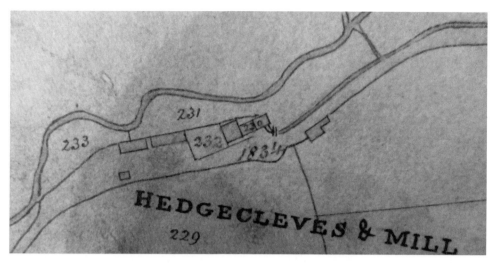

1840 Tythe map showing a leet running to the mill wheel at the eastern end of the property. The road is not defined as it passes through the complex of buildings, but the square Georgian house does have a walled garden plot numbered 232

countless complaints in court, the tolls were not altered. (Tucking Mill and Poughill Mill were up-stream of Cheriton Mill.)

Many leases of property in the area stated that the farmer could only take grain to Cheriton Mill for preparation and indeed, most roads led to the Mill. Since these leases were issued by the Lord of the Manor it is not surprising that he would want the profits from his Mill to be as high as possible.

Cheriton Mill also known as Hedgecleave

Arson or not?

The current Georgian building dates from c1723 but the linhay to the left of this picture is clearly older. Robert Manley of Great Venn Farm purchased the Mill complex from Rev William Harris in 1797 and sub-let it to the Stabbick family and then passed the lease on to his son Robert Manley jnr. A late Victorian water wheel and pit have since been removed from the northern side of the property where the Hollywater runs. A disastrous fire in 1872 destroyed an earlier wheel which stood at the eastern end of the building now known as Millers Cottage where the tenant miller lived and worked. This was said to have been started deliberately by the then tenant, Thomas Fice who was known to have financial problems. As well as the stock he said that he lost there was a box of money kept in his bedroom that was never found. Two floors of the building fell through during the blaze but miraculously, nobody was hurt. Thomas Fice and his wife Sarah and children Sarah Ann aged four, Charles Thomas aged two and William John aged one were in Exeter at the time. They had only recently moved into the property from Sidbury and had no local connections. Fice was the son of millwright John Fice of Modbury but had served his apprenticeship with William Truby at Swanbridge Mill in Sidbury. He took on a seven year lease of Cheriton Mills on 27th February 1871 and Manley had directed him to employ Taylor and Bodley, iron founders of Exeter to first put right all the machinery in the Mill with the promise that he as owner would then take over the maintenance of it during the tenancy. This was an unusual and uncharitable request to make, but it seems that Fice had no alternative but to accept it.

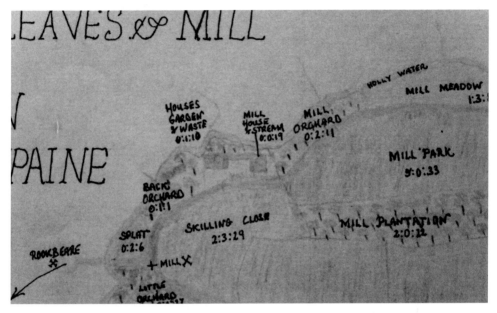

Part of an estate map of Hedgecleave Mill 1797, showing the Mill House and the house and garden when let by Robert Manley to the Stabbick family. The buildings differ from those shown on the Tythe map

The Western Times dated July 16th 1872 reported how Mr Robert Manley who had owned the entire premises for many years had left his house, Hedgecleave which adjoined Fice's Mill House at about 10am on the morning of the fire in order to meet with the Bishop who was going to conduct a Confirmation at Cheriton Church that same day. He returned soon afterwards hearing that the Mill was well alight and already badly damaged. Depositions were made by John and Richard Raymond, Daniel Hodge, Daniel Melhuish, Robert Southcott, Rodney Manley his grandson, Samuel Wootton, Mary Ann Gillard, P C Wood and Sergeant Phillips. P C Percy had reached the burning building at about 11.30

am and stayed there until 5 am the following morning to witness the destruction, seeing the mill stone fall and floors collapse

P.C. Percy sworn, said—I remember the 12th of June; I was between Stockleigh Court and the village when I heard that Cheriton Mills were on fire. I went directly there; it was about half-past eleven o'clock when I got there. I remained all day and until the next morning about five o'clock. I saw the floors fall in, but did not see any bran, meal, or anything else. I was in a position to see if there was any there. I saw the top floor fall in; the second fell first. The water was running over the wheel; the water was a little muddy, not particularly discoloured. I saw Fice on the Sunday, and he told me people had accused him of setting the mill on fire, and he said that was not likely as he had bought two fresh cows, a horse, and a new cart, and had tilled up his garden, and was in hopes that things would go on all right. He said he had lost most all he had got. He said he had a large quantity of meal, bran, and sharps, and a lot of empty sacks destroyed, and about £48 in money. He said £35 was in notes, and the remainder in silver and copper. He accounted for having so much silver and copper by receiving it from people around Cheriton who had paid him for meal, &c., he had sold to them. I asked if he knew the numbers of the notes. He said "no," and that he had taken them from a man in Exeter, but could not tell who. He told me the money was kept in a box in his bedroom. I afterwards searched and sifted the rubbish, but could not find any money, flour, meal, or anything else of the sort.

But there were suspicions about how and why the fire started and locals began to talk about it. Elizabeth Melhuish who happened to be Manley's daughter reported that she had heard Mrs Fice threaten to burn down the Mill because the couple were finding it hard to pay their rent to Manley. Some locals stated that Robert Manley was 'an old rogue … who had sold out one or two before'. Others swore that there was very little flour or meal being produced at the mill by Fice at the time and that he did not seem to have much stock or money to hand. Manley himself testified that there was ill feeling between himself as landlord and Fice as tenant over money that was owed, and that Fice had started to move his personal belongings from the premises.

Elizabeth Melhuish said—I remember being in my father's house (Mr. Manley's) when the altercation took place with the prisoner and his wife, Mrs. Fice. I cannot tell exactly when it was, but it was between the 25th of March and the 11th of April. I heard what Mrs. Fice said, it was, "I'll burn the b—— old mill down sooner than master shall have another farthing, if Tom goes to prison for it." Fice said, "Hold your tongue you old fool, I knew it would be so when you came in. You are like your old father, you can't keep nort." I remember Mrs. Kingsland coming for some barleymeal, it was the Friday before the fire. I don't think there was more than two or three parts of sacks in the mill.

The case was referred to trial, and in July 1872 after all the evidence had been heard and considered, Thomas Fice was acquitted of arson.

But Manley was not satisfied and in September that same year he pursued Fice in respect of £9.5s.8d. owed to Taylor and Bodley for the initial iron-work they had carried out on machinery at the Mill. The court denied Manley the money saying that it was usual for the owner of a Mill to undertake such work at their own expense in readiness for a new tenant. Fice was by then living in Exeter, needing to make a fresh start. He moved the family to Cornwall to find work in his trade. Sarah Fice died whilst they were in St Gluvias, Cornwall leaving him with several children to bring up. Only two months later he married a widow called Elizabeth Jane Sedgeman (nee Francis) and they then moved to South Devon to settle in Plymouth. She had been married to John Sedgeman for a very short time before he died, possibly as a tin miner. In Plymouth, Fice's eldest son, Charles was apprenticed by his father and became a miller himself.

It is difficult to know who was in the wrong throughout this case because each party appears to have had their faults. Some believed that Fice had burned the Mill to harm Manley and to obtain insurance money, whilst other believed that Manley was capable of ruining others. Mr Manley had the property re-built and it featured in a 'for sale' advertisements in the Western Times for 10th July 1874 as 'Cheriton Mills a newly built dwelling house and cottage, excellent homestead, large walled garden, small lawn and shrubbery, and 57 acres 1 rood 1 perch of rich pasture, water meadow, orchard and productive arable land. Possession at Christmas, Completion 25th March next.'

The Georgian House itself does not bear any traces of having been affected by the fire, save that a two storey extension has been built on the southern side, throwing out its symmetry. The cellars beneath are likewise unaffected, so it may be that Manley took the opportunity to improve his side of the property when he re-built the tenanted part.

Fice had not felt entirely comfortable in Cheriton from the start, because on 27th June 1871 he had taken a Mr M Coles to court, suing him for non-payment of a bill for £3.3s.0d. in respect of three sacks of barleymeal that he had processed and delivered to him. Coles reported that he had never received the goods and as he had little money himself, he could not pay anything (Western Times 12th September 1871.) Mr Manley was a man with a reputation, intent upon making money and when he purchased the mill from the estate of Rev William Harris in 1797 there is no doubt that he was determined to improve his own family's fortunes.

Marks of the beam in the cellar underneath the Georgian Mill House

Other crimes reported at the Manorial Court

1454 Thomas Gore for brewing ale, Geoffrey Fore, Walter Browne and Peter Lake for tapping ale by false means. Richard Oxenbere for attacking John Gibbe.

1462 William Parson, clerk attacked John at Combe.

1490 the high way between Buddlemede and Foxcrosse has not yet been repaired and the highway between Wodemore and Whytecrosse is deep in mud and Robert Bobycocke must repair it (Buddle/Bowdell must have been built in the area that was called Buddlemead)

1535 Thomas Langham suffered the highway between Sladeparke and Budlamede to be deep in mud and also his fence overhangs the road.

1535 John Lake suffers the highway between Weston brygge and the east side of Waden … is deep in mud.

1535 John Ford taps ale and gives a fine for licence to the office of tithingman John Forde.

1550 Barnaby Langham attacked Thomas Lake with a dagger but the dagger was not presented at court and the case was dropped.

1551 Robert Voysey permitted the high road from Smythwyll Corner towards the upper part of that close called Brodeclose to be in decay

1595 the bridge between the land of Henry Bellew and Andrew Beere, leading from Cheriton Fitzpaine to Stockleigh English which was in disrepair was to be repaired by both parties (Hollywater crossing)

1596 Thomas Conneby obstructed a footpath in the free hamlet of Sutton Sachfild (Upcott area) leading from Cheriton to Exeter. Another footpath in the said place leading as above is also stopped by Edward Browne to the grave damage of the inhabitants. A place called Shut Ashe is mentioned.

Quarter Sessions

Quarter Sessions were held in Exeter four times a year and a Justice of the Peace attended to hear criminal charges as well as civil and criminal appeals. Unsurprisingly, there are few records of cases involving Cheriton people, and those cases that were heard, usually involved common assault or theft.

1736 Robert Skinner the younger was said to have been assaulted by a whole group of neighbours including yeoman John Webber and his wife, William Colscott, labourer, Joan Knowles, spinster, Mary Hodge, spinster and Elizabeth Coggins, spinster.

In 1740 Robert Down assaulted Susannah Glanville so badly that her right tibia was broken.

But the Lawdy/Parkhouse vs Bright/Wootton case was by far the most protracted and can be found in the Quarter Sessions' records for 1740. That year animosity between families bubbled over and led to an attack upon Jane Bright, wife of John Bright by several others. Husbandman Richard Lawdy and his wife Elizabeth, together with Elizabeth Oldbridge, and husbandman Richard Parkhouse attacked Jane Bright, and one can imagine the fracas with poor Mrs Bright at the bottom of the scrum. Augustine Wootton, yeoman and cooper had his own grudge against the Lawdy family and pitched into the fight assaulting Richard Lawdy. Augustine seems to have been a man with a grudge against many neighbours and his name appears several times in the Quarter Sessions records. For all participants to be in the same place at the same time points towards a social event where alcohol may have been involved. The matter was resolved at Sessions but things between them did not improve. The following year the same people were summoned to Sessions again. This time there were accusations that Augustine Wootton and John and Jane Bright had broken into Parkhouse's garden and stolen an elm plank that belonged to Parkhouse and Lawdy. Lawdy and Parkhouse then retaliated by stealing 'a parcel of sticks fit for stakes of the value of six pence' belonging to John Bright.

Three years earlier in 1737 Augustine Wootton had managed not to resort to violence when Hugh Moxey allowed his cattle to stray and break down his hedge, but in 1750 he had another altercation with neighbours and was reported by Mary White, wife of John for swearing five profane oaths. He retaliated by reporting her for swearing seven profane oaths and both were fined.

In 1752 Augustine suffered flooding to his property and accused labourers Thomas Shapcott and Samuel Upham and William Badcock, yeoman of unlawfully diverting a water course on to the highway from Cheriton Church Town to Tiverton, and digging up and removing stones, earth and soil. The result was that the highway between Lower Down Hedge and Augustine Wootton's house was flooded. The case dragged on with two more men, Richard Campion and William Badcock, both yeomen, being accused of the same misdemeanour the following year.

In 1754 Augustine Wootton and Thomas Taylor were accused of assaulting Martha, wife of Joseph Pope, carpenter. By then the records referred to Augustine as a labourer rather than a yeoman or cooper and one wonders if his fortunes had changed over the years.

In 1754 Hugh Moxey, yeoman was prosecuted for allowing his cattle to run along the highway and break the hedge of Augustine Wotton.

Another salacious case occurred between the Taylors and the Brewers. 1753 Mary Taylor was accused of assaulting Joseph Brewer, a tailor, as well as Mary the wife of William Brewer, a cordwainer. At the same court Mary, the wife of John Taylor, husbandman, claimed that she was assaulted by several members of the Brewer family: the said Joseph Brewer, Mary Brewer and her husband William and white bread baker Robert Brewer and his wife Mary. Their cat fight may well have been fuelled by alcohol whilst the couples were socialising and was likely to have been over jealousies or property. Mary's husband John Taylor was in fact the son of Herman Taylor who had cost the parish so much during his period of lunacy in the 1720s, and one might be tempted to conclude that it was a retaliation attack on the Taylors, but because John does not appear to have been involved in the fracas at all and may not have been present at the time, it was probably not sparked by old resentments about Herman. Mary, already a mother to four children, gave birth to her next baby, John jnr, shortly after the court hearing.

1754 John Yelland, tailor assaulted William Oliver for which he was fined 6d.

Another member of the Oliver family was involved in a case in 1756 when Richard Oliver, yeoman was accused of assaulting and beating Philip Westron at Cheriton Fitzpaine. The witness was Samuel Stempson. As there was no bill against Oliver the charges were probably dropped. Rating lists show that Philip Westron farmed West Burrow in 1749 and 1751 and it may be significant that Richard Oliver had taken on an apprentice, John Crocker to work for him at West Burrow farm in 1754. The two therefore must have worked closely on the farm but again, there are insufficient details to identify the problem. Philip Westron of Dunscombe and West Burrow figures in more than one Chancery Court cases, indicating that he was a man who wanted things his way.

1739 Joan Davy, singlewoman was said to be a common scold and public disturber of the peace.

Theft

In 1742 Margaret Littlewyre, spinster of Cheriton Fitzpaine stood accused of stealing from William Smith a woman's quilted coat, a duroy gown (corduroy), three chequered aprons, one pair of women's shoes, one pair of women's worsted stockings, fourteen women's caps and three women's handkerchiefs to the value of 10/-.

1743 Thomas Taylor, labourer from Cheriton had joined forces with Joseph Coombe of Bickleigh to break into Elizabeth Uppon's (Upham's) house and take 'one iron crock of the value of a shilling, one brass kettle of the value of a shilling, eight pewter plates of the value of four shillings and one brass skillet of the value of one shilling.'

In 1747 William Maunder, cordwainer joined up with Robert Goff of Poughill and Thomas Edwards of Kennerleigh to break into William Newton's house at Poughill, damaging 'the lasting and plaistering' to the value of 20/-. That same year William Maunder also joined up with Michael Rowe of Cheriton and Nicholas Helmore of Poughill to steal seven pewter dishes, six pewter plates, one

Pewter plates

pewter bowl, two iron crocks and two tubs to the value of £3. William Maunder got married to Mary Ocock the following year and must have been influenced to turn away from his youthful crimes for there are no further prosecutions. Their little family however was not a fortunate one with Mary Maunder their first child dying when she was only two years old and their son John Maunder, born 1753 being drowned in a well at two and a half years old when his mother was nursing his four month old brother, William. A Coroner was called to investigate the toddler's death:

1755 30th June, John Maunder a child drowned in a well at Cheriton Fitzpaine.

William and Mary had three surviving children: Robert 1750, William 1755 and John 1757.

In 1753 Anne Hockaday stole a goose from John Hall of Crediton and John Hockaday the elder and the younger of Cheriton Fitzpaine stood surety for her.

1753 Thomas Shapcott, mason, William Badcock, yeoman, Samuel Upham, yeoman and Richard Campin, labourer were charged on November 5th with redirecting the course of the river so as to cause a nuisance to the public and to Augustine Wootton, Lower Down. Each was fined 6d.

In 1836 Four elm planks, a bar of iron, two fowls, a quantity of fruit and a pair of stockings were stolen from William Brown. Those accused, William Newbury, Henry Fray and William Vicary were all acquitted.

Highway matters

The parish had a rota of one or two men responsible for looking after the roads and bridges each year. These men had to find labour and materials to keep pot-holes filled and bridges passable so that daily traffic and trade were not disrupted. They submitted their Accounts to the Overseers of the Poor for settlement at the end of the year. Roads were not metaled and cart wheel ruts caused considerable problems, especially during wet weather when the lanes became waterlogged and holes got deeper. Some parishioners however seemed to take liberties with the roads outside their properties, digging out stones and rubble to maintain their own tracks and buildings and dumping broken carts, dung and household rubbish where others needed to pass.

1734 On January 1st Ann Labdon blocked the common highway leading from the parish church of Cheriton Fitzpaine to Exeter

1750 Edmund Sharland, yeoman was accused of digging, breaking up and making pits in the road from Cheriton Fitzpaine Church to Tiverton. The pits were said to be two feet deep. He also took it upon himself to divert the course of water in an underground gutter which led to other people suffering.

Other crimes can be discovered in the newspapers of the time and the following were considered to be news-worthy:

Assault and theft

1841 Mr Luxton, a respectable farmer returned from market travelling up the hill leading to seven crosses when he noticed several women and two men lagging behind him. He was attacked and robbed of £20 and was unable to put up a fight against so many.

Rape

Little Mary Ann Strong aged ten had been sent on an errand out of the village by her mother in February 1863 and was enticed into a field on the pretext of helping to clean a shoe in the grass by John Lake. She was raped by the sixteen year old who was employed at the time by Farmer Cockram at Burrowcombe Farm. The child carried on with her errand and only told her mother about the crime the following morning which resulted in her father challenging the youth and ensuring that he was brought to trial. Lake was given five years in prison for his crime.

Arson

Over several weeks in the summer of 1830 a number of fires were set in the parish and although there were suspicions as to who the perpetrator was, nobody was ever brought to justice. Rev Arundell had his haystacks set alight and Mr Strong had his house set alight and suffered injuries as a result. Many matches were found in the area. Strong was also attacked as he rode along the highway when a 5lb stone was thrown at him injuring his horse. He felt so uncomfortable in the village that he chose to move away from the area. It is not said where Mr Strong farmed but there was a tenant farmer at Grewe at about this time who was not good at maintaining his hedges or his house and another tenant farmer at Higher Chilton called Richard Strong in the 1820s and 30s. Richard's son John Strong was the father of farm servant Elizabeth Dunn's illegitimate son John, born 1833.

That same summer Mr Melhuish's kennels were broken into and not only were dogs released, but a greyhound had its throat cut and several other dogs were hamstrung. These were dreadful crimes for the village, all the more because they were never resolved.

In 1844 Jane Snell aged ten was found guilty of setting a linhay on fire, belonging to William Stone – an unusual crime for a girl.

1867 Mary Ann Bond, 26 of Cheriton Fitzpaine called Johnny Bastin a groom to court to answer charges of Bastardy in respect of her third illegitimate child, a daughter born in August 1867. Grandmamma Bond had given evidence of a farewell conversation between the two on the staircase as John left the village for a position at Brampford Speke, not intending to return. The court awarded Mary

Ann 1s.6d. a week from Bastin's wages. Mary Ann was living with her Uncle John Channon, who first farmed at Morles and later at White's Cross. Her three children were Caroline 1861, Mary 1862 and Bessie 1868. Mary Ann later earned her living as a laundress in the village. Interestingly, Channon had registered Morles in 1845 as a dissenters meeting house and he was a leading light in the non-conformist circuit.

In 1898 the landlord of the Half Moon was summoned to court as there had been a report of men gambling at cards in his bar. The loser of each round of cards had been seen repeatedly having to buy the drinks and this was considered to be an illegal practice. Robert Melhuish the landlord claimed that he had personally warned the men not to do this and the charges were dropped.

In 1904 a jilted bride turned up at the local Court seeking maintenance for her child from one of the Raymont boys. The banns had been published and two fowls had been killed for their wedding breakfast but the groom did not turn up at the church, disappearing without trace. His brother Albert Raymont had to attend court on behalf of the missing man and Florence Emily Hodge was awarded 2/- per week until her child was fourteen years old. Presumably, in his absence, the Raymont family had to settle their wayward son's debts for him. Happily Florence found herself another husband in 1910 and went to live as Mrs Jesse Burroughs in Heavitree. Her new husband was a bricklayer.

Church authorities and crime

In Cheriton during the 17th century conviction money was extracted from those who fell foul of church and secular laws and Overseers put this to good use by distributing it as part of their duty of care to the poor of the parish. Handing this out publically after a Sunday service, everyone would have known who the felons were and what they had done and it must have acted as a deterrent to most.

In 1662 George Heathman, Elizabeth his wife and their son Henry Heathman were reported by the constable for being absent from church. During the same period the constables also reported seven others for non-attendance on one or two occasions: John Smart and Thomazin his wife, Hugh Thomas and Emilia his wife, Abraham Fursdon, John Lee and Thomas Westland.

In 1662 Andrew Davy was fined for selling cider without a license.

In 1676 Robert Moore was fined 20/- for selling beer without a license and this was distributed as follows:

Peter Langham 1/-	Stephen Winter 1/-
Simon Ham 2/-	William Skinner 1/-
Robert Moore jnr. 3/4d.	Matthew Cudmore 1/-
William Winter 1/-	Davy Uphome 1/-
John Wotton 1/-	Mary Parker 1/-

Those officials who decided that Robert Moore's own relative, possibly his son should receive a disproportionate amount of the money were possibly softening the blow for him. They were carrying out accepted procedures but might not have felt totally comfortable fining their neighbour such a large sum of money. They may well have had beer off Mr Moore themselves at one time or another.

1676 for felling timber without a license £1.

1678 Walter Labdon for absenting for church.

1682 Thomas West for selling cider without license, £1. On this occasion nine poor people benefitted from the fine.

William Skinner for drunkenness 5/-. This was distributed to six deserving poor.

Joseph Pope for selling cider without license, £1, to the benefit of nine people.

In 1685 George Hawkes was ordered to give his contribution of 1/- for absenting himself from church and this money was distributed between George Camp, Mary Smith and John Heard who each received 3d.

In 1694 there was a fine for fishing of 2s.6d.

1700 William Hart gave his contribution for swearing and nine people received benefits from it. Mrs Courtny Mare contributed 6/- which was distributed to six people and three others gave contributions for absenting themselves from church.

In 1713 John Mogford of Nowstone was fined 3/-for being drunk and Edward Heal 3/- for wanting from church. As a result, six people each received 1/-.

A fine was levied against a parishioner in 1718 for carrying a gun and shooting at pigeons.

Mary White convicted Augustine Wootton for profanely swearing 5 oaths 10/- and Augustine Wootton convicted Mary White for profanely swearing 7 oaths 7/-. If we assume that 1/- might represent one profane oath, this imbalance of fines seems to represent that the higher the status of the person, the greater the expectation of their sense of pubic decorum. Augustine may well have been an outspoken character as heis picked up in a Quarter Sessions presentments.

1731 a villager was fined for killing a hare.

In 1743 Andrew Taylor was fined 10/- for suffering John Cruwys, Philip Back and William Cruwys to sit tippling in his house, and the conviction money levied on the three men themselves for tippling in the said Andrew Taylor's house contrary to an Act of Parliament meant that ten people received benefit.

Murder and Suicide

Early in 1792 a murder was committed in the parish.

Monday se'nnight the body of a murdered infant was difcovered by fome children, floating in a pond, at Cheriton Fitzpayne, with a cord tied tight round the neck; the other end of the cord feemed to have a ftone faftened to it, but which was flipped from it, whereby the body floated.
Monday fe'nnight as Mr. John Collie a much-

Bath Chronicle and Weekly Gazette – Thursday 1 March 1792

Overseers of the Poor Accounts 1792

To Mr Turner the inquest of the body of the child's at Combe Hamlet £1.1s.0d.

The child is not named but reading between the lines he or she was more than a baby and might have been a toddler at the time of death. Combe Hamlet was *not* the place we might identify today on northside where North Combe, then farmed by Richard Manley and South Combe, farmed then by Edward Bradford were established. It was, rather, the annexed area of Cheriton parish on the southern slopes of Raddon Hill and now in the parish of Shobrooke. Combe Barton farm or Challiscombe was at the centre of this hamlet where smallholdings Little Combe and Newcombe Woods were clustered. They had been part of Cheriton Fitzpaine parish for centuries.

If the child was local to the hamlet one wonders why it was not identified by name, but it could have been the child of somebody travelling through. Is it possible to conclude who it was from the burial registers? Was it allowed a Christian burial? The newspaper report was dated March 1st 1792. Burials for Cheriton Fitzpaine 1792 are as follows:

Jan 18th William Wootton

March 21st Eleanor Maunder an infant

May 28th Joanna Tancock an infant

July 9th Joan Manley etc.

Given the date of the incident, only the first two entries would be possible candidates. William Wotton's age is not stated but he is not termed an infant or a child which would be the case if he was the murder victim, so it would be worth following Eleanor Maunder a little further. In Cheriton there was a family called Maunder baptising their children but there is no mention of Eleanor:

'To Mary and William Maunder: 1771 John, 1774 James, 1777 John, 1779 Sarah, 1782 William, 1785 George, 1788 Mary Maunder'

If Eleanor was their child, given the three year cycle of their children's births, she might just have been born in 1791.

The alternative explanation is that the child was neither baptised, nor buried in the churchyard and has thus slipped through the paper trail of history. It was common to give victims a grave at the crossroads or at the edge of a farm if they

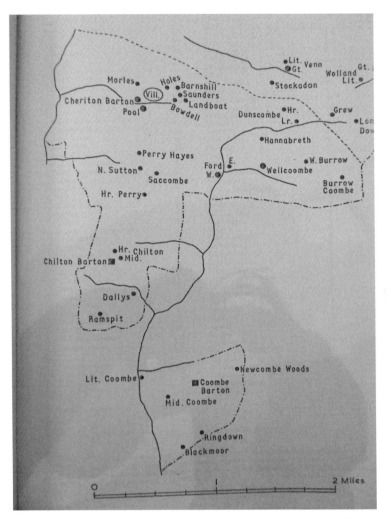

Sketch map by R R Sellman showing Combe hamlet as an annexed part of Cheriton Fitzaine. It later became part of Shobrooke parish

died unbaptised. It is unfortunate that the Overseers gave no further details in their entry.

The evidence of the Poughill parish registers however indicates that it was possible to bury murderers in consecrated ground for in May 1735 one Mary Warren was buried in Poughill graveyard after she had been executed at Heavitree for the murder of 'her bastard child, begotten upon her by Richard Crooke of this parish'.

Suicides

It seems impossible to us that suicide was once considered to be a crime, and those who took their own lives were very often denied a Christian burial. The Coroner was called out from Exeter in the case of a suspicious death in the parish but unfortunately few Coroner's records have survived and the sparse details we have come from newspaper reports, which often contain inaccuracies. Behind each suicide however is a touching human story that has been lost to time.

Emma Sharland was fifty when she hung herself in the loft of her employer's storehouse in 1919. She had worked for Sarah Prior for thirty years as a loyal domestic servant and assistant in the post office and was very much part of the family. She had been ill and in pain for several months and nothing could help her state of depression. The post office was right in the centre of the village and had been a thriving concern when Daniel Prior was alive but Widow Prior was herself getting old and she did the best she could for Emma's future by securing her a coveted place in the almshouses. But Emma did not want to leave her mistress. When she did not rise the next morning another servant went looking for her and discovered the tragedy of Emma's death.

In 1877 Mr John Wotton, Assistant overseer and clerk to the School Board at Cheriton Fitzpaine, aged more than sixty years was found dead in his bedroom. He did suffer from heart disease but he was found hanging there. When the case was reported in the newspaper, it was pointed out that just weeks before another School Board official from a neighbouring parish had also committed suicide.

In 1894 Robert Chamberlain a labourer aged fifty five was missing for work and when William Manning and John Cann gained access to the bachelor's house they discovered that he had hung himself. There was no report of him being in a dejected state of mind at the time.

Both these cases may have been a result of the ageing victims feeling that they faced a bleak and lonely future, but the next case is even more heart-breaking.

In 1785 the 12 year old son of a local farmer was found hanging from a tree having for some time been affected with an unusual dejection of spirits. The boy was not named in the newspaper.

The almost comedy capers of the elderly rector of Stockleigh English, Rev Williams culminated in him shouting out, 'Ha, you villain, your grandfather cut his throat and so will you!' draw immediate attention. Presumably this unkind quip referred to another suicide in the parish. The remarks were directed towards one Farmer Snell whose father Robert Snell was born and bred in Cheriton. Snell snr had married Sarah Roberts in Rev Williams' own church of Stockleigh English in 1782. The alleged throat-cutting dated back another generation when Williams was not officiating in the parish, but he obviously knew about the family's sad history. There is indeed a coroner's visit dated July 22nd 1754, examining the death of one Thomas Roberts in Cheriton Fitzpaine and this could indeed have been Snell's grandfather or great grandfather on his mother's side. For Rev Williams to have dragged out this cruel insult from the past seems ludicrous for a man of the cloth, but by all accounts Williams was an eccentric cleric. He was said to have 'held heterodox opinions offensive to his diocesan, and yet was a good man.' Witnesses hinted that he may well have been about to be asked to quit his rectorship by the Bishop.

According to the Western Times dated 28th March 1840 Rev Mr Williams, rector of Stockleigh English was awarded £25 for a violent assault carried out upon him in October 1839 by a farmer Snell of Cheriton Fitzpaine. The report indicates that there was bad blood between them because Williams had leased out a piece of Glebe land to him and then claimed it back again and started to farm it himself, thus depriving Snell of part of the holding he relied upon to make a living. He also accused Snell of being a rogue who was often up before the judge for petty crimes and he was known to sneer at him and hurl abuse at him whenever they met on the land. Not very seemly behaviour for a man in his mid-sixties, let alone a vicar!

In October 1838 the Reverend was on his horse directing his eleven year old daughter Hannah Maria Williams to drive five cows and a bullock to water from Higher Parsonage Close through Higher Lease, where Snell had a gate. The two men met and argued about the land and about the cattle eating Snell's clover on their way, and there were allegations that William's bull was attacking Snell's cattle. Young Hannah ran home to fetch servants to help and several of them then witnessed Snell violently beating the old man over the head, shoulders and back. It was said that the vicar was badly injured and confined to bed for one or two weeks. Misguidedly, Snell boasted about his actions to James Packer, labourer and William Wotton, glazier of Cheriton Fitzpaine, using some very choice words, and the two men then testified against him in the court.

With so few suicides and unexplained deaths in the parish it is significant that two occurred less than a week apart. One was Thomas Roberts mentioned above as a suicide on July 22nd 1754 and the other was the unexplained death of Philip

Tapp on July 26th 1754. Philip Godbere alias Tapp was born to James Godbere alias Tapp and his wife Elizabeth Marsh in Poughill in 1746, so was only eight years old when he died. The family had lost other children: Hannah in 1752 and Joan in 1753 but these were both infants rather than children and were probably health related. Both Philip Tapp and Thomas Roberts were given Christian burials in their respective graveyards of Poughill and Cheriton.

William Snell appeared again in court records when his carter, John Grant was fined £5.9s.9d. in 1844 for 'violently beating a horse over the head and injuring its eyes.'

In 1882 Henry Newberry a man in his forties attempted suicide, but a neighbour opposite noticed that his light was on at between 10 and 10.30 pm and saw him hanging a rope on a hook in the ceiling then placing the rope around his neck. The plucky woman Mrs Isles a widowed stay-maker, fetched her brother and they rushed round to the house just in time to prevent Newberry from dying. He was arrested but was still threatening to kill himself on the way to Exeter. He was charged with attempted murder of himself and committed to prison for six months. But there is more to Henry's sad story than his desperate act, because he had only just got out of prison having served a nine months sentence for theft, six months of which had been with hard labour. He had pleaded guilty to stealing a quantity of potatoes from Thomas Cole and a stocking from James Chick, with previous offences taken into account. As a skilled thatcher who learned his trade from his father John Newberry, he must have fallen upon hard times and resorted to stealing. After the initial prison sentence his future probably was as bleak as he felt it was, and it was little wonder that he tried to take his own life.

References

1. Manorial Court Rolls, Quarter Sessions Rolls, Newspaper reports and Overseers Accounts have been used to compile the information in this chapter.

Stockadon, Grew and Dunscombe

Stockadon is an important Devon farmhouse which preserves several features of surprisingly high quality. The oldest part of it dates from the early sixteenth century, and according to the listing, it has arch-braced and side-pegged jointed cruck trusses and a smoke-blackened roof, which indicates that it started out its life as an open hall house. In the main room there are crossbeams with elaborately grooved mouldings and ornate stops, similar to those at Pool Barton. These have been referred to as 'ship's timbers', terminology which might indicate that they were salvaged from boats in Exeter or Topsham, but could just mean that they were part of the navy timber crop grown in the area specifically for

ship building. Holes farm was well-known for providing timber for the Navy and there was a designated woodland on the slope between Wilson's Water and Little Coddiford dairy. Richly-moulded oak-mullioned windows have also survived at the property. (Listing NGR: SS8841706447)

A farmstead was situated on the site as early as 1332 when Walter de Stokedon (Stockaton Farm) was listed in the Lay Subsidy Roll, but the property was held in later centuries by various branches of the Scutt family. In the 1524 Lay Subsidy Roll Richard Scutt is listed (G2) and in rate lists for 1664 and 1694 Richard Scutt is listed as living at Stockadon whilst Andrew Scutt farmed at Grew. These two properties, although on opposite sides of the road have been inter-linked for most of their history, forming one estate. Passed from father to son and uncle to nephew through the Scutt family it is impossible to distinguish one member from anther because they also passed down their Christian names.

The Tythe map is damaged at the point where the farmhouse stands but the surrounding fields can be seen. The owners of both Stockadon and Grew in 1840 were the Trustees of Silverton School and the tenant farmer at Stockadon was widow Ann Luxton.

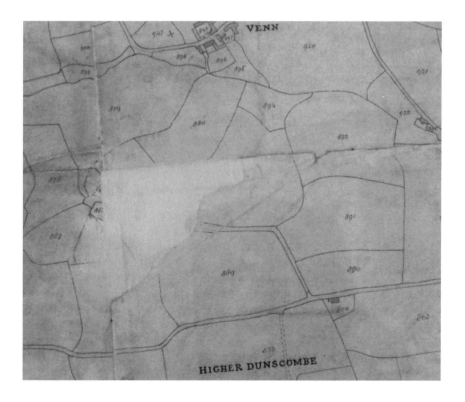

Stockadon

078	Willhay
079	Stockadon Meadow
080	Venn Park
081	Venn Orchard
082	Garden
083	Garden
084	Front Garden
085	Houses Yard and Waste
086	Front Orchard
087	Willhay Orchard
088	Garden Close
089	Gratton
090	Little Denham Field
091	Cappylaw
092	Brim Close
093	Rilley
094	Little Meadow

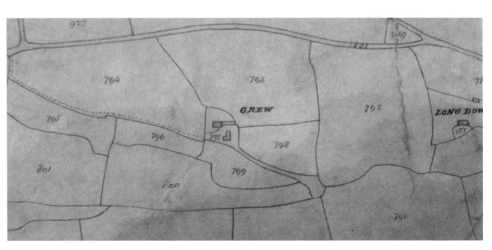

Grew was twice the size of Stockadon at 108 acres.
In 1840 it was tenanted by John Luxton

212

The family dispute over Stockadon and Grew

In 1661 Andrew Scutt the younger of Cheriton Fitzpaine married widow, Alice Croydon of Uffculme in the Church of St Edmund, Exeter. The church is now a ruin but can still be seen on the old Exe Bridge in the middle of what is now a busy road intersection.

The ruins of St Edmunds church on the old Exe Bridge which once spanned the river.

Andrew Scutts' father was a wealthy man and he made sure that his son had a generous wedding gift. Also called Andrew (the elder) he and his wife Grace drew up a document giving their eldest son and his intended wife Alice the properties of Stockadon and Grew alias Yarncombe, together with two cottages that were currently leased out to Charles Baxter and Andrew Dennis (there is a Dennis' tenement in some rate lists), and property in Romansleigh, Marionsleigh and Kitcott (all in South Molton), and in Upcott and Crediton.

Andrew the younger accepted readily and after spending the first few years

A drawing of St Edmund's Street showing the church. The street ran along the top of the bridge across the River Exe.

of his marriage with Alice in Uffculme he was able to move into the property. Their children Grace 1663–74, Rachel 1666, and Andrew 1667–70 were born in Uffculme and Anna and Alice in Cheriton Fitzpaine. Their only son was just three years old when he died, leaving no male heirs in this branch of the Scutt family.[1]

A recital of the marriage portion document was brought as evidence to the Chancery Court in 1726 when there was a family dispute over inheritance.[2] Although the original document had already been mislaid by 1726, it was said to map out the order of inheritance firstly to Andrew the younger (1st son of Andrew and Grace) and his intended wife Alice Croydon, then to their male heirs, and then to any daughters that they might have. In the event of no surviving male heirs from Andrew and Alice, after their deaths the properties were to go to James Scutt (2nd son of Andrew and Grace) and his heirs, and next to Clement Scutt (3rd son of Andrew and Grace) and his heirs, and finally to Robert Scutt (4th son of Andrew and Grace) and his heirs. There is some confusion as to the date of the document and the complainant and the defendants were relying on their memories and upon heresay to recall its exact contents. The complainant who was claiming a right to inheritance was one James Scutt, son of James Scutt,

214

deceased (2nd son of Andrew and Grace and brother to Andrew the younger).

Andrew Scutt the younger left a rather clumsily worded will in September 1695 when he died and at that time his three surviving daughters were unmarried. He failed to make mention of a marriage settlement for the girls and it was this that was used as evidence by their cousin in court. Andrew was said to have stated clearly that he would not settle the premises on one of his daughters on her marriage treaty with 'Mr Hewish a neighbouring gentleman of considerable figure and estate'. This may mean that Rachel, Anna or Alice had been betrothed at one stage to a member of the Hewish family in the village. James further argued that when alive he had heard his Uncle Andrew say that never had any intention of giving the properties to his daughters and that 'in justice' they should go to his brother, James snr. James maintained that he had waited until all three sisters had enjoyed the benefits of the estate during their life-times, fulfilling the wishes of their father and argued that no provision had been made for their heirs either in the marriage portion document drawn up by his grandfather's or in his uncle's badly written will.

The three Scutt sisters (his cousins) all married in Cheriton church on September 28th 1697, two years after their father's death. It would appear that Rachel as the eldest, already aged thirty one, took out a Lease and Release on her ⅓ portion of Stockadon and Grew in favour of her new husband George Westron. But it was Alice who moved into the property with her husband Abraham Langbridge. He was paying rates on the Stockadon in 1704 and the couple brought up their four children on the farm: Scutt 1699, John 1701 and twins Mary and Alice 1704. The land was fertile and with much of it south-facing and well-drained, there were productive orchards and woods. Tragedy struck in 1709 however when Abraham died prematurely leaving Alice with a very young family. Scutt Langbridge did not reach adulthood and the only male heir then was John Langbridge.

Rachel Scutt and her husband George Westron alias Western had set up home in Topsham with their children Philip 1702, George jnr 1705 and Anna 1708. The couple lost three children in infancy (George 1700, George 1703 and Anna 1708).[3]

Anna Scutt and her husband John Davey were probably the couple so named who were living in Tiverton with their only son, John c1707.[4]

Rachel and Anna both died in their forties, and having married late they left young children behind them.

Alice Scutt was the last of the three sisters to die so that in 1722 the future of their father's bequest to them was thrown into jeopardy.

Cousin James Scutt came home to Cheriton Fitzpaine from Tipperary, intent upon claiming his uncle's estates in Cheriton. He believed that with no marriage settlement in favour of the three daughters, he was the next in line to inherit. He was the son of James Scutt, deceased, the second son of Andrew and Grace. As soon as he arrived in the village James approached the tenants of the two cottages, offering them money to accept him as their rightful landlord and then turned his attentions towards Stockadon, Grew and the other holdings. He had lived for many years in Rosscrae in Tipperary, Ireland, and the family had not sent him letters of otherwise contacted him to discuss inheritance.

The defendants who attended court in 1726 argued that Andrew had been frail at the time he wrote his will and it was always his intention to secure the inheritance for his daughters *and* their heirs. The interested parties were: (C11/489/40 1726)

> John Langbridge, son and heir to Alice (Scutt) born 1701
>
> Philip Westron, son and heir to Rachel (Scutt) born 1702
>
> John Davey, son and heir to Anna (Scutt) born c1707, infant, with Philip Westron his cousin acting as his guardian
>
> and George Westron, the only remaining husband of the three Scutt sisters

The court case was recorded on several large parchments and most of the evidence was given verbally from memory as several original documents could not be located at the time.

> For Grew there were recitals of several leases;
>
> 1664 from Andrew Scutt the elder and Grace to their second son James and his wife Margaret
>
> 1674 from Grace Scutt, now widowed to Andrew her first son
>
> 1691 from Andrew Scutt the younger to Elizabeth Scutt and her husband Andrew Taylor
>
> 1698 Elizabeth Scutt and her husband Andrew Taylor to Abraham Langbridge, husband of Rachel Scutt

As with the majority of Chancery Court records, the final judgement is not extant but the actions of the family after 1726 make it clear that the court found against James Scutt the nephew and in favour of the heirs of the three Scutt sisters.

There must have been considerable ill feeling within the family and the best option seems to have been to sell the property to a completely unconnected party and to share out the proceeds.

In 1724 a wealthy merchant from London called John Richards died, leaving a generous bequest of £1,200 to purchase land to be used for the benefit of the poor of Silverton where he grew up and to build an endowed school for boys in that parish. Trustees were appointed and in 1729 they were offered a property that would guarantee a future income of rental and profits: the estate of Stockadon and Grew in Cheriton Fitzpaine. George Westron and the three male heirs agreed to sell for the princely sum of £1,120. Little did they know that these properties would remain with the Trustees and provide a rental income until c1995 when they were eventually sold into private hands (a Mr Benson) – a total of two hundred and sixty six years!

In 1731 The Trustees of Silverton School advertised for tenant farmers, holding an auction of leases for Stokaden, Grew and Grewlands at The New Inn, Cheriton Fitzpaine (It is not clear which Inn this was). John Powe gained the lease for Stockaden and was charged with building a barn and linhay and with finding trees for filling up the orchards and planting them. William Gibbons gained the lease of Grew and Grewlands and was charged with erecting a new living and barn on the premises. William Hewish was one of several signatories.

1732 John Powe held the lease on Stockadon for the next years, paying rent to the Trustees and living there with his wife and children William 1733 and John jnr 1735. During this time he had the inconvenience of having to bring the farm buildings up to the standards required by his landlords and losing a crop of good quality standing timber that was taken to Silverton for the school building. A notebook of building expenses kept by the Trustees records[5]:

1731 John Cross towards work done at Stockadon

1732 Mr Locke for going to Stockadon and at Killerton to choose the bricks 2/-

Christopher Locke for 16 days work for himself and a man at Stockadon and at home for felling timbers, sawing and preparing it for the floor £2.8s.0d.

William Gibbons toward sawing, making and hanging the gates and bars at Stockadon and Grew

£3 for glazing at Stockadon

1733 Andrew Hewish on part for work at Stockadon 5/- and in full for £1.10s.0d.

John Cross for work at Stockadon and Grew 18/-

Thomas Andrews and John Morris for work about the walls of Stockadon barn £8.2s.2d.

John Cross about the roof £3.15s.6d.

1734 James Morrish the mason for work done at Stockadon 10/-

The widow Poufford for nails used at Stockadon 19s.6d.

John Cross for felling and sawing timber used about flooring the schoolhouse £1.19s.8d.

Thomas Andrews about the walls of the barn at Stockadon ...... for William Gibbons, James Morrish and John Cross

1735 Humphrey Holman for carriage of timber from Stockadon for the seating 14s.6d.

Mr Thomas Carpenter 12/- for the fine for lands lying in Stockadon and Grew at Cheriton

This notebook also records the rents paid by John Poe for Stockadon and William Gibbons for Grew up until 1736 when the book ends.

It was certainly not ideal having a consortium of landlords living several miles away and using the profits from an estate to benefit another community, and it caused some resentment and trouble. In 1738 one of the tenants, a Mr Smith defaulted on his rent payment for Stockadon and the Trustees had to resolve the matter by taking out a 'Distress'. In January 1739 they hired a horse for 7s.6d. and rode to Cheriton to confiscate some of Smith's goods and chattels. Their expenses came to 7s.6d. It appears that Smith was ready however and he 'fraudulently' carried away his goods, forcing the Trustees to apply for a warrant on February 1st and to call in the bailiffs to enable them to execute the warrant. These actions cost them a further 9s.6d.

It was not the first time that there was trouble, for the previous year John Powe had defaulted on his rent at Stockadon and the bailiffs were paid £1.8s.6d, for taking out a distress on him. Nor was it the last time, for in 1843 Farmer Strong the tenant at Grew was given notice to quit due to his bad management of the estate. He was said to have damaged hedges and allowed the farm to fall into disrepair. Two years later he was served with a writ for £30 to cover the dilapidation. A new tenant called Mr Back was given £3 for the damage caused to hedges by Mr Strong.

Cheriton Fitzpaine had always been a close-knit community and farming folk in particular pulled together for their mutual benefit. No doubt the Trustees were excellent landlords over the years, but any tenant farmer was bound to feel slightly different from his peers, being managed from so far away with his rents and profits being enjoyed by a neighbouring parish. The Charity Commissioners report on Silverton School in 1830 also make mention of a property called Grove Cottage in Cheriton Fitzpaine, leased by a Mr Drake, it having an orchard and field of about four acres. The house was in a poor state of repair and the Trustees were advised not to renew the lease. The rents from Cheriton properties were at that time being paid directly to the schoolmaster. The rental for Stockadon and Grew that years was said to be £30.[6]

John Richards had wanted a free school that would educate boys 'to read, write and cast accounts' and Silverton School turned out to be a successful venture. In 1830 it was said to be following the Madras system of education. Sitting on the floor or on wooden forms, groups of children would be taught the basics by a variety of monitors. The expert teacher first taught the monitors and then each was sent off to disseminate what they had learned to a small group of their peers. In 1830 there was also a female teacher who taught the younger children, and books for the seventy children attending were paid for by the rector of the parish.

Later tenants for Stockadon and Grew appear in the Overseers of the Poor rate lists for Cheriton Fitzpaine and include:

1741 and 1753 John Labdon
1776–1792 William Lake
1792 William Lake 3½d. for Stockadon and 3d. for Grewe
1807 William Lake

William then passed it to his daughter Ann Lake and her husband John Luxton so in effect the property remained in the family:

1820–1831 John Luxton

1830 James Luxton

Ann Lake was born at Stockadon in 1781 to William and Grace Lake who also had Henry 1771, Mary 1773, Grace 1775, Susannah 1777, William 1779, Sarah 1784 and Charlotte 1787. Her father himself came from the Lake family of Cruwys Morchard.

John and Ann Luxton's only son John was born in 1810 and he grew up to marry Betty Tucker, daughter of Thomas and Hannah Tucker. He and Betty farmed at Grew, Dunscombe and Cotton and when her husband died, Betty went to live at the Cheriton Almshouses.

The 1875 Directory lists John Burridge at Stockadon and Grew.

William Pearcey then took on the farm, advertising for a farm servant in 1902.

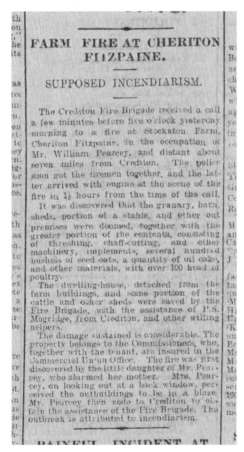

WANTED, competent MAN to drive a good team of horses; wages 13s. week, good cottage, garden, other privileges provided.—Apply, W. Pearcey, Stockadon Farm, Cheriton Fitzpaine.

It was whilst Pearcey tenanted Stockadon that a disastrous fire broke out at the premises in 1907. It was in the early hours of the morning that the granary, barn, sheds and stable caught fire and Pearcey, once woken by his small daughter, saddled his horse and rode to Crediton to alert the Fire Brigade. When they arrived in Cheriton an hour and a half later, the outbuildings could not be saved, and that day Pearcey lost valuable threshing machinery, bushels of seed oats, a quantity of oil cake and about a hundred head of poultry. Thankfully the outbuildings were on the other side if the farm-yard and the farmhouse itself was not damaged. A newspaper article claimed that it was an act of incendiarism but pointed out that the farmer was insured.

Ten years later the lease changed hands again and farm stock and machinery were put up for sale at auction with a persuasive promise that the sale offered 'a good opportunity to persons requiring stock, and the whole is intended for absolute sale, There is plenty of water and shade in the lots of Grew, and a man will see the cattle once a day':

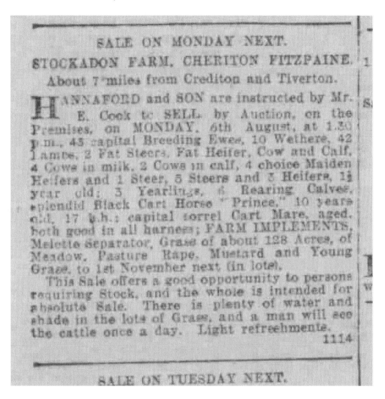

SALE ON MONDAY NEXT.
STOCKADON FARM, CHERITON FITZPAINE.
About 7 miles from Crediton and Tiverton.

HANNAFORD and SON are instructed by Mr. E. Cook to SELL by Auction, on the Premises, on MONDAY, 6th August, at 1.30 p.m., 45 capital Breeding Ewes, 10 Wethers, 42 Lambs, 2 Fat Steers, Fat Heifer, Cow and Calf, 4 Cows in milk, 2 Cows in calf, 4 choice Maiden Heifers and 1 Steer, 5 Steers and 5 Heifers, 1½ year old; 3 Yearlings, 6 Rearing Calves, splendid Black Cart Horse "Prince," 10 years old, 17 h.h.; capital sorrel Cart Mare, aged, both good in all harness; FARM IMPLEMENTS, Melotte Separator, Grass of about 128 Acres, of Meadow, Pasture Rape, Mustard and Young Grass, to 1st November next (in lots).

This Sale offers a good opportunity to persons requiring Stock, and the whole is intended for absolute Sale. There is plenty of water and shade in the lots of Grass, and a man will see the cattle once a day. Light refreshments.
1114

SALE ON TUESDAY NEXT.

References

1. Uffculme and Cheriton Fitzpaine parish registers
2. Chancery Court couments C11/489/40/1726 tell this complex story
3. Topsham parish registers
4. Tiverton parish registers
5. Silverton school notebook
6. The Report of the Commisioners Concerning Charities; containing that part which relates to Devon, with appendix and index. Vol III 1830

Cheriton Barton and Tower Hill tenement

In the 1840 Tythe of Cheriton the extent of land belonging to Cheriton Barton was as follows:

Cheriton Barton				
205	Court Mead	Meadow	3 . , . 9
242	Great Moor Park	Pasture	4 . 3 . 2
243	Little Moor Park	D°	1 . 2 . 10
244	Coney Park	Arable	8 . 2 . 3
245	Higher Oak Field	D°	2 . 3 . 14
246	Great Oak Field	D°	4 . 3 . 7
247	Lower Oak Field	D°	1 . 1 . 2
248	Barton Meadow	Meadow	2 . , . 9
249	Comyns Close	Arable	6 . 3 . 7
250	Northern Kidy Ball	Arable	7 . 2 . 22
251	Southern Kidy Ball	Arable	7 . , . 18
252	Gribble Park	Arable	5 . 2 . 37
253	Gribble Orchard Plot	Orchard	, . , . 27
254	Brimclose Mead	Pasture	2 . 2 . 18
255	Brimclose	Arable	0 . , . 7
256	Grattow	D°	6 . 1 . 2
257	Holly Water Mead	Meadow	3 . , . 30
258	Little Grattow	Arable	2 . 1 . 1
259	Long Orchard	Orchard	2 . 1 . 3
260	Broad Close	Arable	17 . 1 . 34
261	Second Chugbear	D°	12 . 3 . 39
262	First Chugbear	D°	9 . 1 . 17
263	Chugbear Orchard	Orchard	, . 1 . 25

260	Barton Orchard	Orchard		2.	30
269	House and Yard			2.	11
204	Upper Garden			.	32.
205	Middle Garden		.	1	1
			122.	3.	11½

The land lay north of the road to Stockleigh English and west of the road to Stockleigh Mill, starting from Tower Hill crossroads, so much of it was on the south-facing slope of the valley.

Although the owner was listed as the Rev John Hole, the tenant at that time was thirty six year old Samuel Pridham who lived next door to the farm house at Pool Barton. He had grown up at Pool with his brothers Joseph Pridham 1801 and Daniel Tremlett Pridham 1805, and his sisters Elizabeth and Mary. Joseph, the eldest sibling, did not reach adulthood. When their father Samuel snr died Daniel was in a position to buy his own 330 acre farm near Yeoford, called Rock Farm and left the village. That farmhouse is listed and in part dates from the 16th century and standing near Caddiford and Woodland Head as it does, it may be a complete co-incidence that it shares its name with the family's farmstead at Yeo in Sandford which had once been known as Rock and formed part of the Pool Barton estate.

Rock Farm near Crediton, not to be confused with Rock Farm, Yeo (demolished) on the Sandford-Cheriton Fitzpaine border

Deeds held privately by the owners of Pool Barton record the transaction of the Sandford-Cheriton Fitzpaine property known as Yeo and formerly as Rock:

10 and 11.1.1786 Lease and release on lands in Cheriton and Sandford

Joseph Pridham of Rock, Crediton, gent, eldest son and heir of Samuel Pridham deceased and Elizabeth Pridham of Rock, widow of Samuel Pridham

Samuel Pridham of Rock, brother of Joseph.

For the natural love and affection and the consideration of 10/- released all that one messuage called Rock alias Yeo, together with one dwelling house erected thereon in Yeo and also North Sutton in C F formerly in the tenure of James Smart and Roger Peaster being all those dwelling houses, orchards and gardens, barn etc. in CF, also the hallhouse, the new house adjoining the hallhouse, the southern part of the linnay or stable and the tallet over the same, the orchard adj the said house last mentioned and the herb garden and plot adj the house, the halfendeal of the linnay formerly belonging to John Oliver in the inner court, the wall between the hall and the shop formerly belonging to Richard Smart and the privilege to lay straw and make snug before the stable door. Also Oak park, Beare Close, the long hay, the round hill, the Oak park meadow the wester meadow, 2 acres of the wester end of Broom close and the souther part or half of the new hedge made in the said Broom close for the dividing thereof with a way and passage to the said wester meadow and Broom close with the privilege of the mud pond every 2 years etc.

Samuel had inherited the land known as Stock Parks from his father and lived in Pool Barton house with his young family and his widowed mother Ann. Cheriton Barton next door had been carved out of land originally parcelled up with Pool when it was set up as a separate farmstead around 1728, but in his father's time the two properties had been brought together again to create a more productive parcel of land. By 1851 however Pridham jnr had decided to give up the rented section that was Cheriton Barton, and concentrated on farming just 245 acres, managing this with three men and eleven outdoor workers: Sarah Harris, William Moxey and Charlotte Stoneman, adult workers Marie Blackmore, Mary Tucker, Thomas and James Hepper, Thomas Butt, William Please, William Grant and Richard Melhuish, teenage farm hands.

The other 123 acres were then farmed by whoever rented out Cheriton Barton farmhouse. In 1861 this was an older man called Andrew Knapman who lived in the house with his elderly cousin Mary Wooland acting as his housekeeper. Three men and two boys worked for him in and around the farm, two of whom were carters who worked in the outhouses standing around the yard. In addition, he employed William Crook a twelve year old farm servant and Mary Manning a sixteen year old house servant. The numerous out-building around the yard lying to north-west of the house could have also accommodated his live-in workers, and possibly offered shelter to some of the many men employed next door at Pool. When a new tenant was advertised for in 1849 the description was:

'Cheriton Barton Farmhouse, outbuildings and 123 acres of arable, meadow, orchard and pasture with 3 cottages for labourers.'

The three cottages referred to may be the outbuildings around the farmyard but are more likely to be the three thatched cottages known as Tower Hill

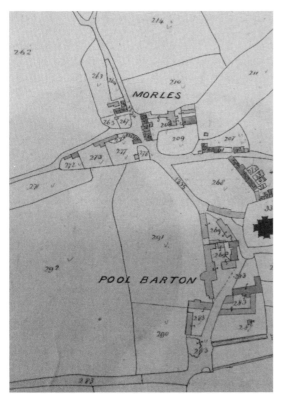

Tenement which owner John Hole also held at the time of the Tythe. Certainly, having cottages to offer workers would have attracted family men with sons and daughters rather than singletons. Tower Hill Tenement cottages are 265, 266 and 267 on the Tythe map and Cheriton Barton House and yard are 269 on the 1840 map.

Cheriton Barton house was built around 1728, but the range of outbuildings probably pre-dates it, being part of the larger and older Pool Barton complex. During recent renovations a small musket ball was discovered embedded in the cut end of a roof beam, the result of a shot being fired at the outside wall of the barn. The musket pre-dates the rifle and was generally only used in combat, so the question of how it got there is tantalising.

The 1569 Muster Roll for the village list nine Harquebusiers or musket-men:

John Kellye, Hugh Card, Ralph Atkyns, Robert Tayler, John Barton jun, Gregory Smyth, David Shepherd, William Atkyns and James Robarts

At that time men in the South West were unlikely to be called up for combat and the Muster was purely a paper exercise, surveying the country for the Crown to find out what capacity there was. Each parish had to put forward one or two Presenters – men of good repute and standing in the community, who were given the task of listing all the eligible men in the area and visiting properties to discover how many horses were available should there ever be a call to arms. Conscientious local Presenters may well have felt it necessary to drill their men, even though it was known that they would not be called upon to enter into active battle. One of the two Presenters for the village in 1569 was William Reynold of Pool, a principled and zealous man who was known to approach all things in a conscientious way. There is every likelihood that musket practise was carried out in his yard and that he took the nine men listed and did his utmost to train them in how to handle a weapon and how to aim accurately.

During the Civil War in the 1640s when there was a more tangible threat of action, and musket practise would certainly have taken place in the village. Pool was still in the hands of the Reynold family at that date (a later William Reynold) and standing at the centre of the village as it does it would certainly have been a meeting place for potential 'soldiers'. Military practise often took place after the Sunday service when all able-bodied men were gathered together in one place and Pool is perfectly positioned, directly opposite the church.

Fortunately, tucked away in the countryside and not on a direct route to major towns, Cheriton saw no action at all during the Civil War, but people were still conscious that they ought to be ready for the fight.

The other possible explanation for this stray musket ball may be that an itinerant soldiers was showing off to the locals. Over the years a few wandering militia men did find their way to the village and stayed for a few days. One local girl claimed that the father of her illegitimate child was 'a soldier called John' and one can imagine the romance of a man in uniform paying her some attention.

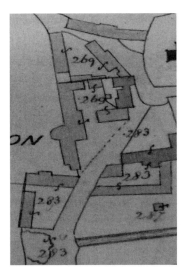

The outbuildings around the yard at Cheriton Barton are numbered 269 on the 1840 Tythe.

The western range of outbuildings at Cheriton 269

The mystery of why a Rev John Duffield Hole owned Cheriton Barton (and also Tower Hill Tenement) in 1840 needs unravelling. At the time of the Tythe he was the rector at Woolfardisworthy which is only a few miles from the village but he was born at Dunsford in 1763. His connection to the village comes through the illustrious Arundell family via his first wife Lydia Arundell, born in Cambourne Cornwall to William Arundell. The couple married in Cornwall in 1794 but had their three daughters in Woolfardisworthy near Witheridge in Devon where John was rector from 1788 until his death in 1841. Lydia was said to be 'lovely in form and mind', and 'universally beloved from the cradle'. These words were written by John in the parish register when he buried Lydia in 1797 just two months after their youngest daughter Penelope was born. John remained unmarried for many years, bringing up his three little girls at the Rectory. Several years later he did marry for a second time and must have thought about securing the financial future of his beloved girls Elizabeth, Lydia and Penelope who were then almost of marriageable age. From c1794 he had held a share in Cheriton Barton which had previously belonged to William Harris, but when he died his estate was broken up and many properties were put up for sale. Just two months before his marriage Hole bought out his partner:

August 18th 1806 The Barton farm, messuage and tenement called Cheriton Barton with the cottage house and garden adjoining the said Barton on the east side therof conveyed from Rev Philip Carlyon of Cornwall to Rev John Hole.

1806 was also the year that Rev Philip Carlyon married and needed to consolidate his property, so he was able to sell his share in Cheriton Barton and concentrate his holdings in and around St Mawgan where he was vicar.

Cheriton Barton taken from the Trim Tram path by the church wall

John Hewish who died in 1766 held a lease on Cheriton Barton from the Rev Harris and sublet it to his daughter Mary and her husband Thomas Wellington to farm. Thomas died young in 1758 and Mary was unable to farm the land with such young children to care for. Her brother Andrew Hewish who had married Sarah Stabbick in 1756 moved in to manage the 123 acres and lived there for many years with his wife and only son John 1761 until he moved to Lower Saunders in the Main road.

Cheriton Barton was not the only property that John Hole owned, and the seven children from his second marriage to Sophia Brassey benefitted on his death from many properties in Devon and Cornwall. Kennerleigh Mill was another local property he had acquired. John Hole died in 1841 aged 78.

His youngest daughter Louisa (from the second marriage, so not related by blood to her father's first in-laws) married into the Arundell family and became the wife of the Rev William Harris Arundell in 1840. Their son Rev William *Henry* Arundell was born in 1841 but was left motherless at the age of four when Louisa died young. There was a second marriage of the Rev William Harris Arundell to Sarah Peach Kettle.

Because Cheriton Barton was only held as an investment by John Hole he never lived there and it always needed to be tenanted. His 1841 Will stated that it was still in his possession and was for the joint interest of the three daughter from his first marriage. By this time Lydia was married to Rev Fothergill of Belstone Rectory and Penelope was married to a vicar's son called William Kettle who was a practising physician in Tiverton (there was probably a family connection

Exeter and Plymouth Gazette March 1849

229

to Sarah Peach Kettle). Elizabeth Ann Hole remained unmarried and very much needed the income from the tenants at Cheriton Barton.

The property continued to be rented out with Lydia Fothergill receiving a yearly rental of £183 which she shared out equally. Andrew Knapman had to give evidence of this fact at a court case in 1877 when Lydia's son, Rev Henry John Arundell Fothergill had his assets assessed in regard of a £2,900 debt. Knapman said that he had started renting the property in 1856, paying Mrs Fothergill directly but when she died in 1872 he paid equal sums to Henry and the remaining sister, Mrs Kettle.

The tenant in 1891 was William H Kelly who hailed from Bridport Dorset. He farmed Cheriton Barton with his wife Louisa and daughters Effe S, Annie L, Annetta, Louise, Evelyn, Astria and Stella, all born in Tedburn St Mary. He was still there in the 1901 census, but the property had changed hands again before the 1911 census.

Rick Fire at Cheriton Fitzpaine

Considerable excitement was caused at Crediton about one o'clock on Saturday afternoon, when the local Fire Brigade received a call to a fire at Cheriton Fitzpaine. Within a few minutes the brigade, with their manual engine and other appliances, were seen galloping through the streets to the scene at Pool Farm, Cheriton Fitzpaine, a distance of seven miles. On arrival the brigade found a large rick of hay, containing about 20 tons, well alight. The owner, Mr. J. Shilston, with his employees and other willing helpers, did what they possibly could to keep the fire under until the arrival of the brigade. A plentiful supply of water was found at the bottom of the Vicarage garden, which required about 1,100 to 1,200 feet of hose to reach the rick. The brigade soon had the fire under control, and they succeeded in saving the farm buildings. The brigade kept hard at work until between eight and nine o'clock in the evening, and saved a portion of the hay. The cause of the fire appears to have been the overheating of the rick. The brigade returned to Crediton shortly before 11 o'clock on Saturday night.

In 1911 the eight rooms were occupied by William Westcott from Tedburn, his wife of twenty nine years Grace, and their three surviving children John Rendle Westcott a teacher, and James and Elsie Westcott. They only had one live-in farm servant but employed other men and boys who lived with their own families in the village. The practise of having live-in workers was changing.

Next door, the fifteen roomed Pool Farm had been occupied by Joseph Shilston since 1894. Whilst he was the tenant of Pool a fire broke out at the property one evening, causing considerable damage to his barns and spreading to the southern end wall of Cheriton Barton house, which had to be repaired. This explains the single storey extension on the present day building where a kitchen has been attached. Other alterations may have been carried out at the same time.

Owners and occupiers at Cheriton Barton

1728 William Maunder and Philip Shapcote

1732 William Hewish

1738–40 John Hewish

1752 the occupiers of Cheriton Barton

1753 Abraham Hewish (John's son who died 1755)

1757 Thomas Wellington (John's son-in-law)

Abraham Hewish the son of John Hewish died without issue in 1755 and the property passed to his sister Mary and her husband Thomas Wellington. Married in 1742 their children were Mary 1745, twins Judith and Alice 1747, Ann 1752, Thomas 1754 who died the same year, Thomas 1755 and Susanna 1757. The property was tailor-made for a growing family and it would have stayed in the Wellington family had Thomas survived into old age, but Mary was unable to continue farming herself with very small children and she had to offer the lease of the property to other family members. So it was that her brother Andrew Hewish (who was involved in the Lower Saunders dispute) acquired Cheriton Barton in 1758 and farmed it himself well into the 1780s, taking on an apprentice to work with him in 1773.

1758–80 Andrew Hewish (John's son)

1788–1799 William Harris with John Hewish jnr tenant

1800 Rev Hole with Richard Mogridge tenant

1803 Rev Hole with Thomas Tucker tenant

1804 John Brewer

Pre 1808 owner Rev Carlyon

1808 owner Rev John Hole

1812-1826 Rev Hole with tenant Thomas Tucker

1830 Rev Hole with Richard Collinhole?

1832 tenant Samuel Pridham

1841 Will of Rev Hole

1843 Samuel Pridham auctioned 50 oak, 12 ash and 9 elms growing on land at Cheriton Barton

1843 Tenant Mr Thomas Melhuish

1849 new tenant advertised for.

Cheriton Barton Farmhouse, outbuildings and 123 acres of arable, meadow, orchard and pasture with 3 cottages for labourers, currently in the occupation of Mr Thomas Melhuish.

1851 tenant John Tucker

1856 tenant Andrew Knapman

1877 tenant Andrew Knapman

881

1891 owner? William H Kelly

1901 owner William H Kelly

1911 owner? William Westcott

Tower Hill Tenement and Tower Hill Cottage

Tower Hill Tenement is not the same as the present day Tower Hill Cottage – that stands today on the right hand side of the road as you climb the hill, but Tower Hill Tenement stood on the left hand side of the road and was demolished to make way for the present day bungalow, Grey Gables.

In the parlour of Tower Hill Cottage there is a fireplace beam with the inscription R H 1641 which may be the initials of Richard Huish/Hewish who signed the 1641 Protestation Returns. The property is listed as part of Morles Farm in the Poor Rates and would have been a worker's cottage. It appears on the 1840 Tythe map as two cottages with a further cottage to the right which has since been demolished. There is a gap between the current extended house and the next property, Honeysuckle Cottage.

The listing for Tower Hill cottage is completely wrong stating that it was built in 1870

Honeysuckle Cottage

Honeysuckle Cottage, by the entrance gate to Morles Farm was where one of the village blacksmiths lived. Until quite recently it was known as Smithy Cottage. The listing for this property dates it from the late 16th century with a re-used beam from earlier in the 16th century. A sale in 1922 of Smithwright cottage included a half acre garden. At the same time the freehold smith's shop and shoeing

Honeysuckle Cottage

forge adjoining the man road was sold on behalf of Mrs Prior. During the 1950s the Scholes family lived at Honeysuckle Cottage.

Tower Hill Tenement

Tower Hill Tenement on the west of the hill has the bungalow called Grey Gables built on the footprint of its original three cottages. The field behind it which stretches up the hill and ends at the junction of the two lanes was also part of the original curtilage and it described as an orchard. Although difficult to till because of its gradient it faces south and would be well-drained. The whole plot was once owned by the parish with tenants paying their rents to the Overseers of the Poor who used the income for the benefit of paupers. They were maintained by the parish with payments for glazing, re-building stairs, and carrying out general carpentry work on doors and thresholds. It is very likely that in 1753–4 the three cottages were used as temporary accommodation for the pensioners of the Poor House when they needed to be moved out of Church House during alterations. The old building had to be brought it up to the level of National standards for a Workhouse and this took the best part of a year to complete. During those months pensioners would have dutifully plodded along the Trim Tram path in their clogs and boots from their temporary lodging at Tower Hill, through Cheriton Barton farm (there were farm buildings on both sides of the lane then) to attend Church services. When not being used to house the poor, other tenants were offered the cottages to generate rental income for the poor fund. The Overseers as landlords were responsible for the upkeep of the buildings e.g. sweeping chimneys, replacing latches and locks etc. Other cottages in their portfolio included all eight dwellings in The Hayes, built on Harris' charity land and the two ends of the Poor House that were rented out when not used for housing the poor. After the completion of the modernised Workhouse in 1753, it is possible that the three cottages that formed Tower Hill Tenement were given up for public rental although Overseers still paid for maintenance e.g. 1801/2 they paid James Pridham 3/8d for repairing the house at Tower Hill.

In 1755 a conveyance describes, 'cottage and garden in churchtown in Chugbear Lane and formerly part of Cheriton Barton now in the possession of Sarah Hewish, widow or Thomas Moggridge her undertenant and *also a cottage, garden and little orchard on Tower Hill in Churchtown in which Roger Hopland formerly dwelt together with a small orchard on the left hand side on the road leading to Stockleigh and now in the possession of Sarah Hewish or her undertenants'*

In 1783 'Sarah Hewish's cottage in Tower Hill' was conveyed from William Harris to James Pridham, mason – on the three lives of James, and James and Peter his sons.

In November 1783 William Harris esq of Keneggie, Cornwall granted a lease of ninety nine years on 'the dwelling house and orchard on Tower Hill' to James Pridham, mason. It was drawn on the three lives of James aged forty, James jnr aged seven and Peter Pridham aged one. Pridham lived there with his wife Mary Edwards and children Betty 1767, Sarah 1770, Charlotte 1773, James 1776–1804, Agnes 1779, and Peter 1782–1854. Peter grew up to become a Sergeant in the East Devon Militia. As a skilled mason James found plenty of work in the parish and held the lease until 1799. He hailed from Cruwys Morchard and does not appear to be related to Samuel Pridham, despite sharing the same surname.

In 1795 'a cottage, garden and little orchard in Tower Hill in the possession of Sarah Hewish in which Roger Hoxland formerly dwelt together with a small orchard on the left-hand side of the road leading to Stockleigh, lately in the possession of Mark Horwell but now of James Chamberlain or Josias Sowden or Robert Chappell his undertenants' and 'a cottage and little orchard on Tower Hill in Churchtown lately in the possession of Mark Horwill etc.' was included

Smithwright's cottage in the foreground and Tower Hill Tenement centre back

in a bundle of property conveyed by lease and release between William Harris, clerk and members of the Arundell family to Daniel Tremlett, yeoman who was developing a portfolio of property in the parish at the time.

In June 1838 the property was advertised as part of the larger Lewcombes and Sander. A farm house and thirty acres was mentioned but the Tower Hill Tenement was given as a cottage and garden held by lease during the life of James Pridham, mason with ⅔ offered on the lives of three people aged 66, 56 and 54 in the possession of Mr Oliver and James Pridham. The remaining ⅓ part being to the life interest of Mrs Ann Oliver. A lifeleasehold property with very few years left to go would have been an attractive acquisition.

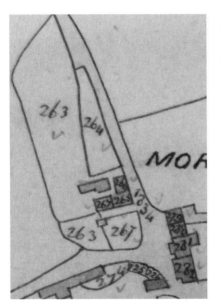

In 1840 Rev John Hole owned Tower Hill Tenement including the orchard and gardens. The whole tenement appears as 263-267 on the 1840 Tythe map:

William Stoneman, John Treble and Thomas Prior each paid rent on their cottages, all of which owned by Rev John Hole as part of the Cheriton Barton estate.

Tower Hill Tenement		
William Stoneman	264	Strap Orchard
	265	Cottage
John Treble Junr	266	Cottage
Thomas Prior	267	Cottage and Garden

This photograph from the 1960s shows the H-shaped footprint of the three thatched cottages in the foreground that formed Tower Hill tenement. The orchard is to the left. A similar footprint was acknowledged when the Grey Gables bungalow was built on the site.

Tower Hill House built c1844 on Lower and Higher Cod Closes

Tower Hill House started life being known as Cod Close cottage and then Tower Hill Cottage before adopting the less confusing Tower Hill House. John Oliver built it high up at the cross roads of Tower Hill and Mill Lane where it commanded good views of the valley below.

'To let a delightful cottage with extensive views, standing nearly in the centre of a field with a good garden in front built within the last three years. Sitting room, kitchen, dairy, pantry, 5 bedrooms, wash house with furnace, pump and soft water, 3 stalled stable and other convenient outbuildings.

If required 5 or 6 acres of excellent land can be supplied John Oliver 1847' John was a cattle farmer and butcher.

A newspaper advertisement from 1852 confirms what the 1851 census shows that John Oliver had not managed to sell his newly built house and was living there with his mother Sarah and unmarried sisters Mary and Sally.

John had downsized considerably and was farming a meagre eleven acres. When their eighty one year old mother died at the end of 1851 the siblings decided to part company and John aged forty seven and Mary forty four went to live together at Park Hill in Dawlish.

The Pridham family

Samuel Pridham jnr rented Cheriton Barton for a time but consolidated his land and concentrated on Pool Barton farm around the time of his marriage to Susan Harris from Crediton in 1846. The couple had their own family, Ann Harris Pridham, Samuel, Harris 1854–1855, Joseph and Lucy Elizabeth, but Susan did not seem to be suited to the farming life and often stayed with her sister and brother-in-law in George Street, Plymouth where he was a wealthy tea dealer and grocer. The Wills household included six servants and two governesses and life would have been much more vibrant than in sleepy Cheriton. Samuel died in 1870 at the age of sixty seven leaving the farm to his son Samuel the third. This Samuel followed in his father's footsteps and was a very good farmer, winning many prizes at Agricultural shows over the years for his stock, He was not afraid to change with the times and in 1887 volunteered to host the trial of one of Hornsby and Son's new digging ploughs. Hornsby and Sons had been awarded a prestigious medal at the 1851 Great Exhibition for their innovative machinery and by the 1880s they were manufacturing oil-powered tractors at their works in Grantham. Later the company produced machinery with caterpillar tracks and this proved invaluable in tank manufacture for World War I.

No illustrations survive of the Hornsby steam digging plough but it may have operated like this system which had a winch on the underside of a powerful steam engine. One engine would drive along one side of the field and the other engine parallel to it on the other side. The plough would be connected to each winch cable and be pulled up and down the field. One can imagine the excitement in the neighbourhood as farmer Pridham proudly hosted a demonstration for fellow farmers at Pool. If he had purchased one of these machines he would have been able to increase his productivity and cut down his workforce. What a contrast it would have then been to the traditional way of ploughing in mid-Devon as described in 1796 by William Marshall in his Rural Economy of the West of England.

'(With regard to ploughing) The style of driving an ox team, here is observable; indeed, cannot pass unnoticed by a stranger. The language, though to a certain degree peculiar in the country, does not arrest the attention; but the tone, or rather tune, in which it is delivered. It resembles, with great exactness the chantings, or recitative of the Cathedral service. The plow boy chants the counter tenor, with unabated ardour through the day; the plow man throwing in, at intervals, his hoarser notes. It is understood that this chanting march, which sometimes be heard to a considerable distance, encourages and animates the team, as the music of a marching army, or the song of rowers … I have never seen so much cheerfulness attending the operation of ploughing, anywhere as in Devonshire.'

Farmer Pridham was in the newspapers again in 1887 when The Tremlett Hunt rode into his garden and killed a 'fine old dog fox'. The Pridham/Tremlett family connection ensured that this was a regular venue for the Huntsmen and hounds and indeed Pool Barton owners hosted meets well into the 20th Century.

The Pridham dynasty in Cheriton had begun in 1799 when Samuel Pridham son of Samuel of Yeo made a very good marriage with Ann Tremlett and in 1889 when Samuel Pridham retired from Pool and moved into The Pynes (Arden House) to become Registrar of birth, marriages and deaths and District Surveyor.

When the Pridham tenure began, the village was at that time dominated by Daniel Tremlett and his family who owned part of the manor of Cheriton Fitzpaine and Trundlemoor and lived at Upcott Barton from about 1767. Ann Tremlett was born at Upcott in 1774 as was her sister Sarah in 1771 but older siblings John 1760, Elias 1762, Mary 1763 and Elizabeth 1766 were all born before they moved into the parish.

In 1787 Tremlett sought a tenant for Upcott Barton.

In 1791, thirty two years into his marriage with Mary Snow, Daniel fathered an illegitimate child with a local girl. He encouraged the pregnant woman to marry a man called John Gosling who lived at Cruwys Morchard who was known to be an 'idiot'. He obviously wanted to avoid owning up to the child and hoped that the neighbouring parish would support mother and baby with her witless new husband. Daniel was not however a popular man and there were complaints made against him for his actions. He was unceremoniously summoned to the court, sentenced to six months in prison and ordered to pay costs of £50.

Tremlett wanted revenge and started an action against the Pennymoor Overseer who had brought the prosecuted against him. William Thorne had married his sister-in-law when he was widowed and had several children by the union. Tremlett prosecuted him for incest. After a protracted ten month hearing the case ended in 1794 with each party paying their own costs.

Tremlett must have been somewhat thick-skinned because his self-importance was not diminished by the scandal. Only two years later he added to his empire by purchasing several farms from the estate of William Harris esq from Keneggie Cornwall who was rector from 1784-94. Morles tenement was leased for 99 yrs in June 1784 for the lives if Daniels' children Mary 21, Sarah 13 and Ann 10 and other acquisitions were a moiety of Stockparks, Moxeys alias Bodleys tenement, Trundlemoor, and part of Holes.

He had already married off his two eldest daughters and he now married Sarah to John Brewer in 1806 and Ann to Samuel Pridham in 1799, giving the couple Pool Barton to farm. A Mrs Tremlett had paid Poor Rates on Stockparks, the land around Pool farmhouse as early as 1751, but it seems that Tremlett was able to purchase the freehold on the property in 1795 from William Arundell (obliged by the terms of his relative's will to assume the surname Harris), who had inherited it from William Harris of Hayne, the Lord of the Manor.

Moxeys Tenement alias Bodleys Tenement

George Bodley took out a 99 year lease in November 1753 from Hon John Harris on a tenement called Moxeys or Bodleys lying in or near Cheriton Church Town. George Bodley married his wife Elizabeth that same year and they brought up a family including Anna 1755, Mary 1756 (d 1758), Mary 1759 and George jnr 1762. Confusingly, Moxey's Tenement was not the Moxeys that we know today in the middle of the village, but was instead two parcels on northside comprising thirteen acres of land running northwards along the left-hand side of the road to Poughill from the area around Homecroft as far as the cross roads, together with two cottages and gardens along a trackway to the west of Court Place, Upham. As such it was a difficult holding and George must have held additional land from which to make a living. The 1753 lease was surrendered on the death of his wife Elizabeth and found its way into the hands of Daniel Tremlett who then surrendered it to William Harris in 1793, agreeing to pay the sum of £180 to Harris and two guineas in gold for Harris' wife. The plot names given in both these leases match exactly those given in a newspaper advertisement dated 1834 offering a seven year lease on Bodleys:

Lot 1 an orchard held by Mr John Hewish (192)

Lot 2 Grattons Mead, an orchard and Long Close (197, 193)

Lot 3 Mead Park and Kelly's Close (191, 190)

Lot 4 Tunnel Close and Presterwell (189, 186)

The two names of Bodleys and Moxeys tenement were interchangeable for many years.

The names of the plots comprising Moxeys Tenement in the Tythe apportionment, then owned by George Tanner and farmed by James Wotton also match those in the earlier leases:

Moxeys Tenement					
163	Sresserwill	Arable	2	.	. 3
186	Sresserwill	D°	1	1	23
189	Turnell Close	D°	1	.	9
190	Hellys Close	D°	2	.	1
191	Mead Park	Meadow	2	.	.
192	Grallow Orchard	Orchard	.	3	21
193	Long Close	Arable	1	3	16
197	Grallow Mead	Meadow	2	.	1
			13	.	31½

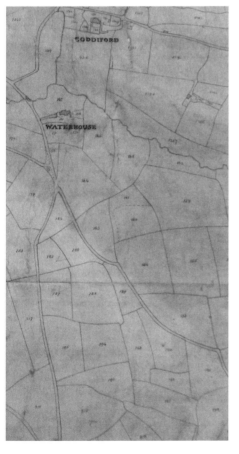

Moxeys Tenement 1840 lay mostly within the triangular shape between the lanes.

Before George Bodley took on the land in 1753 earlier references in the Overseers' and the Churchwarden's Accounts show that it had been in the Moxey family for more than a hundred years.

243

1664 occupiers of Moxeys tenement paid rates

1670 occupiers of Moxey's tenement pad 10d. church rates

1689 William Moxey for Moxey's tebement

1701 William Moxey paid 7d. rates on Moxey's tenement, southside

1713 William Moxey or the occupiers 3/-

1725 occupiers of Moxey's tenement

1728 occupiers of Moxeys tenement

1782 Robert Melhuish for Moxeys

1801 owner Daniel Tremlett, occupier John Rattenbury £1.9s.4d.

1831 owner Mrs Turner, occupier John Hewish, tailor, £1.9s.4d.

The tenement was not the Moxey family's main holding in the parish and they can be found farming at various leasehold properties including Smith Hayne, Peach Hayne, Tucking Mills, Higher Waterhouse and Farthings on northside. John Moxey was paying 2s.6d towards church repairs in 1613 so he must have owned a small farmstead at that time too. Martha Moxey, a widow was living at one of these properties as early as 1664 and Matthew Moxey and Peternell Snow were joint owners of another in 1663. The unusual name Peternell appears again with Petronella Moxey in 1627 when there was a dispute over a nuncupative (spoken not written) will by John Moxey, son. John Moxey snr her husband had died around 1624.

Later owners of Moxeys *Tenement* were John, Hugh and Solomon Moxey. Interestingly there is now a house in the village diagonally opposite the Half Moon Pub named Petronella after a past inhabitant.

Moxeys in the village

Moxeys in the main street is not the same as Moxey's Tenement which lay over towards Coddiford as mentioned above. The question is, how did it get its name, and when were the current dwellings of Little Moxey and Moxeys built? Many villagers remember it as one dwelling with its workroom and shop being owned by Tom Breyley the saddler and motor mechanic, with a petrol pump on the forecourt. Tom also owned a garage and yard called Shutelake in Back Hayes Lane which was later bought by Molly Cotter and then became a store for Martin brothers, builders. Latterly the site has been re-developed with the

building of Dormouse Cottage and Otter Cottage. Tom's shop was often full of villagers passing the time of day, and by all accounts he was a very sociable man with a talent for his craft.

'Breyley' is not a local name and in fact Thomas Edward Gloyn Breyley was born at Northlew and apprenticed as a saddle and harness maker in Hatherleigh, where he worked for some time with Henry Darch in The High Street. When he arrived in Cheriton Fitzpaine to set up his own business he met and married thirty seven year old Mary Ann Prior. Although he claimed to be older than he was, he was actually several years younger than Mary Ann, and inevitably, because of her age, the couple were not able to have any children of their own. He ran a successful business with his wife and encouraged various nephews to live with them as apprentices. In 1911 nephews Alfred and Sidney Breyley from Inwardleigh were at Moxeys as apprentice saddlers. A natural teacher, ten years earlier he had successfully trained his cousin Richard Breyley from Hatherleigh. The Breyleys shared the property with Mary Ann's widowed father, Mr Prior who retained the left-hand side of the dwelling as his own. When he died, sometime in his eighties, Tom and Mary Ann Breyley inherited the whole property. Sadly, Mary Ann died in 1912 aged only fifty five, leaving Tom a widower for many years until his own death in 1945. The whole property was then inherited by Bert Breyley in the 1940s and finally the right-hand side was passed down to Alan and Brenda Fowler (nee Breyley) in 1972. Many memories of Bert and his open-all-hours shop and meeting place have been recorded by those who knew him.

When built, Moxeys was a large dwelling house, and it is not surprising that over the years, one of the rooms at the front has been rented out by a variety of people. In 1926 an advertisement in the newspaper announced that the Midland Bank would be operating a branch at Moxeys, to be open to the public every Thursday from 11am-1pm. At other times the visiting dentist has used the room, and for many years Samuel Pridham rented the room in his capacity of Registrar of Births, Marriages and Deaths. A brass plaque to that effect can still be located in the building. Pridham had retired from farming at Pool Barton and was then living at Pynes (now Arden House) in the High Street.

The house was officially split into two separate dwellings in the early 1970s, the larger to the right retaining the name Moxeys and the smaller, to the left taking on the name Little Moxey. At the same time the orchard at the back of the property and a parcel of land to the rear of Hayes Cottage were sold to a developer called Mr Bedford. Moxey's Close was laid out ready for the construction of the present day bungalows and a two storey house. Original plans set out to widen the entrance to Moxeys Close by shaving off the left-hand corner and indeed, a wall still stands there at an angle, marking the intended boundary.

How had Mary Ann Prior come to inherit Moxeys? She was the eldest child of Emma and John Prior and was born in 1857. The couple also had Laura 1859 and Albert John 1862. John Prior was for many years a mason, working out of Moxeys front yard and helping to build many of the houses in the village. It was John who won the lucrative contract for building the Methodist Chapel which was begun in 1860, but an unfortunate problem with the depth of foundations came to light just ten years later and John must have felt responsible when much work was required to remedy the fault. William Hoskings who died at the age of 85 in 1900 had worked for John Prior as a mason and later on for J and E Prior in the village. Legend has it that he consumed ½oz of tobacco a day which is what he swore kept him healthy until his death. John Prior's son Albert did not take up his father's profession and chose instead to become an apprentice draper in Exeter city, whilst Mary Ann remained at home supporting her parents and not expecting to marry. As the years went by John looked to supplement his income as a mason with work that was less physically demanding, and he also worked as an insurance agent in the area, selling policies to farmers and house-owners and meeting clients in his front room. His wife Emma opened a small shop on the premises, using part of the building that now juts out towards the road, stocking local produce and buying in other necessities for her neighbours. The property was perfectly placed for trade at the centre of the village.

Tom Breyley's arrival in the village was a complete change of fortune for the Prior family, and in particular for their spinster daughter, Mary Ann. His marriage into the family gave him the opportunity to set up his own business as a saddler at Moxeys and he made a great success of it.

John Prior himself had inherited Moxeys through marriage when he made Emma Wotton his wife. Emma was born in 1832, the eldest of John Wotton's daughters. He was a carpenter who later on specialised in making barrels and other wooden containers. It was John Wotton who built Moxeys around the time of his marriage to Mary Ann Berry in 1829. Emma Wotton grew up there with her younger sisters Ellen 1834, Mary Evans 1839, Emily 1844 and Edith 1846 and her brothers Edwin 1830 and Humphrey Berry 1835, Humphrey died when he was just two years old, leaving one son and heir who was destined by tradition to take over from his father. Emma married John Prior in 1856 but because her mother had died just three years earlier, she was left with a brood of younger siblings to look after. There was no question of her leaving the property so her new husband moved in with her and the house was unofficially divided between the two branches of the family. Mary Ann, from a baking family herself, had helped her husband to diversify so that as well as earning a living as a cooper John was also known for making and selling bread in the village. As well as catering for the family, Emma took over her mother's role in the bakery, taught and supervised by her grandfather Humphrey Berry. Humphrey and his wife had been baking in the village for many years and regularly supplied the churchwardens with the sacrament bread e.g. 4s.8d. in 1827. They lived in the southern end of Church House.

It was hoped that Edwin would take over one or other of his father's businesses but he did not enjoy his apprenticeship as a baker and chose instead to branch out and follow his own interests. By the time of John's death in 1860, Edwin had already turned his back on the village and moved to Taunton where he married a school teacher called Frances Dyer. He trained as a Land Agent, being the first generation to start earning their livelihood as a white-collar worker. The couple had just one daughter, Rose Berry Wotton 1859 and with their little girl they lived at 29 East Street, Taunton running a school for young ladies. Number 29 was a substantial property and as many as fourteen young girls between the ages of twelve and eighteen boarded there, with the Wottons. After Edwin's death in

1884 his wife took in an additional three young teachers of English and Music as boarders as well as her young lady students. Rose Wotton grew up to follow in her mother's footsteps and she became a music teacher. She never married and died in Taunton at the age of thirty two.

In his father's will proved in 1860 Edwin Wotton inherited Moxeys with some other property in the village but he had no desire to return to Cheriton and sold some to Daniel Tremlett Brewer and Moxeys to John Prior his brother-in-law. No doubt he invested the proceeds in his own land agency business and his wife's school. Moxeys then legally became John and Emma Prior's and the outbuildings, barn and courtyard garden were ideal for his business as a mason, especially when he landed the contract for building the new Methodist Chapel in 1860.

So, John Wotton, cooper and baker was the original owner and builder of the house now called Moxeys and Little Moxey (numbered 54 on the Tythe map). He was newly married and looking to set himself up in business following in the coopering trade from his father Thomas Wotton. His elder brother James was already running a thriving business in workshops at The Half Moon and his father Thomas was still actively involved. Not only were they making the traditional barrels with which we are familiar today but also a wide range of household and agricultural vessels, including buckets, hogsheads, pipes, butts, butter churns, casks etc. Dry Coopers made vessels to transport tobacco, vegetables, building materials, grain, flour etc, whilst White Coopers and Wet Coopers made containers designed for liquids like water, wine, beer etc. A cooper needed outhouses to store and shape wood, a mini forge to heat up iron hoops, and a ready water source to rapidly cool iron bands. John had needed to find himself premises that would offer these facilities and the site he chose was ideal. Not visible to the passer-by today because of the relatively new-built Moxeys and Little Moxey in front, are the original buildings of a one-time public house which by then was being used as a dwelling house with adjacent buildings. These structures still stand behind the more modern range and comprise a long main free-standing building behind Moxeys, and a smaller one that has been incorporated into the rear of Little Moxey. Originally called The Angel Inn, these buildings were a public house and a tap room. Lost to memory now, the Angel Inn was operating in the first half of the seventeenth century and had been built a field adjoining Lower Saunders, owned at that time by the Hewish and then the Wotton family through marriage. John Wotton would have been able to move into the former pub then dwelling house and start up his coopering business straight away and instruct the builders to start work on a new, purpose-built house for his family at the front. There was a good well of water at the eastern end of the original property and a wide courtyard ideal for a cart and horses to load and turn in. The main access was via Back Lane (since variously named Locks Lane, Doctor's Lane or Jack's Acre Lane) and clients could have placed their orders, collected their goods and watched a craftsman and his apprentice at work. Whilst an Inn, customers could have entered the Angel along the same Lane and bought both food and drink from the landlady. An enigmatic entry in the Overseers of the Poor Accounts/Churchwarden's Accounts for 1744 becomes clear when one knows about the existence of this early Inn for it reads, '1744 Mrs Wessen for the Angel … and putting up £2.2s.0d'. This would be the amount paid to the landlady for providing lodgings and food and drink for someone, or perhaps for hosting the committee meeting or for holding an auction ('putting up' goods for sale). In 1744 that was a considerable sum of money so the event must have been a memorable one. Other entries in the Churchwarden's accounts mention buying wine from a Mrs Webber and this may well be the same person:

'1755/6 Mrs Webber for 13 bottles of tent and 17 bottles of port wine £2.10s.6d.'

'1763 Mrs Webber for wine and a bottle of tent £1.5s.8d.

John Webber had died in September 1755 leaving his widow Mary to continue the business. She was buried in November 1776 so it seems probable that the Inn did not renew its liquor license and then became a dwelling house, formerly known as The Angel. William Segar Bastard, born in Exeter 1789 had inherited an interest in the property at this early date, and as a hop merchant he signed a release of his interests on the building to John Hewish, (farmer of Lower Saunders), John Wotton and John Roberts.

When John Wotton built Moxeys at the front of The Angel/dwelling house c 1828 it would seem that he used the older building to the rear as a bakery. By the time the Priors took on the property however it seems that the Angel building had lost its residential status and was just a workshop. Later deeds refer to the building merely as 'the shed,' whereas earlier deeds had refer to it as 'the building formerly known as The Angel Inn, now used as a private dwelling. The whole tenement was auctioned by Helmores in January 1871 and the description of the cottage building at the rear was still that it was 'formerly The Angel Inn.'

This provides a timeline for the structure giving the information that it was firstly a pub, then it was lived in as a cottage and finally it became just a shed or workshop. Today the main building has been divided in two parts and is shared between the owners of Moxeys and of Orchard Bungalow. A very large cooking range at the western end may have been used by the Wottons and Berrys when they were operating a bakery from the premises, and two doors opposite each other on the northern and southern sides are a memory of when customers at the Inn would have moved freely into the bar and out into a yard and garden. The document states that the newer buildings of Moxeys were considered to be at the *back* of the Angel Inn and not in front of it as we might say, hinting that the entrance to the Inn had been on the northern or eastern side as it faced into Mr Hewish' orchard (the grey buildings north of buildings 54 and 55 on the 1840 Tythe map).

Buildings 54, 55, 56 and 57 were not there at the time of The Angel Inn but Back Lane continued to be a well-used route for workers, carts and cattle going up into the fields and orchard beyond in Victorian times.

1840 ownership:

54 Houses and garden owned and occupied by John Wotton

55 Cottage and garden owned by James Stabback, occupied by Samuel Dave

56 Cottage, yard and garden owned and occupied by James Stabback

250

57 Cottage and garden owned by John Hewish jnr,

58 Cottage and garden owned by James Stabback, occupied by Philip Moggeridge

59 Cottage and garden owned by James Stabback, occupied by William Davey

60 Orchard owned by George Tanner, occupied by John and William Oliver

25.3.1791 for '2 cottages with the garden and orchard' between William Harris and John Moxey, yeoman on the three lives of John and Ann Moxey and their son John may refer to the old Angel Inn and tap room at a time when they had become dwellings. If so, this might solve the mystery of why the newer property has been called Moxeys.

1794 Cottage in Churchtown, a 99 year lease conveyed in consideration of £7 by William Harris of Keneggie to John Moxey on his life, his wife Anne's and their nine year old son John's.

If John Wotton took over the property c1831 shortly after his marriage and then built the large dwelling house in front of it, he may have decided to use the name of Moxeys then.

N.B. An auction of the leases of Stokaden, Grew and Grewlands was held at 'The New Inn, Cheriton Fitzpaine' in 1731. Was this the Inn at the back of Moxeys or perhaps the Half Moon.

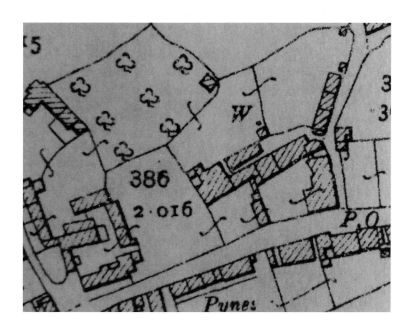

251

1801–1811 Land Tax paid by John Moxey on a cottage owned by Daniel Tremlett 4/-

1821 Land Tax paid by Mary Moxey on a cottage owned by John Brewer 4/- (John Brewer married Daniel Tremlett's daughter Sarah Tremlett 1806))

1831 Land Tax paid by Mary Moxey on a cottage owned by Sarah Brewer 4/- (widow of John Brewer)

Bakeries in the village

Whereas all farmhouses in the area had a bread oven, many cottages in the village had to rely upon neighbours who had the facilities to bake bread and supply it to them. Some put the women in their families to work, baking daily for neighbours whilst they continued in their various trades. Others took on the business full-time themselves and were able to meet the needs of numerous villagers, delivering to those who lived in outlying hamlets. Humphrey Berry and his wife were baking as early as 1827 and they also supplied sacrament bread to the church. They lived in the cottage attached at the southern end of the Poor House numbered 24 on the 1840 Tythe map, using the large bread oven that still juts out into the churchyard. Their daughter Mary Ann Berry took the trade with her when she married John Wotton, builder of the modern day Moxeys and Little Moxey. The two families probably also baked in the large range in the old building behind Moxeys that had once been The Angel Inn.

Married couple John and Ann Drake both aged sixty five were also operating as bakers for the village and its surroundings in 1841. They had John's younger brother Samuel aged sixty living with them in what is now called The Old Bakehouse, no doubt helping with the heavy work lifting sacks and kneading dough. A cousin called Matilda Drake, aged fifteen was also listed at the property in the census.

A property had been left to John and Ann in their father John's will dated 1818, but it was not The Old Bakery where they were running the business in 1841. The cottage bequeathed to them was left on the proviso that John jnr kept it in good repair and if he did allow it to become ruinous and failed to do anything about it within three months' notice given by the Trustees, it was to be taken by the Trustees and the lease sold on or the building otherwise used for the good of the Poor. John was also tasked with 'new building the oven' in the said house and with putting the thatch in good repair immediately after his father's death. John snr's signature was extremely shaky and he stated that he was very sick and weak in body at the time and was seventy six years old. In his will he also left three sacks of best wheaten flour to be given to John jnr at the end of the month and mentioned the 'kitchen chamber where I now sleep', and 'my bed'. John snr, who was a thatcher had held a lease on the property in Churchtown from Rev Arundell as early as 1795. Because of the clear involvement of the Trustees with the property mentioned in the will this property can be identified as the cottage at the northern end of the Workhouse, described in a later lease as:

'House with rooms, chambers and buildings lately erected and added thereto with the court, and a passage at the north end of the workhouse with stabling and outhouses. Robert Maunder coedwainer, now deceased to John Drake, for the use of John Tuckett 1833.'

This property is number 27 on the Tythe of 1840 and was a cottage attached at the northern end of the Poor House, later halved in size to allow for a wider entrance to The Hayes and then amalgamated into The Old School building. By 1841 John Drake jnr had sold the lease to William Pitt and it was occupied by John Bradford. So it looks as if after inheriting the lease on the property, John either decided that the work required was too great and sold the lease on straight away, or carried out the work and as his business expanded, moved out to the bigger premises in the high street known today as The Old Bakehouse. At the time of the 1841 Census this was the only property in the village owned by John Drake jnr, baker. With his brother Samuel however, he also jointly owned a cottage at Long Down near Foxes Cross.

The Drakes were the second generation to live in the village, having descended from a family established in Cruwys Morchard for at least seven generations before that (John Drake 1500–1552.)

By 1851 John Drake was calling himself a 'retired baker' and the business had been picked up by James Thorne a baker from Broadclyst, married to local girl Sarah Bradford. The Thornes lived in the main road of the village with their only daughter Elizabeth, having lost their two year old daughter, Mary Ann in 1853, and they ran a business there until the 1880s. Also producing bread were

*The Old Bakehouse in the high street – the earliest date on the deeds
is 1800 but the building date is unknown*

John Wotton, also working as a cooper and living at Moxey's, and William Wotton.

Quite by chance another James Thorne arrived to live in Victoria House from Cruwys Morchard sometime after 1851. The 1861 census names him then as a shopkeeper and draper, whilst later entries call him a draper, grocer and baker. Because of his namesake living so close by, this James became known as James B (Bidgood) Thorne. His wife Jane from Woolfardisworthy was several years younger than him, but the couple had only one child, Edwin Thorne born in 1862. They were active Bible Christians, meeting in a designated cottage in the village until numbers in the congregation swelled and it was apparent that a chapel was required. In 1845 a house where John Channon, yeoman lived was registered (this was probably Morles Farm), whilst in 1850 Henry Cross, Dissenting Minister registered a house in the possession and occupation of Robert Crook, tanner at Upham. J B Thorne sold the plot of land next to his property for the princely sum of £60 and the building of the Chapel began around 1860. Mason in charge of the project was John Prior of Moxeys, using his front yard to store

255

stone and equipment for the huge building task. The chapel was completed at a cost of £280 including £60 for the freehold land and was officially opened on October 21st and 22nd 1860.

The building of Cheriton Fitzpaine Bible Christian Chapel began in 1860

1910 Thorne's bakehouse and shop on the left-hand side of the road and their home, Victoria Cottage opposite on the right-hand side.

Delivery carts were stored in what is now Swain's shop out of shot to the right of Victoria Cottage, and horses were led through to stabling at the rear.

In later years Edwin son of James B Thorne became a Sunday School Superintendent and funds were then raised for the addition of a schoolroom on land also offered by the family. Edwin, who learned the trade from his father kept the business running, taking on his own apprentices, William Manning, James Great and Thomas Spencer in the bakery and Annie Great in the shop. Delivery wagons were housed in what is now the post office and shop, next to Victoria Cottage, and the oven and shop were in The Old Bakery opposite. Later on, ovens were also installed in the Post Office building. With its central position in the village it was well-placed for trade. Edwin's father James Thorne 'sweetly passed away' in 1891 and his funeral was held at the Bible Christian Chapel, attended by 150 mourners. Edwin was married to Bessie Ann Webber and they raised three boys, Granville James, Herbert Edwin and Arthur James Webber.

Granville J Thorne continued as a grocer at The Old Bakehouse during the Second World War.

1955 Note the post box in the wall of the house called Sweetbriar (alias Glebe Cottage) on the left-hand side and the entrance to the stables on the right

The census lists a Post Office, with six rooms, run by Daniel and Sarah Prior immediately after the entry for the eight roomed Victoria House occupied by Edwin Thorne. There has been speculation as to whether Prior's Post Office was in Post Office Lane at this date but the evidence of the census seems to suggest that it was in the High Street, either next to or opposite the Thornes, and certainly in the vicinity. A sad death occurred at the property in 1919 when Emma Sharland aged fifty when hung herself in the loft of her employer's storehouse. She had worked for Sarah Prior for thirty years as a loyal domestic servant and assistant in the post office and was very much part of the family. She had been ill and in pain for several months and nothing could help her state of health or depression. The Post Office had been a thriving concern when Daniel Prior was alive but Mrs Prior a widow was herself getting old and she did the best she could for Emma's future by securing her a coveted place in the Almshouses. Emma Sharland did not want to leave her mistress however and when she did not rise as usual one morning another servant went looking for her and discovered the tragedy.

1870 there were four bakers in the village, Philip Mogridge, John Newberry, John Prior and James Thorne. In 1902 there were just two, Harry Lock and Edwin Thorne, whilst in 1935 just Lock's son-in-law Reginald Charles Elworthy made and sold bread.

Harry Locke served the village with his shop and bakery in the early 20th century, operating from the large double-fronted premises on the corner of what is known either as Doctor's Lane or Locks Lane, leading up to Jack's Acre. Harry came from Sandford with his brother John and late in 1881 he married a Crediton girl called Harriet Fielding. It is difficult to imagine how the two met since earlier that same year Harriet was far away in Newton Abbot serving as a parlour-maid in the household of a vicar. Once settled in Cheriton however, Harriet aided her new husband in his business and bore Edith 1883, Lilian Olive 1895 and Ernest Harry 1889. In the 1911 census the family was sharing their seven rooms with a shop assistant and two fifteen year old apprentices, Walter James Alford, son of a thatcher and Ernest John Moor.

In the 1930s Harry's daughter (Lilian) Olive continued to run the shop with her second husband Reginald Elworthy. Her first husband Tom S Mildon from Upcott Barton had been badly wounded in the First World War shortly after their marriage when serving as a private in the Coldstream Guards. His stomach wound never closed satisfactorily and Olive and her sister-in-law Loveday

Mildon nursed him daily for many years whilst he did his best to contribute his skills to the bakery business. He eventually lost his fight for life in 1922 and his exhausted and heart-broken sister Loveday Mildon then appeared to give up on herself. She died from influenza only a week later. Olive Mildon married Reg Elworthy in 1926 and they made Green Close their home.

Watkins Chapple became the Postmaster at Pynes House where he lived and post was collected and sorted there before being delivered on foot or by bicycle. Bill Price took over from him and eventually moved the post office opposite to the shop we know today run by Roy and Stella Swain.

A reference to Post Office Lane comes in 1932 when Albert John Raymont who lived there was fined for riding his motorcyle without lights and with ineffective brakes. It is known that a post collection box stood at the end of this little road and a memoire written by a villager who was a child in the 1930s mentioned that, 'The Post Office was at the end of the lane which is still called Post Office Lane (Mr Castle's house now)', so this is presumably the present day Lane End Cottage.

Post Office Lane opposite the Half Moon pub which used to run through to Landboat Farm. Lane End Cottage is the first building. Note the arched brickwork at the foot of the garden wall which denotes a culvert or gutter

Pynes or Gidshay and the Oliver family

The name Pynes is a very confusing one when it comes to tracing property in the village, for several houses have used that name over time and there is today a Pynes Terrace, a Pynes Close, a Pynes and a Little Pynes. The property that stands in the main road opposite Locks Lane which leads up to Jack's Acre is now called Pynes House, but it was not the first to use this name. The Firs, a few doors down the road was also called Pynes at one time in its history, but the original dwelling to be given the name Pynes is the present day Arden House. The Sheldrake family decided to rename the property when they moved in to avoid confusion. But even before this house was completed there was an ancient tenement called 'Gidshay or Pynes' which passed down through the Oliver family. The timeline for this tenement which included several parcels of land as well as a dwelling can be tracked in the Poor Rate lists:

1678–1713 1d Poor rate levied of the occupiers of Pynes tenement

1751 John Oliver paid 1½d Poor rate on Pynes. This could be one of two John Olivers producing children at that time in the village viz John father of John 1718, William 1720 and Richard 1725 and John father of Richard 1732, John 1734, William 1736.

1765 Benjamin Brewer paid Church rates on Pynes, Poor rates on Pynes and a town living, and Land tax on Voyseys tenement and a town living. William Oliver that year was paying on Bowdell

1782 William Harris esq of Keneggie, Cornwall owned Pynes with Mrs Oliver occupying Pynes

1787 William Oliver took an apprentice for Pynes

1788 William Oliver was the occupier of Pynes

In 1788 the Oliver family petitioned for use of a pew measuring 6'4" long, broad and high. It was realised in 1790 that much of the church seating was in decay and needed renewal so the authorities looked favourably upon local individuals who approached them offered to pay to build llocated seats.

1791–1795 William Harris owner, John Oliver, leaseholder of Pynes

1796 William Oliver c1720, butcher left a Will in which his sons John and Richard inherited his estate called Pynes.

1800-1815 Richard Oliver took on apprentices for Pynes

1808 Richard Oliver, yeoman of Pynes in the parish petitioned for use of a 'seat in the north aisle' together with a seat 'immediately behind'.

1831 Richard Oliver 1766 appears to have complete ownership of the property as he then left a will in which his children William and Edward were to inherit Pynes. Other children also received bequests:

William 1799 and Edward 1809 were to inherit his two houses 'now building in the village on the north side of my present house' together with timber lying in the orchard to complete the building, and £20 each out of the surplus of Pynes when sold. Edward was to have first choice of the houses. Was one of the houses Wreylands extension or was it present day Pynes House opposite Locks Lane? The other was definitely what today is called Arden House, and was originally named Pynes together with a large garden and stable?

John 1804 and Mary 1799 were to inherit The Ring of Bells 'now in their possession'.

Thomas who was under age was to have 'the house and garden that extends to the hedge on the south side from ---- on the north side adjoining the village now occupied by William Cruwys'. William Cruwys aged 70 lived at Landboat in 1840 with his wife Jane and one would think that he was established there for some years, making this the property mentioned in the will. The garden may well be part of Bowdell's land.

Richard 1802 and Sarah 1806 were to have the house where Elizabeth Prior lived with 'part of the garden now occupied by William Cruwys on the west side of the gutter, part of Pynes' What was the gutter and was this a stream near Landboat?

William was left 'the dairy and chamber over it situate on the left side of the passage leading in from the village together with part of the garden on the eastern side of the wall, south from the gate leading in from the same'. This was probably Cross cottage/dairy farm which does lie on the left of the narrow part of the road that allows access to the village. Cross farm was owned by Rev Arundell and tenanted by Samuel Brewer at the time. A garden on the right could have been the plot on the corner where Oxford House was later built in c1839. It remains a mystery as to where 'the gate leading in from the same' was.

N.B. In the 1840 Tythe William Cruwys 1771 and his wife Jane lived at Landboat. Elizabeth Prior had died 1839 but was married to William Prior d 1815 leaving her with nine children. She was also called Betty and had been Elizabeth Pridham from Stockleigh English.

1830s William Snell took an apprentice for Pynes

1832 Sarah Oliver is listed as owner and occupier of Pynes so perhaps the terms of the will had not yet been carried out.

Pynes (Arden House) is number 21 on the 1840 Tythe map, which shows the glass verandah running along the front of the property on the side facing away from the road. At this time it was in the possession of Nicholas Tuckett together with cottage number 23, the left-hand end of present day Crab Apple Cottage.

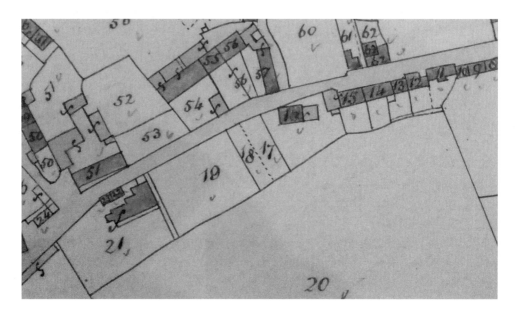

Cottage 22 (part of Crab Apple Cottage) was then owned by William Browning and these were tenanted by Robert Maunder and others.

19 is the plot where Pynes Terrace was later built

16 is present day Pynes House opposite Locks Lane

After Richard Oliver died in 1831 and his property was divided up between his children, some portions were offered up for sale out of the family.

1835

Lot 1: Dwelling houses, barn stables, gardens and several closes of meadow, orchard, pasture and arable land in the occupation of Mr Osmond (Pynes House opposite Locks Lane) Tenant Thomas Osmond had married Hannah Ridler in Exeter in 1833 and the couple had Anna Maria 1834 and Bessey Ridler 1837. In 1840 the owner and occupier of this house was James Prior who also owned the three cottages that later combined to create Church Cottage and other houses in the village.

Lot 2: A dwelling house and garden in the possession of Mrs Sarah Oliver

Lot 3: A dwelling house in the occupation of Mrs Elizabeth Prior

Lot 4: A dwelling house in the occupation of Mr Robert Maunder (Arden House formerly Pynes)

Lot 5: An extensive garden in the possession of Mr John Bradford (was this plot 204 that Bradford tenanted in 1840?)

Lot 6: A large barn, stable and curtilage with other outbuildings in the possession of Mrs Oliver

Lot 7: An extraordinarily rich watered meadow of 4½ acres fertilised by the drose within the village, now in the possession of Mrs Oliver (next to the Old Smithy bungalow at the bottom of Church Town)

Lot 8: A very productive orchard of ¾ acre in the occupation of Mr John Oliver (was this 60 on the Tythe? and where the wood for the two 'in building' houses came from?)

Lot 9: A field called Cod Close being 3¼ acres of prime pasture in his occupation

Lot 10: Higher Cod Close being 2¾ acres of productive arable land in his possession (these two were at the top of Tower Hill between Mill Lane and Coddiford Hill)

For all of these the interested parties should apply to Mrs Sarah Oliver or Mr Andrew Hewish at White's Cross.

Pynes (Arden House) was bought and tenanted out to the local doctor and surgeon Mr Josiah Body. When he died in 1841 the newspaper advertisement for the auction of the property reveals that it was a very desirable residence for the day, facing out towards Rev Arundell's island and boasting a lawn of four acres. The views and nuch of the garden were forfeited when Pynes Close was constructed:

for building on.

Lot 4.—All that substantial new built DWELLING HOUSE, situate near Lot 3, now in the occupation of Josiah Body, Esq., Surgeon, as yearly tenant (at moderate rent) ; containing Parlours, Sitting Rooms, Surgery, two Kitchens, Pantry, five Bed Rooms, Dressing Room, Water Closets, Verandah in front, covered with zinc, and laid with excellent flagging, sixty feet in length; Stabling, with all other necessary and convenient offices. The Garden and Walks near the House are admirably laid out, in front of which is a Lawn of Four Acres, parted off with the most modern iron fencing, now in the occupation of the owner. The House commands a beautiful view of the Lands of the Rev. W. H. Arundell, with the Timber of fine growth, and the luxuriant and thriving Plantations, which, with a southern aspect, impart to this Property a grandeur of feature not to be surpassed by any House in the neighbourhood.

Lot 5.—All that valuable and luxuriant MEADOW, in front of

Western Times 1841

The magnificent verandah eventually started to pull the house apart and it was necessary to remove it in the 1970s. A post or two still remain in situ. The beautiful views across parkland have been partially obscured by the building of Pynes Close at the southern end of the gardens.

In 1841 the Overseers agreed to amend the rates as follows:

Meadow part of Pynes £16

House occupied by William Body £12 (Pynes/Arden House)

Garden occupied by Wotton jnr £2

Part of Holes occupied by W J Tucker £20

Holes House and fields £6

Pynes (Arden House) became the home of Samuel Pridham after 1889 when he gave up farming and moved out of Pool Barton with his wife Louisa and become District Road Surveyor and Registrar of Birth, Marriages and Deaths. He

used one of the rooms in Moxey's nearby as his office and there is a brass plaque
to that effect held by the current owner of Moxeys.

Sale particulars for Pool included

Lot 1 Pool Barton, Stockparks, Sutton and Yeo in Sandford totalling more
than 253 acres lying in three vales with water running through each, and a most
comfortable residence and outbuildings, all with slated rooves together with
outlying thatched cottages (possibly Tower Hill Tenement). The sale also boasted
a quarry of excellent building stone and about a mile of river bordering the
property, appealing to the shooting and fishing fraternity,

Lot 2 was the smithy occupied by Mr Geen.

Later that year it was announced that Mr Pridham was declining business
having let the farm but he still wanted to sell two bullocks, horses, implements
and one hundred empty hogsheads and pipes.

Having settled comfortably into his new home at Pynes, Pridham offered his
newly widowed sister Mrs Annie Harris Hole a place to stay. She arrived in 1900
from her former home, Manor Farm in Stawell Somerset because her husband
Albert had died in 1899 leaving her with six children to bring up. At the time of
the 1901 census the youngest daughter Anna Pridham Hole was away boarding
at Seaton House School in Mutley Plains, Plymouth. With her at Pynes however
were four of the children, Amy Elizabeth, Henry Robert and Edward Albert and
Ellen Harris. Whilst staying at Pynes her second eldest daughter Amy Elizabeth

Hole fell sick and lost her life aged only 17. Just seven months later her daughter Ellen Harris Hole also died - she was barely fifteen years old. The Pridhams were said to be devastated at the loss of their two nieces, especially since they had offered the family a temporary safe home at Pynes to recover from the grief of losing their father.

Annie Harris Hole moved to Beaconsfield to keep house for her cousin and Samuel Pridham lived on at Pynes until his wife died in 1923 and another capital sale took place. The house itself was described then as south facing with a veranda overlooking the lawn and a very good vegetable garden. It had three reception rooms, a kitchen and larder downstairs with six bedrooms a dressing room and a w.c. upstairs. At the rear stood two cottages, (Crab Apple Cottage) and there was a two stall stable, a harness room and trap house. These still stand as the wing at the eastern end. The property had a good water supply, a meadow and two fields of arable land. Samuel Pridham was leaving the neighbourhood to live with his sister Annie Hole who had herself retired to Westbury Park in Bristol. He died there in 1928 and was buried in the parish of Wick St Lawrence aged almost eighty years.

In a separate sale some of his household effects were offered comprising antique and modern furnishings, antique china, glass, Sheffield silver, brass candlesticks and pans. His nine year old bay mare of 13.2 hands and a dog-cart also needed to be sold.

Pynes included the two cottages by the roadside and one is men-

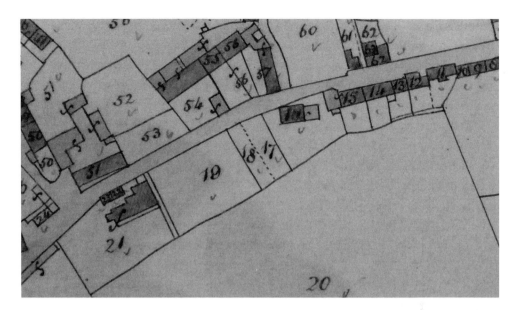

tioned in 1943 by W A Cheriton of Pynes when he advertised in the newspaper for a man for general farm work and offered a cottage and garden as part of the deal.

The property was put up for sale again in 1894 as a result of the death of Dr G L Thorne and unbelievably included in his effects were surgical instruments and a stock of drugs – one hopes that they found their way into the right hands. A telescope, and library of books, a pair of buffalo horns and a camera, chemicals and printing frames given a real insight into the doctor's interests in life. A bay mare and 4-wheeled carriage were included in the sale together with a nearly new carriage umbrella and a mowing machine.

Number 16 on the Tythe map is what today, is named Pynes House, not to be confused with Arden House, the original Pynes. It is Grade 2 listed and the description is as follows:

This listing is for present day Pynes House and not for the Pynes now Arden House belonging to the Olivers:

7/25 Pynes House including Coach-house adjoining to west and front railings

House and adjoining coach-house (now garage). Early C19. Plastered cob or rubble; rubble stacks topped with C19 brick; slate roofs. 2-room house with central staircase plan facing road to north. Coach-house with hayloft over adjoining to right (west). Gable-ended house with end stacks is built up on a stone platform and set back slightly from road. 2 storeys. 3-window front, originally symmetrical. Central 6-panel door, the upper pair glazed, and late C19 gabled porch with chamfered posts and small brackets at the top and shaped bargeboards. To right late C19 bay window with canted sides containing horned sashes without glazing bars upsets symmetry. To left of door and both sides at first floor level are C19 2-light 2-pane casements and centre first floor is pointed arch-headed stair window with Gothick glazing bars and including small diamond pane leaded glass. Stone platform projects forward to street and carries low iron railings with the plain pointed tops bent back towards the house. Rear elevation includes 16 pane sashes. The adjoining coach-house is slightly lower than the main house and projects forward onto the street. It includes a C20 garage door and a C19 plank door to left and, at first floor level, a loading hatch to former hayloft. Listing NGR: SS8690306213

Present day Pynes, opposite Locks Lane (not the original and older Pynes House owned by the Olivers and Pridhams which is now called Arden House)

Pynes Terrace

1889 Sale of several cottages abutting the main road in the centre of the village which included those in Pynes Terrace

Lot 1 a 3 room cottage and outbuildings with two pig styes, a shed and a wc and a garden now in the occupation of Mr Gillard

Lot 2 two cottages each with three rooms and a garden with wc, one now in the occupation of Mr Alford and the other vacant

Lot 3 two cottages each with three rooms with one garden and a wc in the occupation of Mrs Conybere and Mrs Berry.

The auction was held at The Ring of Bells on May 10th 1889.

From the parish registers:

Edward Oliver mar Mary Smart 1672 C F and they had John 1673, William 1677 and Richard 1680

John Oliver mar and had John 1718, William 1720 and Richard 1725

William Oliver mar Mary Huckley in 1703 CF and had Mary 1706

Richard Oliver mar Jane Grant in 1793 and had John 1795 and Richard 1711

Possibly the Olivers above came from William 1720 who mar Ann Wilson Stockleigh English 1755 etc.

Pynes is always entered as 'occupiers of Pynes 1d from 1678 rate lists until Oliver is named in 1792

1701 Edward Oliver and Simon Hewish for a property on southside 2d.

1726 John Oliver and Mary Hewish 2d.

1737 John Oliver for North Sutton Highways Officer

1739 John Oliver for Bowdell

1751 John Oliver for Bowdell

1788 the Oliver family petitioned for use of a pew measuring 6'4" long, broad and high

1791 William Oliver for Bowdell 5d.

1791 John Oliver for Pynes 1½d.

1796 Will of William Oliver leaves Pynes to John and Richard. Richard had one child by this time.

1808, Richard Oliver, yeoman of Pynes in the parish petitioned for use of a 'seat in the north aisle' together with a seat 'immediately behind', presumably for his wife and children. By this time Richard had six children.

1831 Will of Richard Oliver leaves Pynes to William and Edward

Ann 1795 mar William Passmore of Cadeleigh

William 1797 died of a suspected heart attack on his way home from Tiverton in 1841 where he had taken tea with his brother Thomas, then schoolmaster at the Union Workhouse. William was found still clutching the reigns of his horse on the road home and the horse was just standing still. He died in 1841, and although he was the eldest and destined to inherit from his mother, she died in 1844 so his share was re-distributed amongst his siblings. He was not married. From his father Richard who died in 1831 he had inherited half of Pynes including one house in building, north of Pynes and the dairy and chamber over on the left hand side of the entrance to the village together with a garden on the right.

Mary 1799 who inherited half of The Ring of Bells pub from her father in 1831 and remained unmarried but she may have had an illegitimate son, Edwin in 1832 who died the following year. She had jobs as housekeeper etc. and eventually lived with her unmarried brother John and then retired with him to Dawlish

Richard 1802 mar and inherited from his father half of Elizabeth Prior's house in the village and a garden used by William Cruwys, part of Pynes. He moved to Axmouth and eventually emigrated to Ontario, Canada in the mid-1850s.

John 1804 remained unmarried and lived at one stage with his mother Sarah. He inherited from his father half of The Ring of Bells pub in 1831, and from his mother in 1844 Cod Closes at the top of Tower Hill where he built a cottage c 1846. He advertised this for sale in 1852 whilst he was living there and again in 1857 when he had retired to Dawlish with his sister. John was a butcher and smallholder.

Sally or Sarah 1806 inherited from her father half of Elizabeth Prior's house in the village and a garden used by William Cruwys, part of Pynes and from her mother money. She remained unmarried and moved to Stockleigh English and then to Cadeleigh where she lived with a Passmore nephew.

Edward 1809 mar Mary Chamberlain and emigrated to Ontario Canada in 1856. He had also lived in Thelbridge with his family. He inherited from his father half of Pynes and one of the houses being built in 1831 and from his mother in 1844 money.

Thomas 1812 was the youngest and his father ensured that his inheritance of a house where William Cruwys lived (possibly Landboat) was looked after for him within the family until he reached the age of majority. His mother left him money in 1844 when he had moved from Tiverton Union Workhouse to Stockenteignhead. He was a teacher whilst he was in England. He emigrated to Ontario Canada in the 1850s with his wife and family.

The Firs

The property known now as The Firs was built after the Tythe map of 1840 and was first occupied by Thomas Skinner and his wife Jane who appear there in the 1851 census. Thomas had held a gamekeepers licence from as early as 1838 in the parish. He was probably the illegitimate son of Mary Skinner from Cruwys Morchard who made his career as a butler with the Arundell family at the Rectory. So successful was he in his work and with his marriage to Jane from Glamorgan that he lived at The Firs as an annuitant until his death in 1882. He may of course have received an income from his putative father who is not known. The Overseers Accounts for Cruwys Morchard record that 'Mary Skinner's boy' was schooled from 1810–1812 at a yearly cost of 7s.6d. and he is the only child so mentioned. In addition, an entry in 1805 states that Mary Skinner gave the Overseers the sum of £10 towards the cost of her lying in and maintenance, indicating an unseen and unidentified father who wished to provide for his illegitimate son. Mary was in receipt of support for and had been

The Firs

given amongst other things, canvas and thread to mend her clothes, a gown, petticoat, handkerchief, apron and bonnet.

Jane died in 1883, and Thomas died in 1882. Their gravestone reads:

Top Plinth: Thomas Skinner died Nov 28 1882 aged 79 years

Bottom Plinth: Jane Skinner died February 23rd 1883 aged 82 years

Grave 716291

Their house was then occupied by Ann Wotton a widow in her forties and her nephew William Diamond a boot and shoe maker, both born in Hartland. They are listed in the 1891 and 1901 census returns but by 1911 Ann had died and William was there on his own, said to be living in three rooms at the property. During their occupancy the extension to the right was added, bringing an outside well into the house. A later tenant was the doctor who used a second set of steps to bring patients into his waiting room. These have since been removed.

Mrs Elworthy – daughter of Lock the baker and widow of Tom Mildon lived at Green Close next door and later on a passageway through to land at the back on the western side was covered over and built into the house, hence the differing roof levels and window positions that can now be seen from the road. Two pairs of semi-detached houses formed what we now call Pynes Terrace.

Lock's shop had a two storey extension built on at the left hand side which obscured the view enjoyed by The Laurels.

Morles and Hedgecleave and others

Morles Farm

Brewer Daniel Tremlet	William Roach	272	Cottage and Garden
Brewer John Tremlet	John Churchouse	276	cottage
Brewer William	John Treble	275	cottage
Brewer Elizabeth	Christopher Meggridge	277	cottage and Orchard
	Samuel Wotton	278	Garden
		279	cottage
	Mary Channon	280	cottage
	Henry Lake	282	cottage

			Morles Farm
Brewer Daniel Tremlett	John Channon	200	House Outhouses and Yard
Brewer John Tremlett		209	Garden
Brewer William		210	Home Orchard
Brewer Elizabeth		211	Well Hay
(continued)		212	Yonder Orchard
		213	Middle Field
		214	Rack Close
		215	Forth Close
		270	Yonder Morles Mead
		271	Hither Morles Mead

1840 Tythe Apportionment

Excluded from the block of property were 281 a cottage between Tower Hill cottage and Honeysuckle cottage which has since been demolished and 273 a smiths shop and orchard which is where Tan yr og has been built, both belonging to John Brewer snr and occupied in 1840 by Thomas Squires.

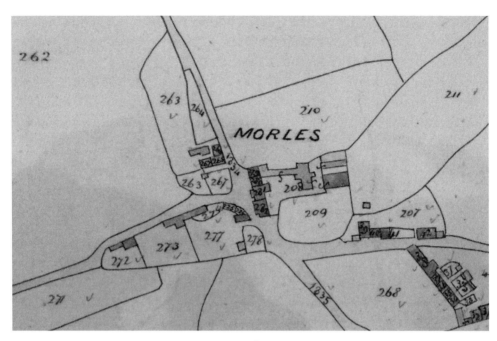

1840 Tythe map

In 1795 the block was owned jointly by Daniel Tremlett Brewer, John Tremlett Brewer and William and Elizabeth Brewer. Christopher Mogridge had taken on the lease from his father Thomas Mogridge for the property numbered 277 a cottage and orchard in Chugbear Lane, and William Roach was tenanting 272 a cottage and garden (Dunns). These properties are immediately identifiable in a lease of 1795 from Daniel Tremlett:

'Cottage house and garden in Chugbear Lane formerly part of The Barton called Thomas Mogridge's tenement

Cottage house and garden

two cottage houses, garden and orchard

Cottage house

Cottage house and garden

Cottage house and small orchard on Tower Hill

Small orchard on left hand side of Hollywater Road

Small orchard up Tower Hill'

Together with this block of land were Moxeys or Bodley's Tenement, and Morles moiety of Stockparks (four closes comprising twenty four acres).

The consideration for the freehold of this entire property was the sum of £785. Daniel Tremlett passed this down to his Brewer grandsons who both carried the middle name of Tremlett.

The farm was split up in 1907 when it failed to sell as an entire lot and then comprised

Lot 1 Morles which was withdrawn from the auction at £900

Lot 2 Dunns Cottage a detached freehold with fruit and vegetable garden was withdrawn at £295

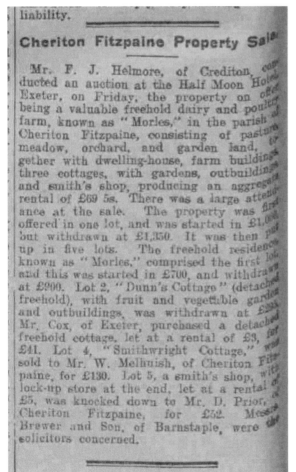

liability.

Cheriton Fitzpaine Property Sale

Mr. F. J. Helmore, of Crediton, conducted an auction at the Half Moon Hotel, Exeter, on Friday, the property on offer being a valuable freehold dairy and poultry farm, known as "Morles," in the parish of Cheriton Fitzpaine, consisting of pasture, meadow, orchard, and garden land, together with dwelling-house, farm buildings, three cottages, with gardens, outbuildings, and smith's shop, producing an aggregate rental of £69 5s. There was a large attendance at the sale. The property was first offered in one lot, and was started in £1,000, but withdrawn at £1,350. It was then put up in five lots. The freehold residence known as "Morles," comprised the first lot, and this was started in £700, and withdrawn at £900. Lot 2, "Dunn's Cottage" (detached freehold), with fruit and vegetable garden and outbuildings, was withdrawn at £295. Mr. Cox, of Exeter, purchased a detached freehold cottage, let at a rental of £3, for £41. Lot 4, "Smithwright Cottage," was sold to Mr. W. Melhuish, of Cheriton Fitzpaine, for £130. Lot 5, a smith's shop, with lock-up store at the end, let at a rental of £5, was knocked down to Mr. D. Prior, of Cheriton Fitzpaine, for £32. Messrs. Brewer and Son, of Barnstaple, were the solicitors concerned.

Western Times September 1907

Lot 3 a detached freehold cottage bought by Mr Cox of Exeter fro £41

Lot 4 Smith wright Cottage sold to Mr Melhuish for £130 (Honeysuckle Cottage)

Lot 5 a Smith's shop with lock-up store at the end was sold to Mr D Prior of Cheriton Fitzpaine for £32

In 1908 a sale of chattles was announced including a black oak kitchen table, antique inlaid mahogany chairs, a grandmother tall clock in a hand-carved oak case, outdoor effects, a single screw cider press and empty pipes and hogsheads etc.

1923 Mr Robert Harris sought to relinquish his business and advertised an auction of live and dead stock, implements, furniture and effects etc.

1924 part Morles being a small holding of a cottage and two rich meadows three acres in all was auctioned.

1927 The Hammetts put up for sale of a smart pony 13.2 hands high and a Rallicar with rubber tyres and harness, nearly new. A Ralli car was a traditional type of horse-drawn cart, named after the Ralli family. The vehicle was commonly used as a general run-around for families. It had back-to-back seating with space under the seats for luggage or shopping bags.

This sale was as a result of old Robert Harris' death at the age of ninety six. He was a man who loved riding with the hunt and only six years previously when he had had his horse die under him, although several miles from home he insisted

on carrying the saddle and bridle home on his back, refusing all help offered on the way. Not bad for a ninety year old!

1942 Mr and Mrs W Hammett of Morles suffered the tragic loss of their son Alick who died aged thirty two. Alick and his wife Dorrie had been running Hedgecleave Mill and it was Mr Hammett who was called upon to put the property up for sale that same year. Hedgcleave offered eighteen acres of arable land and thirty nine acres of meadow and pasture with a good house and ample buildings. The sale on March 15th revealed that their son had been intent on keeping up with modern technology because as well as three horses, farm equipment and a stock of poultry the inventory also offered a Triumph motorcycle and sidecar, a 1937 Ford 10 horse power motor car, a car trailer, a Morris lorry, a Tractor Sweep, a Butt cart with rubber wheels, a Bamlett mowing machine, and a McCormick self-binder. There was also a gent's bicycle and a wireless 'in working order' on offer.

Alick had married Doris Miller of Marsh Farm only six years earlier and the couple had one little daughter, Rita. He had suffered several months of a painful illness before dying, and many parishioners attended his funeral speaking highly of him.

Mr Vinnicombe put this testing advertisement in the Western Times dated November 1925. One wonders what the applicant had to do to prove their worthiness.

'In loving memory of dear Charlie Matthews who was killed in action Oct 12th 1917. Charlie was the son of Mr and Mrs Harold Matthews of North Coombe Farm, Witheridge, and as an Australian he served with the Australian Light Horse as a lieutenant. An In Memoriam notice in the newspaper included this verse;

'God bless our dear one, now laid to rest,
At his post for his loved ones he did his best.
Brave and kind-hearted, like a soldier he fell.
All those who knew him can speak of him well.
Never forgotten at Hedgecleave, Cheriton Fitzpaine or Sunnyside, Poughill.'

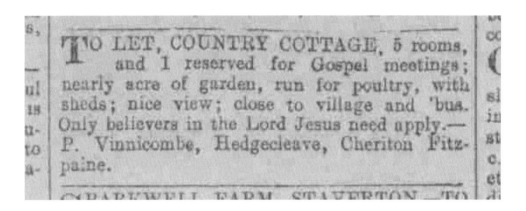

East and West Hayne

1660 Richard Clogge's will was proved in which he left West Hayne to his new wife Mary on the proviso that a barn was built there. Walter, Richard, Thomas and Ann Clogge are mentioned. 'West Hayne otherwise Perry'. In 1693 Mrs Mary Hewish held 'Cloggs' and paid 3d. In 1728 Andrew Hewish held 'Clogs' and Perry and half of Smith Hayne.

1678 occupiers of East Hayne
1689 occupiers of East Hayne, and William Morrish
1708 occupiers of East Hayne and Ann Morrish

1731 John Read for Hayne, William Hewish esq for East Hayne, George Rendle for Hayne

1764 occupiers of East Hayne, and widow Norrish

1779 owned by Edward Hewish esq through his father Mr William Hewish of Pool's Will.

1792 John Norrish for East Hayne, John Norrish for West Hayne

1797 owned by Elizabeth Hicks, daughter of the vicar Nicholas Hicks through her cousin Edward Hewish's Will.

In 1830 the lease on East and West Hayne farm was offered in an auction for the term of ten, fourteen or twenty one years. Described as 'a capacious farm house' with curtilage, labourers' cottages and 90 acres of land, lately in the occupation of Mr William Morrish, the farms lay together within a ring fence.

1840 the owners were brothers Edward Hewish Adams 1787 and Charles Adams 1793 who were the sons of John Adams and Ann Coffin who was herself descended from Ann Hewish. Edward was fantastically rich as a result of his business as a goldsmith in Exeter and lived in Heavitree in Southlands House,

Great Hayne Farm house

Magdalen Court with his wife Charlotte South 1788 and his unmarried sister-in-law Ann South. Their children included Charlotte Jane 1815, born the year after their marriage at Dartington, Ann Hewish and Caroline 1818, Lucy South 1819, Edward Hewish jnr 1829, twins Alfred and Matilda 1823 and George Hewish 1828. Before moving out to the leafy suburbs the couple had lived in the parish of St Stephens in the city of Exeter. The tradition of preserving family surnames is a helpful one and leads directly to the Hewish family and the wills of Edward Hewish 1779 and then his cousin Elizabeth Hicks 1797 who passed East and West Hayne down the line to Ann Adams. As with all married women Ann's inherited property became her husbands by right and he then willed it to two of their sons, Edward and Charles Adams. The house that the family built in Heavitree even incapsulated Charlotte's family name of South. Southlands has now been carved up into flats but was for many years the home of Magdalen Court School which has since moved to premises in Victoria Park Road.

In 1890 the freehold of Great Hayne farm was put up for auction but was not seen to be a good buy and the auctioneer struggled to drive the price up from its low start of £2,250. Farmer May put in a bid of £2,985 but the property of ninety acres and an ancient farmhouse within a ring fence, let at a yearly rent of £145 was withdrawn from the market and disposed of privately.

1906 Hayne was offered for sale having 'been in the occupation of Mr William Norrish for many years'. This meant that the farm had been farmed by the Morrish/Norrish family for period of about three hundred years! At the time of the auction it boasted a good farm house, pound house, extensive outhouses and 85 acres of very excellent arable, meadow, pasture and orchard land. The farm was said to be in a very high standard of cultivation. Anyone interested in the farm was invited to apply to Mr Trebble 'at Hayne village' in Cheriton Fitzpaine. Such was the community at Hayne with its busy farmyards and enclave of workers' cottages that it was often referred to as Hayne village.

By 1927 less productive parcels of land had been sold off and Great Hayne had been reduced to a smaller farm of fifty four acres with a house and various buildings let on a yearly tenancy to Mr Davey, but at auction it again failed to reach its reserve.

A lane connecting Cotton Farm to Great Hayne still exists and is called Cotton Lane.

2015 the farm has diversified and offers Bed and breakfast accommodation to holiday-makers. Its internet advertisement states: 'Hayne Farm The farm has been occupied by members of the same family since the 1870's and has 120 acres of farm land, mainly used for sheep and beef cattle.'

North Combe Farm, northside

North Combe farm was a viable holding with a good water source being sixty four acres at the time of the 1840 Tythe. The early mention of North Combe by name appears in rate lists of 1734 when John White paid his dues on the farm. In 1756 it was Joseph Comber, in 1782 John Martin, in 1788 Richard Manley and in 1795 the farmer was James Channing. At the time of the Tythe it was occupied by tenant farmer Francis Stoman and jointly owned by Ann and Ebener Morrison, Elizabeth Hammett and Rebecca Orchard. All of these parties were non locals and the property was an investment holding for them.

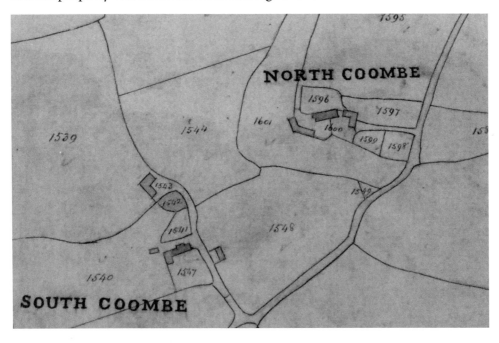

Standing in the lea of the hill behind, North Combe had four or five stock-yards around it where animals could be corralled and tended. A newspaper extract from the Exeter and Plymouth Gazette in 1924 shows Farmer Bending advertising for sale a cow in calf, a colt, steer, turkeys, fowls, hay, mangolds, swedes, grass and a poultry house on wheels. Like most properties in the area it was a mixed farm.

South Combe Farm, northside

South Combe was farmed by Henry Sweet in 1757, Edward Bradford in 1780–95 and Robert Voysey 1801/2. It was a larger concern than North Combe, covering ninety six acres in 1840 when it formed part of extensive land holdings in the possession of the Sharland family. James Squire farmed the land in 1841.

The Index of Tree-Ring Dated Buildings in Devon, revised June 2015 has a felling date of 1329+ for re-used jointed crucks built into the extension of a house of 1464–5 (ref SS 8900087) for South Combe.

In 1828 Southcombe, a farmhouse and 95 acres was offered for rent and was tenanted then by Mr Veysey.

In 1854 James Squire who was tenanting the farm had some trouble with one of his farm hands who stole some bark from the tannery and was given a four month prison sentence. Joseph Madge did not learn his lesson however and he was back in front of the judge in 1854 having stolen some hay. As a boy, Madge was a farm hand for Squires at South Combe

In 1918 South Combe was put up for sale by its then owner Mr A Southcott and it was advertised in the Western Times dated October 25th. The cob and stone-built house boasted six lofty bedrooms and a front lawn, but of particular interest were the many outhouses that were described in detail. With ninety seven and a half acres of productive pasture, arable and orchard lands it was a very attractive lot.

Peach Hayne

Peach Hayne was occupied by Richard Manley in 1753, the year that he married. He farmed there until at least 1774, taking on Great Venn farm in 1770. In 1774 The lease of Peach Hayne (along with those of Court Place, Smith Hayne and a cottage and Stockley meadow) was put up for auction in 1774 when Richard was said to be the existing owner. It was to be a short lease of seven or fourteen years.

1792 George Luxton for Peach Hayne

In 1904 William Tuckett the owner advertised for 'a trustworthy man able to do all kinds of farm work for wages of 13/- together with a cottage, garden and potato ground.

1833 good reed for sale at Peach Haynes.

1836 Farmer Paddon was advertising for someone to help with milking and indoors duties.

1947 his descendant Mr M Paddon was looking to sell his live and dead stock at auction.

Of particular interest to us today is the list of implements offered for sale, along with an eighteen month old sheep dag: 'A rubber tyred flat bottom cart with lades and side rails and brakes, a chest wagon, a set of spring harrows, Acting reed comber, banking plough, horse hoe, hay sweep, Deering mowing machine, Bentall 3-knife chaff-cutter, Bamford Lion hay kicker, Talbot 20 furrow tractor plough, stone roller, reaping machine, set of breeching harness and various other lots.'

The Tannery at Upham

Industry on northside, Cheriton Fitzpaine flourished under the Sharland family in the 18th and 19th centuries. They developed a tannery business at Upham, damming and managing the watercourse above the tan-yards in order to form pits for the treatment of hides, and installing a grinding mill to process the oak bark collected as a by-product from carpentry and cottage building.

Peter Sharland 1738 the first tanner in the family was apprenticed to a William Bradick, tanner of Bickleigh. William Sharland his yeoman father 1713 lived at Waterhouse with his wife and children, William 1731, Jane 1734, Peter 1738 and Mary 1741, but he had died by 1751 leaving his widow to pay a poor rate of 5¾d. on the property.[1,2] Peter's uncle Edmund Sharland, yeoman, paying 4d. on a nearby farm (probably West Upham) fell foul of the law in 1749 when he was accused of digging up three feet in length of the road from Cheriton Church to Tiverton, breaking it up and making pits two feet deep in it. He was also accused and found guilty of diverting the course of water in an underground gutter, presumably for the tanning business.[3]

When Peter had completed his apprenticeship he worked at Loxbeare but then set himself up at Waterhouse as a farmer a tanner.

The work processes carried out at Upham Tannery would have mirrored those at the Grampound Tannery in Cornwall which figures in this photograph of Jack and Cyril Allen scraping hides stretched over forms in the outside yard.[4]

Peter married Jane Mogrige 1750 of Witheridge in 1773 and they set up home at Lower Waterhouse bringing up their children Jane 1774, William 1776, Peter 1778 (died), Catherine 1780, John 1782, Peter 1784, Edward 1785, Elizabeth 1787, Mary 1790 and Thomas 1792. Almost unreadable now there are gravestones

leaning outside the east end wall of Cheriton Church showing that a Thomas died as an infant in 1792 and Mary in 1805 at the age of sixteen. Peter Sharland became a respected man, building up a successful tannery business and serving for a time as Churchwarden. With his eldest son William he was selected to stand on a committee protecting the interests of tanners against a proposed leather tax in 1812.[5] He was selected to manage Poor's Stock which was the invested income from Furse tenement, part of Andrew Scutt's charitable bequest, used to pay for the education of a poor boy chosen from the parish.

Peter retired from the business, eventually dying at the ripe old age of ninety one in 1829 and William Sharland his eldest son took over the tannery business at Waterhouse. William followed his father's example by marrying a Witheridge girl Elizabeth Comins, and the couple had three children Thomas Melhuish Comins Sharland 1813, Elizabeth 1814 and Mary Ann 1816. The rather complicated name they gave their first child reflected the fact that Elizabeth was the daughter of Ann and Thomas Melhuish Comins of Witheridge, a gentleman solicitor and head of a successful family that produced an attorney, an accountant and a solicitor. The Comins had married into the Melhuish family, patrons of the living of Witheridge for centuries, and Rev. Thomas Melhuish was vicar there from 1745 until 1793. The melding of these two illustrious families was obviously something that they wished to honour when they named their son.

As the tannery business flourished in Cheriton, more and more people were attracted to the area and the population grew substantially, so much so that new cottages were required in the immediate vicinity to rent out to tannery workers. This in itself generated work for villagers who were carpenters, masons and thatchers. General labourers would have received a wage for felling and preparing trees, cobbing, and haulage work. The village enjoyed an extended period of prosperity that was for once not tied up with agriculture.

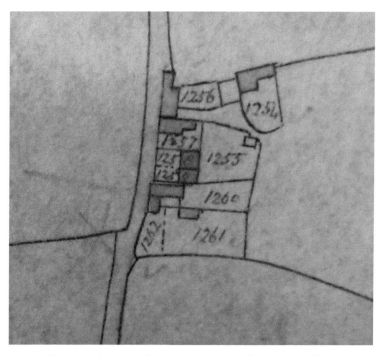

1840 Tythe map of 1260 Balle Cottage, alias Well Cottage built c1610 and several newer cottages providing accommodation for the tannery workers

With reasonable rents and modern living conditions, families who lived at Balle hamlet developed a mini-community of their own on the eastern side of the road to Upham, just beyond Redyeates. The hamlet included a small smithy.

Ball, owned by Thomas Beedell:
1254 cottage, outhouse and garden, John Balsom
1255 cottage, outhouse and garden, Roger Reed
1256 cottage, outhouse and garden, John Brookland

Owned by Ann Edwards:
1257 cottage, garden and smiths shop James Clogg
1258 cottage and garden, William Sharland
1259 cottage and garden, John Tibbs

Owned by John Cadeleigh Manley:
1260 cottage and garden, Robert Mare
1261 cottage and garden, George Greenslade
1262 cottage and garden, Betty Greenslade[6]

Some workers still walked up from the village to the tannery but many others enjoyed living just a stone's-throw from the tan-yards either in 'the Buildings', or in Upham itself and in particular, at Coleman Cottages which were close to the entrance to Cotton Farm. Upham was a thriving hamlet.

Jobs at the tannery were many and varied meaning that men, women and children could earn a wage from the Sharlands, stripping oak bark from tree trunks delivered by local farmers; operating the grinding mill to powder the bark; collecting urine from farms and cottages (both human and animal products were essential in the tanning process); trimming hides and scraping the hairs and flesh from them; soaking leathers in the pits fed by the managed watercourse; drying and softening the finished products by applying animal fats, and carting materials to and from the tannery. Oak bark was stored in hovels or stacked up in the yard under straw thatches until it was needed. The effluent from the tanning process, a foul-smelling liquor by all accounts was taken to fertilise the fields around the tan-yards owned and farmed by the Sharland family. With a prevailing south-westerly wind conveniently taking smells away from the tanner's residence, it was the inhabitants to the north of the tannery who were most affected.

1841 census, Lower Waterhouse
William Sharland, tanner
Elizabeth Sharland, wife
Thomas Sharland, son
servants, John Greenslade b.1806, William Ellis b. 1821, Charlotte Pleace b.1821, Mary Keen b. 1826
N.B. William had taken Elizabeth Pleace on as an apprentice when she was only eleven years old in 1832. She was the daughter of Robert and Elizabeth Pleace.

As an honest, upstanding member of the community, William Sharland spoke up for those he felt had been wronged. A report in the newspaper for 1840 records his testimony on behalf of a tanner colleague from Cullompton named Selward. William and his son Thomas had been travelling inside the Beehive coach two miles from Taunton, with Selward riding on the top box with the driver. Sometime into the journey part of the horse-harness broke, and instead of staying with the coach and four, the driver jumped from the step (or was jerked off it as he late claimed), lost contact with the reins and allowed the vehicle to speed off downhill where it hit a bank and overturned, pitching the passengers into the road. [7]

A contemporary coach and four.

Selward suffered life-changing injuries as a result of the accident and both Sharlands gave their opinion, that had the driver stayed on board, the crash could have been avoided. They observed that three of the four horses were actually blind (something that was not denied by the owners) but believed, as experience horse-handlers themselves, that the team could have been controlled by the driver had he stayed on board during the incident, which happened when they were travelling at about six miles per hour. The judge decided in favour of the newly-disabled tanner and awarded him the sum of £500.

By 1851 William and Elizabeth Sharland had retired from Waterhouse tannery and moved out of the village to lead a very comfortable life in a newly-built house in St David's Exeter – number 1, Peamore Terrace. The area around Bury Meadow was being developed with rather grand Victorian houses, one of which was James Templeton's Mansion House School in St David's Hill. The plots were well situated being close to the city, boasting fine views over Haldon Hills and enjoying substantial gardens. William died in Exeter in 1855 aged seventy nine, and Elizabeth in 1859 aged seventy four. There is a plaque to both of them on the wall in Cheriton Church. At the time of his death, William was calling himself a 'landed proprietor'. The tannery business had certainly paid him well.

Sharland memorial on the south wall inside Cheriton Church

William's brother, Peter jnr was also a tanner but, having no children of his own he chose to go into business with his nephew, Henry Wippell at the tannery at the Green in Woodbury.[8] He died a wealthy man and left nearly £7,000 in 1842.[9]

Edward, the third surviving brother started working as a tanner at Broad-hembury, marrying Sarah Rowe of Sampford Peverell in 1810 and producing a large family of his own, but then he made the move to Fareham in Hampshire in 1825.[10]

William's only son Thomas Melhuish Comins Sharland succeeded to what had become a thriving business in Cheriton around 1838 when his father retired to

Exeter and immediately married his first cousin Ann Sharland, daughter of his Uncle Edward Sharland. The two branches of the Sharland family strengthened their business ties with the marriage and it is evident that both Thomas and Ann travelled back and forth to Hampshire on numerous occasions.

By that time Edward was running a thriving tannery in Wallington. It was a larger concern than the Cheriton tannery, and with far better transport links to ports and cities, London in particular, it managed to operate for much longer. When Edward's son Henry died on 25th March 1875 he left the considerable sum of £30,000, made in business in Winchester, but when his son Edward jnr tanner of Fareham died on 20th February 1886, he left a vast fortune of £49,095. 9s.0d.! His executor was one James Wippell tanner, also of Fareham.[11] Edward had married into the Wippell family of Alphington, marrying for love but also for business.

Edward, the story goes, set out from Devon to Hampshire in a carriage lent by the local squire.[12] In convoy behind them came at least thirty retainers, travelling in a variety of farm carts. On arrival at Wallington Edward left his wife Sarah with the children and returned to Devon to tie up some business affairs, blissfully unaware of the fact that local tradesmen did not trust the fact that a woman had been left in charge of the business! In desperation she sent her eldest son, aged only twelve at the time, on a horse back to Devon to fetch Edward. He returned immediately to reassure his new workforce. Once accepted by the community, the Sharlands became well known for running an efficient business and looking after their many workers. Like the rest of his family in Devon, Edward was an active member of the Fareham Church and indeed, when a fire broke out in the building in 1840, he was directly responsible for saving it from destruction. On receiving the news from workers that there was a fire, he instructed 'green' hides to be carried from his tan-yards and laid over the roof and walls to protect them from the heat. A human chain of workmen then ferried buckets of water from the river to keep the hides damp. This action suffocated the flames and the Church was saved.

It was inevitable that Edward Sharland's children would be involved in the business in some way or another and his eldest son Peter became a successful leather merchant, operating out of Winchester. He lived in Silver Hill right in the centre of the city.

1851 census, Lower Waterhouse, Cheriton Fitzpaine, Devon
Thomas Sharland, married, 225 acres employing 10 labourers on the farm and 39 labourers in the tannery
Henry Sharland brother-in-law and assistant in the business 1824
Servants, Loveday Ellis 1825 and Maria Fisher 1825

1851 census, Tan-yard North Wallington, Fareham, Hampshire
Edward Sharland, married, farmer employing 27 men and 6 boys
Edward Sharland 1818, Thomas 1822, Jane 1827, Elizabeth 1829, Harriet 1835, Maria Edney, cook and Ann Edney, house-maid

1851 census, 9, Silver Hill, Winchester, Hampshire
Peter Sharland 1813 leather merchant
Sarah Sharland, mother 1791
Ann Sharland, sister 1819
Sarah Dowling 1813, servant

Ann remained close to her family after marriage and the 1851 census return shows her away from Cheriton visiting her brother Peter in Winchester. Their mother had travelled up from Fareham to be there too. Sadly, Ann died in Cheriton Fitzpaine only four years later, leaving William with no heirs to the business. Each of her male siblings was settled in his own successful business and there were no other Sharlands interested in taking over the Cheriton site. Thomas had to look for another wife if he was going to keep the tannery in the family.

1432 House, yard and garden
1433 Woodcock Orchard

Surprisingly, he looked again to Fareham for a wife and this time it was Mary Kiln, fifteen years his junior, who was living with her two brothers Isaac Henry and Albert, and her sister Eliza in West Street. Their much respected parents Isaac and Anne Kiln had recently died and Isaac, a brewer in his early thirties was providing for them all. The family brewery was sited in Malthouse Road a stone's-throw from their house. The Sharland/Kiln marriage took place in Fareham in 1859.[13]

That same year Thomas brought Mary back to Lower Waterhouse in the

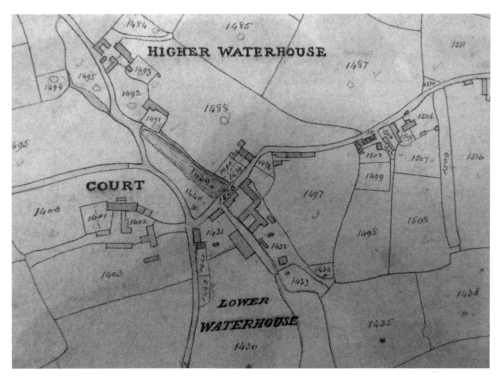

Lower Waterhouse – owned and occupied by William Sharland, 1840 Tythe map

hamlet of Upham, Cheriton Fitzpaine. It was a comfortable house approached along a circular drive with a monkey puzzle tree in the centre, and pleasant grounds planted with trees and shrubs.[14] The Tythe map shows a sizable orchard at the rear called Woodcock Orchard. With a good income and servants, Mary would have lived a secure but quiet life and there is evidence in the 1861 census that she liked to entertain her young friends from Fareham at the house. At that time Thomas was employing 32 men and one boy in his joint tanning and farming business.

1861 census, Lower Waterhouse
Thomas M C Sharland
Mary Sharland, wife 1829 Fareham
Selina Vasper, unmarried, Lady, 1853 Gosport
Alexander Clarke, unmarried, Gentleman, 1839 Fareham
Loveday Tucker, housemaid, widow, 1824, Sarah Hucker, cook 1837 and William Cosway, foreman tanner, 1805

It is apparent from this entry that Loveday Ellis, a servant with the family ten years earlier had in the meantime married a Mr Tucker, but had been recently widowed.

Leather from the Upham yards was of a high quality and it was not sold locally. Mr Sharland travelled around the country finding the best outlets for his product and took advantage of close family in Winchester and Fareham to set up business contracts. Leather was a sought-after commodity in the 19th century being used extensively for shoe-making, gloving, saddlery, luggage, upholstery and many other things, and a fine quality product could command a very good price. The process of tanning was a slow one with hides being soaked for months at a time in each pit but needing attention daily. A king-pin in the successful running of a business would have been the site foreman.

The Sharlands' outdoor pits would have been very like these at Rhaeadr Tannery.[15]

The tan-yards had a series of deep pits in which hides were hung, suspended from horizontal batons. After a time the hides were lifted out and transferred to the next pit for another period of soaking: tanning with oak bark was a particularly slow process. Even the preliminary stages took time, because the oak bark needed to be collected in the spring and summer and then thoroughly dried for several weeks before it was ready to be ground up into small chips and infused in water to create the tanning liquor.

Hides were prepared by scraping and shaping prior to curing, and after tanning and drying they required oiling, trimming and bundling up for sale.

Jack and Cyril Allen preparing hides indoors at Grampound Tannery in Cornwall[4]

In 1851 there was a theft from the yards at Upham. A legal case was reported in the Western Times in March that year, prosecuting one Thomas Coles for stealing 77 lbs of leather from the tannery and selling it unusually cheaply to a Crediton shoe-maker called George Elson. Elson was complicit in the crime because he knew that Coles had been a publican and had no ties to the leather industry, but he had gone to his house in Rack Street and haggled to purchase the goods from him at the knock-down price of 9d. per pound (the true price was 13d. per pound.) The cobbler, hoping to make a profit for himself then offered it up for sale at The Ship Inn in Goldsmiths Street, Tiverton for a price so low as to raise suspicion. The theft was exposed and Coles was brought to trial. Examination of the butts by Henry Sharland, site manager and brother-in-law of the owner Thomas, showed that the bends had probably been taken from the yard before they were totally dry. He was able to identify working marks on the ends of most pieces, and could point out where processing marks had actually been cut out of others. [16]

Indoor sheds where hides could be dried gradually

Henry reported that he had not noticed a theft, but that this particular batch would not have been sold in Devon anyway and was destined for markets in Liverpool and Manchester. The thief was prosecuted and no doubt Sharland stepped up security around the premises after that.

The family shipped in bales of untreated hides to add to their local supplies, using the Exeter canal as their preferred route. After unloading cargo in the newly improved Exeter Basin, duty would be paid at the Customs House and the goods transported to the village on long, horse-drawn wagons. The route was a tricky one and Sharland did all that he could to improve the journey each way. He donated £500 toward road alterations in Exeter so that his large wagons could travel more easily and avoid sharp bends. This resulted in the Bonhay Road we know today being carved out between Head Weir Mill and St David's railway station. In 1861 he held the Overseers of Shobroke to account for their failure to remove ice from Raddon Hill in the winter thus making 'traffic impractical'. He won the case and the Overseers were charged costs and ordered to keep the highway clear for him and for others using the route.[17]

As an industrialist he was constantly looking to the future and was not afraid to invest his money in improvements. An 1863 for example a sale particular for one of his farms in Cruwys Morchard mentions that he had recently outlaid a large sum of money there on drainage and improvements. In 1866 his manager Henry Sharland gave evidence at the Select Committee of the House of Lords along with other local tradesmen when the proposed Exe Valley Railway was discussed. He said that the tannery was capable of producing between 300 and 400 tons of leather each year and required about 100 tons of drugs etc. in the process.[18] Their hides were wholly foreign and were currently brought to Exeter or Topsham rather than to Bristol and the narrow gauge line connecting Tiverton to Exeter with a station at Bickleigh would be most advantageous to the tannery.

Sharland was an honest but shrewd business man with a keen sense of justice and he did not tolerate bad practice. Newspaper reports for 1860 and 1861 show that he was fully prepared to have men prosecuted for not doing their jobs properly. John Brewer was fined 9/- for sleeping in his wagon and not having proper care of his horses, whilst John Yeo was fined 10/- for riding the shafts of his master's wagon.[19]

Before Thomas and Mary could have any children to inherit the business, Tanner Sharland died unexpectedly, aged fifty. He was at the height of his career and had everything to look forward to, but no-one in the family to succeed him. Tanner Tom had left almost £45,000, showing that the business had been a lucrative one, but poor transport links may well have put prospective buyers off. His widow Mary and the extended family had no choice but to take out an advertisement in the Daily Express dated May 1863, offering twenty cottages and two residences for let at the tannery premises.

In 1865 Lower Waterhouse was offered to let, being described as 'a genteel dwelling house with stables, coach house, gardens, summer house, conservatory etc. late the residence of T M C Sharland esq. For particulars apply to Mr Robert Manley, Farleigh, Cheriton Fitzpaine.' (Western Times 13th January 1865)

Mary Sharland returned to her native Fareham with her share of wealth, but she fared no better there, marrying a curate called Francis Chidell in 1870, but dying less than eighteen months later in April 1872.

The Sharland family tomb stands at the eastern corner of Cheriton Church.

For a while there were efforts to keep the tannery at Upham working in some way, and flax was treated in the lower of the two yards, but the business never regained the success it had enjoyed under the Sharland family.

The population of Cheriton dropped from 1,200 in the 1850s to just 610 in the 1890s.[20] The demise of the tannery would have accounted for much of this and whole families were forced to leave the area and find other employment elsewhere. Dwellings between Upham and Wells Cottage deteriorated and were dismantled or demolished, and in 1939 Lower Waterhouse suffered a catastrophic fire.[21] The site was re-developed with 'new' houses being built. As the tannery fell into disuse there was no further need for the ponds and pits in the tan-yards and the river dam was removed allowing the water to flow along its original course again. The site is now a builder's storage yard called Pond Yards.

Mr Thomas Sharland was known to be honest, generous and religious and people living in the Upham area looked for a way to remember him after his untimely death. As a result a porch was erected at the front of the Upham Independent Chapel and dedicated to his life. The site of this chapel is now called Broadclose, Chapel Hill. Sharland was not expecting to die, and just three weeks before his death he had been going about his business as usual, looking to the future. He had placed an advertisement in the Exeter Flying Post to sell a farm called North Loosemore in Cruwys Morchard that he had recently improved; the new Bonhay Road had just opened and he was looking forward to making good use of new route, and with his new wife he was looking forward to the prospect of a having a child to introduce to Waterhouse and the business he cared so much about. His sudden death brought to an end more than a century of tanning on the site at Upham.

Following the tradition of keeping things in the family, the man charged with calling in debts and carrying out the terms of Thomas' will was his own cousin, Thomas Melhuish Comins jnr of Witheridge, solicitor.

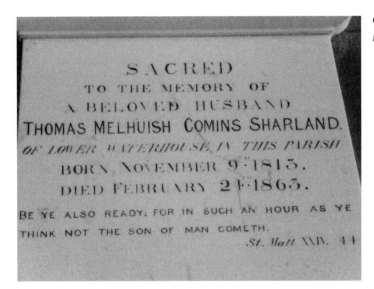

On the south wall inside Cheriton Church

Across country in Wallingford Fareham, his Uncle Edward Sharland continued business as a very wealthy tanner, employing 34 men, 5 boys and 6 women in 1871. But in Cheriton all of Thomas Sharland's property was put up for sale in 1864. Together with the well-stocked tanyards which came with eleven cottages and a grand house, Thomas had owned Lower Waterhouse, West Upham farm of 110 acres, Cotton farm of 63 acres, South Combe farm of 96 acres, two cottages called Gate Cottages at Upham and three cottages at Balle. The auction was to be held in September 1864.[22]

TO TANNERS AND OTHERS.
CHERITON FITZPAINE, DEVON.

MESSRS. HUSSEY and SON have been favoured with instructions to SELL by AUCTION, at the Globe Hotel, Exeter, on FRIDAY, the 23rd day of September next, at Three o'clock in the Afternoon, all those extensive and substantial TANYARDS, DWELLING HOUSES, COTTAGES, and several good FARMS, now let to respectable tenants, together, or in the following lots, late the property of Mr. T. M. C. Sharland, deceased. The Tanyards are replete with every convenience; the tan-pits will contain from 8 to 9 thousand kides, and the drying and bark sheds are of ample dimensions, with good water power, and well supplied with bark of excellent quality.

Lot 1.—A very compact and highly productive FARM, called "West Upham," containing 110a. 2r. 17p. of watered Meadow, Arable land and Orchard, which is let to Mr. Frantis, for a term of 14 years, from 29th September, 1854. With this lot will be sold a good DWELLING HOUSE, TANYARD, and all convenient Offices, Bark Mill by water power, extensive ponds, and all requirements for carrying on an extensive business, and about seven acres of meadow land and orchard, in hand; and also, 11 Cottages and Gardens. Immediate possession may be had of the Dwelling House and Tanyard, and seven acres of land.

Lot 2.—A most desirable FARM, called "Cotten," with a good House and Homestead, and 63a. 1r. 35p., of watered Meadow, Arable Land, and Orchard, let to Mr. John Squire, for a term of Fourteen years, from Christmas, 1857. With this lot will be sold three cottages and gardens adjoining the farm, lately held by the owner.

Lot 3.—A genteel DWELLING HOUSE, the late residence of Mr. Sharland, with dining and drawing rooms, 8 bedrooms and dressing-rooms, water closet, kitchen, back kitchen, larder, dairy, beer, cider, and wine cellars, in front of which is a lawn with conservatory, summer-house and gardens, well stocked with fruit trees, and shrubs, &c. With this lot will be sold a capital Tanyard, bark barn, drying sheds, bark mill by water power, mill pond, and all conveniences for a tanning trade; also five cottages, and 19a. 2r. 19p. of first-class Meadow and Pasture land. Immediate possession may be had.

Lot 4.—Two COTTAGES, called "Gate Cottages," with Gardens, 0a. 1r. 5p.

Lot 5.—A compact FARM, called "South Coombe," containing 96a. 2r. 0p. of watered Meadow, Pasture Arable land and Orchard, with a good Farm House, and nearly new farm buildings, in the occupation of Mr. Samuel Cleave, for a term of Fourteen years, from 29th September, 1854.

Lot 6.—Three COTTAGES at the Ball, with Gardens.

The whole of the above Property is Freehold, and in good repair, having been occupied by the late Mr. Sharland and his father, where a handsome fortune by the trade was made by them, and it affords a good opportunity for a man of capital and energy to do the same. The lots 1, 3, 4, and 5, are Land-tax redeemed.

Lots 1, 2, 3, and 4, will be first offered in one lot, if not sold, will be offered in lots as above stated.

For viewing apply to Mr. BLATHERWICK, on the premises; and for further particulars to Mr. GIBBINGS, Tanner, Chichester; to

T. MELHUISH COMINS, Esq.,
Solicitor, Witheridge;

References

1. Cheriton Fitzpaine parish registers
2. Cheriton Fitzpaine Overseers of the Poor Accounts
3. Devon Quarter Sessions for West Budleigh hundred
4. Jack and Cyril Allen at Croggan's tannery ref 20100223 http://photos.grampound. org.uk/photos/php?from=30&numb=30&kw=tannery
5. Exeter Flying Post 20th August 1812
6. Cheriton Fitzpaine Tythe Apportionment
7. Western Times March 28th 1840
8. Brighouse, Ursula W, Woodbury. A View from the Beacon 1998
9. Will of Peter Sharland 1829 1078/IRW/S/491
10. Sampford Peverell parish registers
11. Wills of Henry 1875 and Edward 1886 Sharland on Ancestry
12. Privett, George L, The Story of Fareham
13. Fareham parish registers
14. Carr, Jean, Cheriton Fitzpaine Our Village 1998
15. Rhaeadr tanning pits – post card owned by the Clwyd-Powys Archaeological Trust
16. Exeter and Plymouth Gazette 8th March 1851
17. Western Times 23rd February 1861
18. Tiverton Gazetteer 20th March 1866
19. Western Times 25th August 1860 and 10th August 1861
20. Population taken from the Census returns
21. Exeter Express and Echo 31st January 1939
22. Western Times August 19th and 24th 1864

Domesday Properties – Coddiford, Dunscombe, Cotton and Upcott

In the Domesday Survey of 1086 the following are recorded:

Cheriton, Upcott/Stockley, Coddiford, Coombe, Chilton and Dunscombe.

A total of 75 men were recorded which would probably represent about 310 people in all. They were able to derive a good living from the well-watered, fertile lands, by grazing sheep, harvesting timber and ploughing for grain and root crops. The ancient Britons had built hill forts in the area and as families broke away from these tribal centres they found parcels of good land in the lush valleys.

Their name, Dumnonii means 'deep valley dwellers', and the evidence of their settlement remains in the landscape where Bronze Age and Iron Age hillforts can still be seen. In and around the parish of Cheriton Fitzpaine are Cadbury hillfort, Yedbury hillfort, Raddon top, Berry Castle hillfort an Iron Age castle near Puddington and another just west of Poughill.

The manor of Cheriton was owned by the Stanton family and then brought by Margaret, daughter of Elias Fitzpaine through her marriage to John Asthill. According to the notes made for his Survey of the County of Devon by Tristram Risdon between 1603 and 1630, it was then passed via their daughter Joan Asthill, into the Kelly family.

Upcott was owned by the Radfords and then by a James, a John and then another James Courtney. It then passed to John Moore.

The Lay Subsidy Roll for Cheriton in 1332 lists:

Ralph and Thomas de Ferlegh (Farleigh Farm)
Richard and Roger atte Cotonne (Cotton Farm)
William and Peter de Upcote (Upcott Barton)
Stephen atte Ford (Ford Farm)
Alexander de Wodeland
Joan de Chileton (Chilton Barton)
Geoffrey and Henry Uphom (Upham – Court Place)
John atte Forse (Furse tenement)
Walter de Stokedon (Stockaton Farm)
Richard de Moggherigg
John de Sutton (Sutton Farm at Perry Green)
Elias FitzPaine (possibly Coddiford)
Thomas de Smythsheies (Smith Hayne Farm)
Robert and William atte Fenne (Venn Farm)
William de Welcomb (Wellcombe Farm)
John de Churiton (Cheriton or Church Town)

Such a list is astonishing because the names of many present day farms can be recognised more than seven hundred years later: Wellcombe, Ford, Sutton, and Chilton Barton on southside and Venn, Smith Hayne, Stockaton, Upham, Upcott, Cotton, and Farley on northside. It is interesting to note that Christian names were still the primary means of identification in the 14th century and that 'surnames' were the tag of where they lived. Several centuries later the farmsteads that we know today stand on the very same sites that these men farmed. The only place name unfamiliar to us in the 21st century is that of 'Wodeland'. Sutton was the name given to the farm at the bottom of Dovers Hill on the Perry Green site. Another early farmstead in that location was Saccombe which was demolished by the Yeandle family in the mid-20th century and stood on the eastern side of Dovers Hill, opposite Perry Green.

Coddiford

Coddiford was established as a farmstead in 1086 and although not mentioned by name in the later Lay Subsidy Roll it is most likely that it was the property that Elias Fitzpaine farmed in 1332 whilst he was Lord of the Manor. It had been a significant farmstead in the 1086 Domesday Survey with seven ploughlands, four villeins, four bordars and five serfs, and it was a well-watered and well-sited parcel of land.

The current buildings are fairly late in date and the Historic Buildings listing for the farmhouse and adjoining cottage state that the earliest features date only to the early 17th century:

> Good interior. The earliest features apparent in the main block are the early C17 oak plank-and-muntin screen on lower side of passage - ovolo-moulded and scroll-stopped muntins with central recessed panels, original doorway at rear end – and contemporary moulded oak rear passage door frame (now converted to a window). C17 fireplace in hall of volcanic ashlar with hollow-chamfer ovolo-moulded jambs with runout stops. The rear pentan includes round-headed oven door (now a window) and a carved stone showing a square within a diagonally set square. Possibly C17, 2 plain chamfered hall crossbeams. Late C17 or early C18 kitchen block has plain chamfered crossbeam and large rubble fireplace with oak lintel, its soffit chamfered with straight cut stops, and oven doorway (now a window).

> Cottage interior much rebuilt circa 1970, but preserves plain chamfered beam at south-west end and C17 rubble fireplace with oak lintel soffit-chamfered with scroll stops. Lintel is inscribed 1492 FP, presumably by a modern hand.

The inscription of '1492 FP' on the lintel in the cottage deserves some investigation. It might indicate that an older beam has been re-used in the building but the general belief is that it has been inscribed by a modern hand. In the 1524–5 Lay Subsidy Roll the only surnames beginning with the letter 'P' are those of John Pyne, William Payne, Andrew Payne, John Pawlyn and William Pole. The 1543 Roll lists John Payne, Andrew Payne and John Pawlyn. The 1569 Muster Roll has Joan Payne and Thomas Pownsford. It is not known whether any of these people had connections with Coddiford however. Another possibility is that the initials 'F P' stand for the surname 'Fitz Paine' which was originally written as two separate words. Roger and Matilda Fitz Paine had held the manor of Cheriton in 1256 paying 'a sore sparrowhawk' for it. John Fitz Paine held it in 1316, Elias Fitz Paine in 1332 and Juliana Fitz Paine held ⅓ of the manor in 1346.

Later Lords of the Manor of Cheriton Fitzpaine were absentee landlords with no main residence in the parish so there has never been a Manor House as such. Through inheritance, they held the manor as one of many in their portfolio of property, sending representatives to collect leasehold rents from the farmers each quarter. It was rare for a Lord of the Manor to spend time in Cheriton and several relied upon the rector that they sponsored to supervise and meet the needs of the population. Often that nominated rector was also an absentee, living for only part of the year in the village and paying a curate to take care of parish matters. The result was that farmers enjoyed a security of tenure and were readily able to act just as if they owned their farms, passing the land down through their families as lifeleasehold properties without the landlord interfering. Coddiford became one of these estates and has been farmed successfully over the centuries.

Later owners of Coddiford

A deed from 1579 mentions Anna Cruise, widow of John of Cruwys Morchard esq owning Coddiford with her son, also named John. At that time it was sublet to Robert and Thomasin Warren and Anna stated that she had bought it from Henry Champernon esq. If the line of direct succession to John jnr failed then the property was to revert to Anna's other sons, first James and then Arthur Cruise. The estate was referred to as Cadford:

> 1 October, 21 Eliz 1579 Deed 1159. Enrolment 8 October
> Cheriton Fitzpaine – Agreement by Anna, wyddowe of John Cruise of Crewesmorchard, esq. with John Cruise of Rakenford, gentleman, Alexander Morrish, clarke, and Robert Webbe, yeoman, that she will enfeoff them of the tenement called Cadford in Cheriton Fitzpayne in the tenure of Robert Warren in the right of Thomasyne now his wife with all houses, dovehouses, loftes, curtilages, gardens, landes, tenements, pastures, woodes, waters, commons, rents etc. thereto belonging which Anna purchased of Henry Champernon Esq. desced. and the Feoffees will be seized of the tenement to the use of Anna and John her son and his lawful issue failing which to James Cruise, John's brother and his like issue, failing which to Arthur Cruise another brother and his like issue, failing which to the right heirs of Anna if John or James or Arthur during his tenure attempts to alienate the tenement except by a lease not exceeding 3 lives the use to him shall cease and the Feoffees shall

stand seised of the tenement to the use of the next brother or the right heirs of Anna. The rent reserved upon the lease to Thomasyne Warren shall be paid to Anna during Anna's life.

The description gives some idea of what came with the farm: 'all houses, dove-houses, loftes, curtilages, gardens, landes, tenements, pastures, woodes, waters, commons'.

The names of later owners are lost to us because entries in the Overseers of the Poor rate lists just mention the 'occupiers of Coddiford' with the property rated at 3d., with Coddiford Leas at 2d. (modern day Leys farm). In the mid-18th century however members of the illustrious Hewish family owned Coddiford with John Hewish in 1736 and Thomas Hewish in 1751. In 1792 John Parkhouse paid the 3d. due on Coddiford.

Access to Coddiford was often compromised by the state of the bridge near Waterhouses and by the flow of the river. The bridge needed constant repair and was on the list of things to maintain given to the Highways officers each year. It was not only a vital connection to Coddiford and Leys but also to Tucking Mills, Upcott and the village of Poughill. In 1859 the Vestry met to consult over building a new bridge at Coddiford Water.

1866 Great and Little Coddiford were to be let for a term of 10 or 14 years along with Waterhouse and 119 acres:

Lot 1 Great and Little Coddiford being a very good farm house, a dairyman's house and a labourer's cottage

Lot 2 Waterhouse, being a farm house and outbuildings

Both within a ring fence and occupied by Mr Marwood Stone and Mr Mare

Little Coddiford is known to us today is the property adjacent to the main farmhouse, but it was originally the name given to a dairyman's cottage situated in the field to the south east of the farmstead. It was reached by one track from Waterhouses and another from the lane running along the northern boundary of the estate. These trackways have become designated footpaths but the buildings were demolished after the Second World War and there is little trace of them now. During the war the Griffiths family were evacuated to the village and spent some time living in Little Coddiford.

305

The Griffiths family were evacuated to Little Coddiford in World War II

Little Coddiford (the labourer's cottage or Dairyman's house) has since been demolished, but in the Second World War Jack Griffiths and his family were evacuated there and although facilities were very basic, they had happy memories of their nine month stay. They later bought April Cottage in Backhayes Lane. The name of Little Coddiford has since been given to the dwelling next to Coddiford farm.

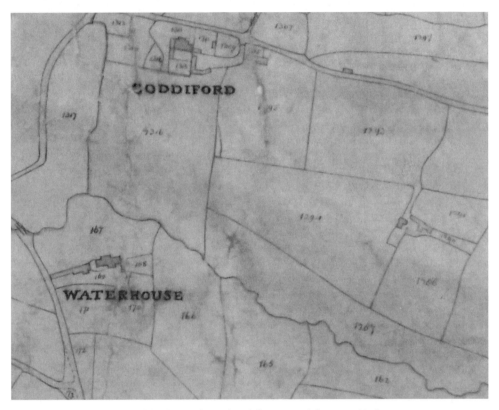

Little Coddiford is to the right of this part of the 1840 Tythe map,
south east of the main farmstead

The footpath from Coddiford Hill across the fields to Little Coddiford still exists, although the buildings have long gone. Anyone walking it today might wonder why it suddenly vears to the north as it joins up with the top road from Coddiford Farm. It can be seen on the Parish Map of Cheriton Fitzpaine showing rights of way and County roads, 1:10.000.

Related facts

1896 the wedding took place at Broadclose Methodist Chapel of Mark Tucker and Louisa Raymont the daughter of Samuel Raymont of Coddiford Barton. The bride wore a navy dress and hat and her sister as bridesmaid wore silver grey.

1896 a fatal accident occurred on Coddiford Hill when Mr Turner fell under the horse that was pulling his covered bread cart as he drove it round the corner from Hedgecleave Mill and clipped the corner. He suffered catastrophic head injuries and his body was carried to Little Coddiford to await a post mortem. He was driving without lamps and had two passengers on board at the time who were uninjured.

1901 there was a friendly neighbourhood warning to keep to the right when driving along Coddiford Hill because of the long arms of trailing briars and brambles.

1908 the small-holding of Coddiford and Farthings was advertised with a good farm house, a labourer's cottage and 112 acres of prime orchard, meadow, pasture and arable land. Mr Nott was the tenant at the time.

1919 Coddiford and Farthings were purchased by the tenant Mr William Isaac for the sum of £2,500. He purchased West Ford farm (105 acres) in 1928 for the sum of £2,900 and moved there with his wife. Her death was announced in 1941. She died at Laburnhams, Cheriton.

Jumping forward to the 20th century, a BBC initiative named Domesday Reloaded included this passage about Ray Sanders who was farming Coddiford in 1986, nine hundred years after the Domesday Survey:

> 'Coddiford Farm, mentioned in the original Domesday Book, is now farmed by Mr Ray Sanders. He has owned this 220 acre farm for 35 years. Mr Sanders and his two sons work the farm, not forgetting his faithful dog who helps by rounding up the cows. When he first bought the farm all the work was done by horses. Now it is done with six tractors. The fields are larger than they were as several hedges have been dug up to make it easier to use modern machines. Ray Sanders has 102 milking cows and gets from 2 to 8 gallons a day from each cow. The cows are milked at 6 a.m. and 4 p.m. and the 350 gallons of milk are collected each day by a tanker and taken to a factory to be made into cheese.'

CHERITON FITZPAINE FARM GUTTED

Strong East Wind Fans Blaze

EARLY MORNING ALARM

Plaster falling from the ceiling on to their bed awakened Mr. and Mrs. C. R. Ford, occupants of Lower Waterhouse Farm, Cheriton Fitzpaine early on Tuesday and closer investigation revealed that flames were licking along the rafters. Immediate steps were taken to inform the Crediton Fire Brigade by Mr. Mildon, of neighbouring Lays Farm, who was informed by the Fords.

The Brigade arrived under Chief Officer W. A. Cherry but their efforts were unavailing, and the farm, which is an old building, was gutted. Outbuildings and cattle were saved.

One side of the roof was thatched, whilst the other was constructed of corrugated iron The fire originated in a chimney beam, and a strong-east wind fanned the flames on to the thatched portion of the roof. This burnt fiercely, and the building was destroyed within a short tim'

Apparently the beam had been smouldering for some time, but nothing was noticed until the plaster started falling. Mr. and Mrs. Ford retired at 11 p.m., and were awakened at three a.m.

The farm belonged to Mr. Isaac, of Cuddiford, Cheriton Fitzpaine.

The Brigade returned to Crediton about eight a.m. Assistance was rendered by P.C. C. Anstey, of Cheriton Fitzpaine.

1939

Higher and Lower Dunscombe

Dunscombe estate was mentioned in the Domesday Survey for Cheriton and it lies in a well-watered valley running alongside the southern edge of the road from Cheriton to Cadbury, about a mile outside the village. In 1086 it supported three plough lands, two serfs and three bordars. It was one of the smaller farmsteads in the parish at the time with Upcott topping the list, Coddiford next and the village, third. A 'ploughland' was the amount of land that eight oxen could plough; a bordar was a peasant who had a cottage or a few acres to farm but who also had to work part-time for the lord of the manor; a serf was an unfree peasant with no land of his own who worked full-time on the lord of the manor's lands.

Rate lists for 1678–1700 list an Agnes Dunscombe, widow and then the property was taken on by William Langworthy in 1701. By the 1730s the estate

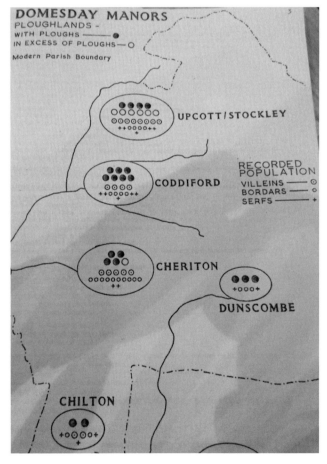

A sketch map drawn by R. R. Sellman 1978

310

had been split into two separate farmsteads, comprising Higher Dunscombe (the older of the two) and Lower Dunscombe. There is no trace now of the buildings and farm-yard of Higher Dunscombe, but the ruins of Lower Dunscombe were recently re-developed and are once again a dwelling. On the 1840 Tythe map, both farms were flourishing:

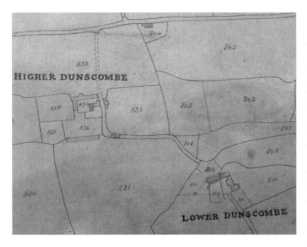

Towards the end of the 19th century the older of the two farmhouses was left to deteriorate and was then ploughed back into the soil. It is always surprising how little remains when a cob building is demolished, merely raising the ground-level of the site where it formerly stood. Looking at this 1937 sale particular, the site of Higher Dunscombe farmhouse is orchard plot 415.

Knowing that there was once a bustling farm-yard there, explains the route of the surviving track-way which makes a 90 degree turn before it reaches the lower farmstead and also accounts for the name *Lower* Dunscombe still being used.

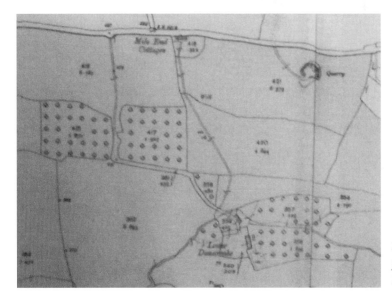

20th century sale particular for Lower Dunscombe farm

311

The Scutt family was closely connected with Stockadon and Grew which both share boundaries with Dunscombe, so it was inevitable that they would also farm Higher Dunscombe at some time. Being leaseholders however, they were not in a position to include it in the estate sold to the Trustees of Silverton School in 1729. Philp Westron 1702, son and heir of Rachel Scutt and George Westron was to be found farming there when he returned to the village from Exeter, having spent his early working life in the city as a tailor. He bequeathed the leases on Dunscombe and Westborough farms in his will proved 1772, mentioning his brother George Westron jnr who was married to Elizabeth Brock (with children Margaret, Elizabeth and George), and his 'sisters-in-law' Mellony and Katharine Wind. He also referred to a 'cousin' called Alice who was married to a Mr Prydham. Philip also held a piece of land in Christow called Christow Woods which he had purchased from his relative John Brock. Remembering friends in Exeter he also provided for John Kelly and his mother Susannah and John Luke, ironmonger of Exeter.

Philip may have purchased the leases on Dunscombe and Westborough with his share of the money generated by the sale to the Trustees. He was a wealthy man and gained importance in the parish, sitting on the committee responsible for the renovations at Church House in 1753 when the building was brought up to spec as a Poor House-cum-Workhouse. He may well have been swayed by his own self-importance however because a complaint was made against him at the Quarter Sessions in January 1756 for 'carrying away a quantity of straw, the

312

property of Richard Oliver of Cheriton Fitzpaine, yeoman. (QS/4/1756/Easter/RE/39) He was bound to appear at the next Session, but unusually, the person who stood surety for him was not 'of the parish'. William Gloster was the keeper of the South Gate prison in Exeter, and while he may have been a long-term acquaintance from the time Philip lived and worked in the city, it was rare for a defendant not to select a local person to trust their innocence and put forward a sum of money.

Quarter Sessions records also reveal that Richard Oliver attacked Philip Westron in 1756. The two men worked alongside each other with Philip paying rates on Westborough farm and Richard Oliver taking on an apprentice there in 1754.

South Gate, Exeter housed a prison for debtors and a Bridewell until it was demolished in 1819. A new prison was then built in Queen's Street. William Gloster and his wife moved around several parishes in Exeter and baptised children in St Thomas the Apostle, St Mary Major and Holy Trinity.

The Stabbick family also had connection to Dunscombe and Westborough in the 18th century.

Names associated with Higher Dunscombe:

1705–42 William Langworthy for Dunscombe

1750 Humphrey Tucker Higher Dunscombe

1750 John Drake apprenticed to Humphrey Tucker of Higher Dunscombe

1767 George Bodley

1781 Henry Esworthy

1824 John Tuckett

Names associated with Lower Dunscombe:

1734 Thomas Parkhouse

1744 John Dyer

1758 Richard Pubb

1771 Henry Esworthy

1790 Alexander Dundass

1804 Robert Manley

1824 George Gater

1833 John Luxton

1843 80 acres of orchard, tillage and pasture called Lower Dunscombe and Dinham was offered for sale. The tenant was John Luxton.

Cotton Farm

Richard and Roger atte Cotonne (Cotton Farm) 1332 Lay Subsidy Roll.

1734–51 John Hurrell

1756–1778 Andrew Hewish

1793–1808 John Brewer

1824 John Downing

1842 death of Mr George Luxton yeoman aged 72

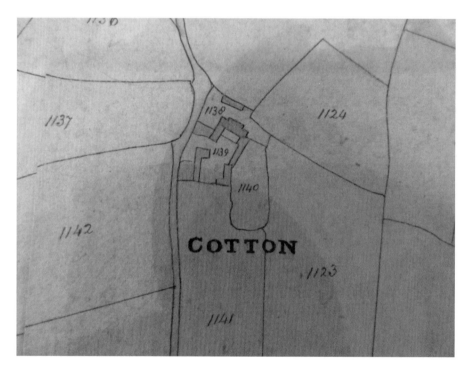

Cotton was only 36 acres at the time of the 1840 Tythe when George Luxton owned and farmed it. The ancient trackway called Cotton Lane runs south from Cotton to Hayne hamlet, and a later public footpath connects the farm to Peach Hayne and the road to Upham. It is very close to Smith Hayne farm but the two businesses have managed to co-exist for centuries.

Upcott Barton

Much has already been written about Upcott Barton and the Radford murder and I can do no better than to refer the reader to published material including *Upcott Barton* written by R L Thorpe in 1993 and to the history complied by the last owner, the late Charles H B Cole, some of which appears in the 'about/ history' section of this website:

http://www.upcottroundhouse.co.uk/about-glamping-devon/history-of-upcott-roundhouse/

Other Post Domesday Farmsteads

Furse Tenement

Furse Tenement, an old estate that is mentioned in the 1332 Lay Subsidy comprised between forty and fifty acres on northside, close to the boundary with Cruwys Morchard. It was purchased in 1717 with '£210.15s.0d. and one broad piece of gold' from charity funds and other bequests called Poor's Money and Courtney's Gift, in order to increase revenue for the Trustees.

James Courtney in his Will of 1590 had stated that his four copyhold tenements in Newton St Cyres were to be sold for the benefit of Cheriton's poor. The sum of £240 was then invested and money regularly distributed in the parish. Later Trustees decided to change tack and invest some of the money in a farmstead that would generate a regular rental with the residue of Courtney's bequest and other donation being used to buy 3% consols, some in the name of Thomas Parkhouse. That farmstead was Furse, lying between North Combe and Brindiwell on the eastern boundary of the parish.

Furse had been in the possession of one family for more than six generations and gave its name to their descendants. Roland de Cumba was the earliest owner, followed by William de la Furse, Robert Furse and John Furse. The Furse family hailed from south Devon and had always been charitable to the poor. In the 16th century Robert Furse of Dean Prior started a family tradition of bequeathing one cow to his heirs, stating that income from it must be donated to a charitable cause. They acquired Furse in Cheriton Fitzpaine sometime in the century.

In 1717 descendants released the property to the Cheriton Trustees when John Worth of Worth in Washfied and Edward Dicker, yeoman of Upton Hellions sold it to the parish for the sum of £200. Worth was a wealthy Tiverton merchant who was the local MP from 1710 and also served as a County Lieutenant. Furse had come into his possession through his marriage to Elizabeth Furse in 1705 but he decided that the estate was of little use to him and of no sentimental value. A pragmatic man he decided not to stand for re-election in 1715 when he was opposed to a commercial treaty with the French that might damage his family fortunes and he turned his interests back to the wool trade, off-loading Furse Tenement two years later to release some funds. There may well have been an inherited 'rider' on the sale of the property because of the Furse family motto to help the poor and this might be the reason why Worth sold it to the Cheriton Trustees rather than a private buyer.

John's interests lay very much in Washfield where his family had built a substantial country residence, replaced in 1985 by a later house. The Worths had always traded in wool and Henry Worth had purchased Bolham Mill as early as 1595.

The earlier Worth House in Washfield near Tiverton

After the purchase, Furse tenement was let out by the Trustees of the Cheriton charity to a succession of tenant farmers who bid at auction for the lease:

William Mitchell 1731
Nicholas Stone 1745

317

John Seaman 1762

John Drake 1777

John Squire 1791

Thomas Mogridge 1802 for a yearly rent of £28

John Balamy 1832 etc.

It was the practise of the Trustees to collect the quarterly rent, to take out expenses for maintenance and to distributed the remaining money to the poor of the village on the following Sunday. This may have happened in the church porch itself, or else on the Vestry steps.

Described at auction in 1802 as 'a house, garden and between forty and fifty acres' Furse was Moggridge's home for twenty one years and then his lease was extended for a further fourteen years. It was said that the house was regularly repaired by the Trustees and was 'in a good condition'.

The wealthy Hewish family took an interest in the Furse charity and in1730 Mr William Hewish of Pool gave the Trustees of Furse a sum of £6 to be placed out at interest by them so it would always be possible to educate one poor boy in the parish. In 1779 Edward

PEACH HAYNE, CHERITON FITZPAINE
PLEASE NOTE: WEDNESDAY, April 16th.

HARRIS & CO., having been favoured with instructions from Mr. M. Paddon, will SELL by Auction at the above the under-mentioned LIVE and DEAD FARM STOCK, comprising:—

SHEEP.—58 Grand Devon Longwool and Closewool Ewes, with very promising lot of Dorset Down Cross Lambs, and 2-Tooth Dorset Down Ram (bred by Mr. Joyce).

CATTLE.—5 Rare Devon Cows with calves, Shorthorn Cow in calf, Devon Cows and 1 Heifer in calf (two of which are due at time of Sale), 5 Young Barreners, 3 Rare Devon Steers from 2½ to 3 yrs. old; and 9 Grand Maiden Heifers about 2½ years old (outliers); 2 Devon Heifers and 2 Devon Steers about 18 months old; 5 Devon Steer and Heifer Yearlings.

HORSE.—Bay Gelding, 13 years old, 16 h.h., quiet and good in all gears.

PIGS.—Large Black Young Sow and 9 Farrows.

POULTRY.—60 Black Leghorn and Light Sussex Cross Hens, 1946 hatched, in lay.

GOOD SHEEP DOG, 18 months old.

IMPLEMENTS AND MACHINERY.—Rubber-tyred Flat Bottom Cart with lades and side rails and brakes; Chest Wagon, Set of Spring Harrows, Acting Reed Comber, Banking Plough, Horse Hoe, Hay Sweep, Deering Mowing Machine, Bentall 3-Knife Chaffcutter, Root Pulper, Turnip Cutter, Bamford Lion Hay Kicker, Talbot 2-Furrow Tractor Plough, Stone Roller, Reaping Machine, Set of Breeching Harness, and various other Lots.

Sale at 1.30 p.m.

EXETER MARKET.

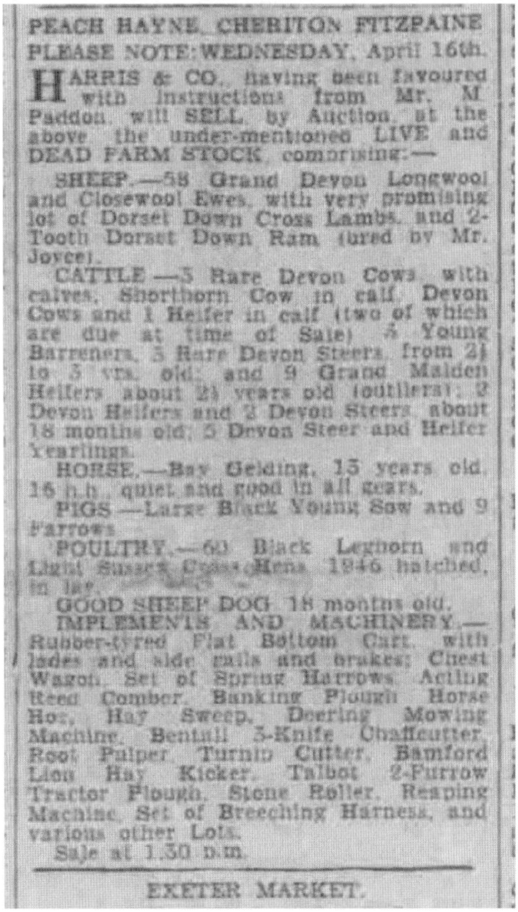

1947 sale of stock at Peach Hayne including farm machinery

Hewish son of Mr William Hewish also left money to the Furse Trustees for the Poor of Cheriton.

The Poor Rate value of Furse tenement was halved from 4d. to 2d. in the 18th century, suggesting a change in size but by the time of the Tythe it had grown to sixty four acres.

1842 saw a disastrous fire at Furse Farm and it was destroyed. £150 was borrowed to rebuild it and the Trustees of the charity managed to repay the debt in 1852 with the help of £100 worth of the Consols that they had previously purchased.

Smith Hayne
Thomas de Smythsheies (Smith Hayne Farm) 1332 Lay Subsidy Roll.

The cider press at Smith Hayne Farm

1731–1742 Mathew Moxey

1758–1770 Edward Bradford

1787 1801 Robert Lendon

1812 William Norrish

1827 John London

The estate of the late Mr Edward Chamberlaine was put up for auction in May 1844. Advertisements pointed out that the lower part of the estate of 116 acres was capable of great improvement by undertaking drainage. Another selling point was the presence of a stone quarry on the estate. It had been for many years in the occupation of Mr Luxton.

Venn

Robert and William atte Fenne (Venn Farm) 1332 Lay Subsidy Roll.

Venn has for centuries been divided between Venn and Little Venn and tenants have been as follows:

Venn	Little Venn
1720 Andrew Paine	1738 John Labdon
1733 Hugh Payne	1743 Charles Bagstor
1734 William Langworthy	1764 Joan Bagstor
1744 Henry Waters	1786 Richard Manley
1763 Samuel Cozens	1793 Robert Manley
1779 John Southwood	1833 Sarah Manley
1793 Betty Southwood	
1801 Thomas Southwood	

When Little Venn and its adjoining cottage were listed in 1985 the main building was said to be mid-18th century which may be when the larger farmstead was divided into two separate holdings. Land on the site however was being actively farmed in 1332.

In 1864 a sale took place of Venn, 'a modern built commodious farm house with all the needful outbuildings in the occupation of Mrs Harriet Manley and her undertenants.' The watered meadows were of superior quality with a good proportion of the young and highly productive orchard. Apply Mr James Waller.

Another sale in 1889 advertised livestock, implements, household furniture, dairy utensils and hay along with 10 sheep, 12 bullocks and a rick of clover hay.

Whites Cross Green
1865 Lot 2. 2 good cottages, a pound house. Orchard and garden containing c1½ acres in occupation of Mr Bradford and one other

East and West Ford Farm
Stephen atte Ford (Ford Farm) 1332 Lay Subsidy Roll.

1455 Thomas Page alias Thomas atte Forde held property in the manor that would then pass to Nicholas Radford of Upcott.

1558–1579 a Chancery Court papers record a dispute between members of the Manley family over East Ford and Westborough. Thomas Manley had died leaving the two properties and 200 acres to his son and heir John Manley of Cruwys Morchard. Andrew and Edith Manley appear to have 'casually' lived there for several years having been granted life-time leases from a William Mayne, Gent and John Pynse. Fourteen years after the death John wanted Andrew and his wife to vacate the premises and after 'gentle' requests for them to present deeds as to their right to be there, John Manley had to take the matter to court. (C3/124/54)

In 1879 the lease for East and West Ford Farm was advertised, being 160 acres of meadow, pasture, orchard and arable land with an excellent dwelling house in the occupation of Mr James Troake. Apply to dairyman George James to view the property. It was announced that the highest tended would not necessarily be accepted,

Lot 1 West Ford farm on the left hand side and a cottage on the opposite side of the road 89 acres 1r2p

Lot 2 East Ford Farm on the right hand side 70a.0r.11p.

Perry
1850 Mr T Strong was the proud owner of a beast called King of The Valley who was paraded around the district and shown to farmers who were interested in improving their stock. The horse stood 16½ hands high and was dark brown with great muscular strength and at six years old he had won the coveted Premium prize at the 1848 Agricultural Show.

Hannabeth
The name Hannabeth is a corruption of the earlier Hennebeare.

In 1821 Hannabeth was offered for sale in two lots: thirty acres and a good farm house called Hannabeth, and 17 acres with a good farm house called Over-land Hannabeth. All the land was said to be in 'a high state of cultivation' and was in the occupation of Mr John Jackman who could be contacted at neighbouring Dunscombe House.

Bowdell

1821 Bowdell was offered for sale, being 98 acres in the occupation of Mr John Jackman together with six dwelling houses attached, belonging to the same also Hannabeth a farm of forty two acres

One month later the cottages had been sold off and Bowdell and Hannabeth were re-advertised for sale. Bowdell this time was describes as being 'in a high state of cultivation'.

Holes Farm

1838 Mrs Edwards was the tenant farmer when Samuel Pridham esq and Mr J Brewer offered the lease on Holes -a dwelling house and 17 acres of arable, meadow and pasture land

1859 a crop of timber was sold from Holes and North Yeo

1875 The freehold estate of Holes was put up for sale by Emma Hewish a week before her marriage to Tom Cole in June 1875. Her father John Hewish who had farmed it for many years had just died. It comprised:

> a good dwelling-house with convenient farm buildings, and about 50 acres of very productive orchard, arable, meadow, and pasture land, situate near the village of Cheriton Fitzpaine, and for many years past in the occupation of the late Mr. John Hewish, the owner. Possession may be had at Michaelmas next.

When the farm did not sell Tom gained the authority to dispose of the farm by his will and the couple set up home there themselves having a daughter, Winnie the following year.

The farm was well-known for its good crop of timber, specifically Navy oak and as his father-in-law had let business slip somewhat during his final illness, Cole decided to fell the timber and auction it off. In 1876 he advertised:

Fifty-two prime Navy Oak, twenty-one Ash, and thirty Elm Trees to be SOLD, by Auction, at the Half Moon Inn in the village in lots as described in hand-bills circulated in the neighbourhood.

The Auctioneers beg to state that this is an extraordinary lot of timber (particularly the oak). The whole being long lengths, large dimensions, and first rate quality, and well situated for removal. The same may be viewed the day previous, and morning of sale.

Emma and Tom Cole then let Holes out to a tenant and in 1878 moved into Barnshill, a farm with 46 acres

1881 Mr Prior, a butcher sold stock from Holes farm

1913 The Priors advertised for a respectable girl for in-house duties to be treated as one of the family.

1936 Leonard Prior the well-respected butcher died and there was a sale of household effects and butcher's equipment. The son of James Prior he set up his butcher's business when he married in 1871. Before her marriage, Leonard's mother Louisa Payne had been at first a lady's maid and then a housekeeper to Mr Bellew at Stockleigh Court. His father James Prior snr was born in Stockleigh Pomeroy, learning his trade as a butcher and farmer at Stockleigh Mill alongside his Aunt and Uncle and little cousin Eliza Yendall. His Aunt had been widowed early so he and his brother William Prior would have had the opportunity to take on additional responsibilities and improve their skills at a young age. His own father had been a dairyman at Little Chilton. Leonard was buried in the family vault at Stockleigh Pomeroy.

1937 February, Holes Farm was advertised in several lots as:

A five bed dwelling house and one acre of land £375

A corrugated iron roof store abutting the main street £2

Three thatched cottages with large gardens, 2 with possession, £115

And Lots 4-10 comprising pasture and arable land 24 acres.

Barnshill

Tom and Emma Cole had responded to this advertisement when they took on Barnshill Farm:

To be let by Tender for a term of five or ten Years from Michaelmas next, all that desirable farm called Barnshill, comprising a convenient dwelling-house with suitable farm buildings and carpenter's shop. About 46 acres of the above consist of very prime meadow, orchard, old pasture, and arable land. – Applications to view should be made to Mr. S. Searle, the tenant, on For terms of letting and further particulars apply to the owner, Mr Saunders, Rashleigh Barton, Wembworthy.

The owner does not bind himself to accept the highest or any tender. – Dated Crediton, 20th April 1878.

At Barnshill Emma gave birth to a stillborn son in July 1879.

The 1881 census states that the couple were then farming 96 acres and employed 2 men and 1 woman which indicates that he had continued to use the acreage at Holes farm in addition to the Barnshill land. Only five years later, however, with Emma's mental health deteriorating, Tom Cole began to think about selling up:

Sale of 120 sheep, 21 bullocks, 6 horses, etc live and dead stock together with a rick of hay, a rick of oats, implements, apples, cider and a portion of the household furniture.

Sheep – 50 young Devon long-wool breeding Ewes, 20 fat sheep (part wethers), and 40 lambs.

Bullocks – 5 capital dairy Cows in full milk, 2 Heifers in calf (time nearly up), 4 two-year-old Steers, 4 Steers, 2 Heifers (18 months), 4 yearlings.

Horses – "Merry," chestnut cart mare, 8 years old, 16 hands in foal; "Prince." Chestnut cart horse, 5 years old, 16 hands (These two make a splendid pair, and can be thoroughly recommended and are good in all harness); "Nipper," grey cob, 8 years old, 15 hands good in saddle and harness, a perfect hack; a chestnut colt out of "Merry," by Mr. Bamsden's horse, and a sucker by the same; bay cart colt, rising three years.

Pigs – 2 young breeding sow.

Brindiwell

Built in the early 1600s the property was a cross passage long house facing south west close to the border with Cadeleigh. After a fire in 1940 it was renovated but the oak plank-and-muntin screen on both sides of the cross passage survived. Edward Hewish inherited it from his father Mr William Hewish who then bequeathed it in 1779 to his cousin Elizabeth Hicks. She then passed it on in 1797 to James Coffin of Linkinhorn, Cornwall, related through his mother Anne Hewish.

1734 William Hewish

1736 Nicholas Stone

1756 Thomas Moggridge

1796 Peter Sharland

1812 James Frost

1829–1840 Mrs Jane Frost

1763 Mary born to Thomas and Sarah Mogridge of Brindiwell

1931 death of Ellen Hullard, wife of Ernest Hullard died at Brindiwell, The service was at Upham Methodist Chapel. The Hullards had previously lived at Redyeates and at Upham Cottage. He started his working life as a carter.

Higher Holn, Upham

A dwelling house, workshop and premises and 40 acres of land on the north of a field called Barnes Close, belonging to the Holne estate.

Henry Stone, wheelwright lived there in 1877 with Sydenham and Philip Francis of Court Barton, Upham being owners.

Wife Jane Stone and father John Stone

In 1882 *Backhayes* Meadow occupied by James Prior and Backhayes garden occupied by Daniel Prior in the village were offered for let together with Mrs Greenslade's orchard at Wilson's Water near White's Cross tenement.

The Retreat

1796 William Harris, rector to Philip Moggridge

1822 Four married daughters and heirs of Philip Mogridge to Thomas Tucker

1832 Thomas Tucker to his married daughter now Luxton and to George Sharland

1835 Sharland, Luxton, Collihole and Bodley to Andrew Hewish, tailor

1840 Tythe Map Property 13 occupied by Andrew Hewish snr, tailor and Property 14 occupied by Richard Hewish, tailor

1852 Andrew Hewish's son John Hewish to Rev Arundell

1877 Rev Arundell rents Robert Melhuish a plot of land for 10/- pa

1886 Rev Arundell sells the house to Robert Melhuish, shoemaker

1907 Melhuish's son Reg Melhuish to Mabel Annie Prior

1912 Mabel Prior married Thomas Pride

1917 Mabel Pride to Elizabeth Sanders, tailor

1925 plot of land part of Pynes Meadow from Arundell to Elizabeth Sanders

1939 Eizabeth's widower Albert to live there rent free

1867 Albert Sanders to George and Rosamund White

1988 The Whites build a two storey extension on The Retreat

1974 The Whites also acquire the garage formerly smithy at four ways crossroads This property has since become a dwelling called Bary Cottage.

Andrew Hewish 1773, a tailor was the son of John Hewish and Elizabeth Pearce and he married Rebecca Elsworthy around 1796. Their children were John 1796, Mary 1799, Annie Agnes Lavinia 1802, Richard 1803, Andrew 1805, Thomas Henry 1811, James 1812, Henry 1814 and Thomas James 1815. In 1835 he paid £76 for the lease of The Retreat where he lived with his wife and youngest son Thomas who was also a tailor, until his death in 1846. Next door lived Richard Hewish a tailor, a fourteen year old relative also called Richard Hewish and Ann Oliver aged sixty five.

On Andrew's death the property passed to his eldest son John Hewish who kept it for a while and then sold the lease to Rev Arundell in 1852. John, known as Old Jack in later life was committed to the Union Workhouse in Crediton where he was on the night of the 1871 census. He died later that year aged seventy five. His sister Mary had emigrated to Nelson, New Zealand and his brother James to Victoria, Australia.

Next door to The Retreat is present day Sweetbriar, but until at least 1993 the house was called Glebe Cottage.

New Housing in the village

1903 saw the sale of a freehold property called Bank Cottages comprising one newly-built stone-built three-bed cottage with a slate roof and two smaller cottages. The larger had been occupied by Elizabeth Hooper deceased and it included a small entrance hall with tiled floor, a kitchen and a parlour. There were outbuildings and a stable and coach-house and yard with a good carriage entrance from the street. The two smaller cottages were occupied by Leonard Webber, a police officer and Mrs Fewings and had their own gardens.

On a 1993 map there is a Bank House in Post Office Lane which runs alongside the children's play-ground. This might be the property mentioned above.

A scheme to erect a stock of four new houses was started in 1924 by an investor called Mrs A H James of Exeter. She soon met difficulties over a satisfactory water supply for the dwellings and left the project half finished. She left the buildings in September 1925.

Inns and Public Houses

1688/9 paid to the Smiths and underdwellers for beer and cider the 25th November £2.6s.0d.

1763 Mr Spettigue the curate towards the wine £1.10s.0d.

1770 Mrs Brake for year's supply of sacrament wine £2.13s.4d.

Mrs Brake for sacrament bread 4/-

1790 John Brake paid liquor duty on cargo from 'The Sarah' from Rotterdam

1800 the Rev Arundell for wine for the sacrament £3.10s.0d.

1801 John Ledger's bill for wine for the sacrament £4.17s.1d.

The Ring of Bells Inn

1831 will of Richard Oliver left The Ring of Bells Inn 'where they now reside' to his children John and Ann Oliver.

1881 and 1891 Joseph Pearn was the licensee and gardener, living there with his wife Sarah Blake Pearn (nee Langworthy) and his children Sarah, Samuel and Claude.

1899 The new licensee, Mr Densham applied for a one hour extension of his licence in September ready for the Harvest celebrations.

1900 the landlord William Henry Densham was unable to meet his bills and a meeting was held for his creditors. He had run the pub since 1897 having no money of his own when he married his wife Mary Ann Hill in 1887. All furniture in the property was hers.

1901 A temporary license was granted to Robert Melhuish of the Half Moon Inn for The Ring of Bells.

1903 A skittle alley was erected close to the road, but the police had frequent complaints of bad language used by those who visited it.

In January 1910 this old Inn with the posting establishment belonging to it changed hands with Mr Gunn leaving and Mr R E Veasey becoming landlord. It had been put out to tender for alterations and repairs in 1903.

1917 Richard Veasey was killed on active service in the First World War. He had left his wife in charge of the pub. He had married Maud Meta Hill in 1910. Their child Laura Annie Voysey died tragically at the age of 8 in 1918 and their other daughter Ellen Kathleen Voysey died aged 18 in 1932. Maud Meta Voysey herself died in 1955 aged 70 years

The Deanery magazine reported:

> 'A Service in memory of the late Richard Ernest Veysey was held at the Church on a Sunday evening, many were present to pay a last token of respect.'

Buried: Arras Memorial in Pas De Calais, France. He was a Private 27752 with the 6th Battalion Somerset Light Infantry.

Nationality: British Details:

28th April 1917. Age 34. Son of Humphrey and Jane Veysey of East Batsworthy Farm Creacombe; husband of Maud Meta Veysey of The Ring of Bells Inn Cheriton Fitzpaine Crediton Devon. Bay 4.

1940 a large shed offering good storage at the premises was offered for let. This may have been the skittle alley.

The Half Moon Inn, formerly Cross Farmhouse

The listed building entry includes details that it is now a Public house but was formerly a house, probably late 16th century or early 17th century with later alterations. It was a 3 room cross-passage house facing east and stands at the entrance to the village at the crossroads. It is not known when it became an Inn but a license to sell alcohol was issued to Isaac Wotton in 1771 'at the sign of the half moon'. For its early life it was the main dwelling for Cross Farm with a spacious farm-yard behind and a range of useful outbuildings. Its fields lay to the west and south, and animals were regularly brought into the Dairy for milking across land which is now Drake's Meadow.

Once a pub, the outbuildings were used for a variety of trades and the licensee often hosted livestock auctions in the rear courtyard. Access to the yard would probably have been between the main farmhouse and the dairy cottage, now called Cross Cottage, or through the field where Drakes Meadow now stands. Farmers met to enjoy a drink or two and exchange stories and opinions as they placed their bids. Property and farm equipment was also auctioned on the premises, the earliest recorded being the sale of Thongsleigh Mill in 1799.

1889 the landlord Mr Melhuish applied for an extra hour's licence on the day of the Harvest Festival, September 24th so that those with carts and horses who were put up at the house would not have to leave the dance early to attend to their horses.

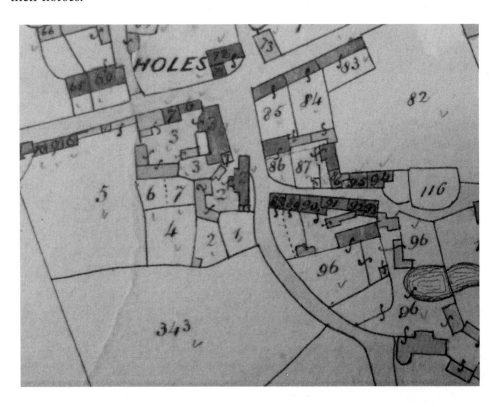

Like so many properties in the parish The Half Moon was owned by the Lord of the Manor and leased out to locals. The Rector on occasion also the Lord of the

Manor, through marriage or inheritance and Rev William Arundell Harris held both offices at the time of the 1840 Tythe survey. Rev William Harris Arundell therefore owned plots 1-5 and leased them out to Samuel Brewer:

1 Cottage, outhouses and garden

2 Cottage and workshops, garden and outhouse

3 Half Moon Inn, offices, outbuildings, yard and garden

4 garden

5 orchard and sheds (known as Half Moon Orchard and later sold to Tom Breyley and then developed as the Nunn's House etc.)

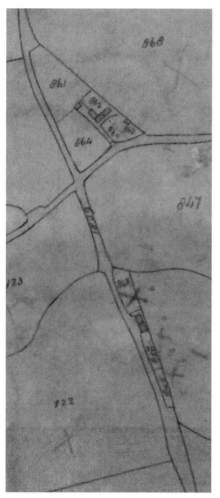

These plots were still called 'Cross Farm'. Ann Edwards had acquired the two cottages (6 and 7) on the north side of the courtyard and rented one out to Samuel Brewer and the other to William Elsworthy. The garden plots for these were separated from them and stood on the far side of the yard. As the outhouses were developed into small businesses it was seen necessary to gain access to them from the main road and that is why the end cobb wall of building number 6 has been shaved away to create an odd-shaped house.

Cross Farm also came with three cottages and gardens numbered 848, 849 and 859 on the Tythe situated near the football ground at White's Cross.

848, 849 and 859 were part of Cross Farm, lying to the south of Whites Cross crossroads

331

In 1751 'Cross' is still listed as a farm under the name of John Hewish in the Overseers' list but in 1755 the Churchwardens settled 'Mr Wotton's bill of 5s.6d.', for wine and again in 1758 they incurred 'Expenses about Humphrey Wotton's Inn by order, of 2s.6d.' It would appear therefore that the farmhouse was serving as a pub as early as 1755.

Humphrey Wotton hailed from Poughill and he married Mary Grant from Cheriton Fitzpaine at St Martin's Church, Exeter in1689 and moved straight back to Cheriton to have Humphrey 1690, Augustin 1695, John 1698, Grace 1701, Augustin 1704, Mary 1706, Mary 1710, Joane 1714 and Thomas 1717. Humphrey Wotton jnr 1698 may have been the publican mentioned in the 1758 accounts. His brother John1698 had a son called Isaac Wotton 1730 who is probably the man who took out the license 'at the sign of the half moon' in1771, the year his own son Isaac jnr was born.

In 1708 Thomas Gibbs was living and farming at Cross Farm paying a rate of 3d. John Hewish is listed in 1741 and Andrew Hewish from c1750–1778. Cross Farm included the fields to the south of the main road and up Lag Hill, but once the decision was made to apply for a license, land was sold off and only the few fields closest to the property remained. The present day Cross Cottage was developed as a dairy and a few cows were kept being brought in to be milked using the trackway to the rear in Drakes Meadow. John Brewer 1793–1808 may well have run the pub and continued to farm the slimmed-down farmlands but eventually Cross Cottage was sold off and the farming side was left to the new owners of that property. All later licensees of The Half Moon have found it necessary to diversify, running extra businesses from the workshops behind the main building. Whether shoe and boot makers, wheelwrights, coopers, or motor-mechanics, the landlords have made the most of the premises. From time to time animal stock markets were held in the back yard and property auctions often took place there. An auction of timber was held at the Half Moon Inn in April 1808.

Cross Cottage meanwhile developed as a small but thriving dairy business.

Rev Daniel Arundell as Lord of the Manor owned the Half Moon Pub and then passed it to William Harris Arundell and then on to Frederick William Arundell. Frederick William Arundell born in the village to William and his wife Sarah Peach Arundell in 1849 later adopted the surname Sanders and farmed 256 acres at Pilton, Pinhoe. In 1874 he sold the Half Moon to Henry Hooper, innkeeper and it was then in the occupation of Mr Hewish. Henry Hooper of Barnshill farm then sold it to William Turner of The Artillery Inn, Holloway Street, Exeter and it was passed down through the family to Edward Turner an ironmonger's assistant. He passed it to the Shilston family and then William Shilston of Leys Cottage a steam engine proprietor sold it on to Alice Holmes James and William Henry James in 1920.

In 1901 Robert Melhuish died as a result of heart failure brought on by 12 months dosing of 'chloral' which he took because he found it difficult to sleep. His inquest was held at The Ring of Bells Inn but he was the licensee of The Half Moon Inn. He also worked as a shoe and boot maker, living at The Half Moon with his wife Mary Webber, and his children Lucinda, Reg, Ethel (a school teacher), George and Margery. The verdict was accidental death.

An Un-named Inn

An un-named Inn was operating, none too legally in the village at the start of the 18th century as evidenced by the following entries in the Overseers' Accounts when conviction money was taken from them and re-distributed to the poor:

> 1717/18 Andrew, William and Richard Taylor paid conviction money when guilty of not selling statute measures
>
> 1720 Richard Taylor for ale when Davie was in keeping 1/-
>
> 1743 Conviction money was paid by Andrew Taylor, contrary to an Act of Parliament, for suffering John Cruwys, Philip Back and William Cruwys to sit tippling in his house on the Sabbath day.

The Angel Inn

An enigmatic entry in the Overseers of the Poor Accounts/Churchwarden's Accounts for 1744 becomes clear when one knows about the existence of The Angel Inn for it reads, '1744 Mrs Wessen for the Angel ... and putting up £2.2s.0d'. This would be the amount paid to the landlady for providing lodgings and food and drink for someone, or perhaps for hosting the committee meeting or for holding an auction ('putting up' goods for sale). In 1744 that was a considerable sum of money so the event must have been a memorable one. Other entries in the Churchwarden's accounts mention buying wine from a Mrs Webber and this may well be the same person:

'1755/6 Mrs Webber for 13 bottles of tent and 17 bottles of port wine £2 10s 6d.'

'1763 Mrs Webber for wine and a bottle of tent £1 5s 8d.

John Webber had died in September 1755 leaving his widow Mary to continue the business. She was buried in November 1776 so it seems probable that the Inn did not renew its liquor license and then became a dwelling house, formerly known as The Angel. William Segar Bastard, born in Exeter 1789 had inherited an interest in the property at this early date, and as a hop merchant he signed a release of his interests on the building to John Hewish, (farmer of Lower Saunders), John Wotton and John Roberts.

Appendix

Details of interest to genealogists are included below:

Reynold family
Documentation shows the family in Pinhoe in the early 16th century with Thomas and John then making the move towards Cheriton:

1525 Lay Subsidy: John Reynolds G3 Crediton, Thomas Reynolds W1 Crediton, Thomas Reynolds G12 Pinhoe, Richard Reynolds G6 Pinhoe, James Reynolds G2.5 Pinhoe, William Reynolds G2 Pinhoe,

Pascoe Reynolds W1 Broadclyst

1535 May 4th Martyrdom of Richard Reynolds at Tyburn

1537 appointment of Thomas Reynold appointed as rector of Cheriton and Michael Reynolds as rector of Pinhoe

William Reynold established himself and his family in the village, taking on farmlands including Pool:

1545 Lay Subsidy: William Reynolds 4 Cheriton Fitzpaine, Robert Reynolds 10, Tedburn St Mary, Thomas Reynolds 5 Tedburn St Mary, Henry Reynolds 1 Tedburn St Mary, Richard Reynolds 10 Pinhoe,

Richard Reynolds 1 Pinhoe, James Reynolds L3 Pinhoe, Simon Reynolds 1 Exeter St Thomas Apostle

1555 Richard Reynolds, gent of East Ogwell sold his farm called Thongsleigh on Northside, Cheriton to Thomas Maunder, husbandman of Cruwys Morchard

1559 will of Thomas Reynolds places: John Reynolds of Sandford, Richard Reynolds of Cheriton Fitzpaine and sons Heiron, Edmund, William, James and John plus daughters, Richard Reynolds of Pyn

1560 Agnes Reynolds married Clement Scutt. Over the next seven years there was a dispute about dowry money and property promised by William Reynolds her father.

1569 Muster Roll – William Reynolds was one of the Cheriton Presenters, William Reynolds G7 Cheriton Fitzpaine, Agnes Reynolds G7 Pinhoe

1570 will of Jerome Reynolds of Winchester, physician – born and baptised in Pinhoe

1591 Richard Reynolds was a tithingman for the Cheriton Fitzpaine

1592 Agnes Scutt, widow complained against Andrew Reynolds in the Court Roll

1595 Andrew Reynolds was a tithingman in the village

1596 A stray animal was reported in Richard Reynolds' land in the Court Rolls

1599 Richard Reynolds one of the twelve jurors at the court

1600 John Bartlett appeared at the court accused of attacking Richard Reynolds

1613 Richard Reynold 8s.8d. for Pool towards the repair of the church

1613 Andrew Reynold 1/- towards the repair of the church

1613 Henry Reynold 2s.8d. towards the repair of the church

1641 Protestation Returns: William Reynolds of Buddle Cheriton Fitzpaine, William Reynolds of Poole Cheriton Fitzpaine, Bartholomew Reynolds Cheriton Fitzpaine, William Reynolds jnr. Cheriton

Fitzpaine, John Reynold Cheriton Fitzpaine

1666 William Reynold's will was proved leaving Pool Barton to his wife, Mary and thereafter to his daughter Anne the wife of William Hewish and their son William Hewish, and remaindered to his son John Reynold, his deceased daughter Mary Lee's children John, William and Ann, and to John Harris of Hayne, esq.

1683 will of Andrew Reynolds of Exeter mentions his aged father William Reynolds in Cheriton, a tenement and cottage in Cheriton Fitzpaine – cottage occupied by Matthew Kelland (a Kelland meadow was still tythable in 1840 in the annexed part of the parish near Combe Barton in the south)

1686 William Hewish jnr appealed to reduce his hearth tax as a result of totally demolishing one of his four chimneys

By the end of the 17th the Reynolds had given up farming and had moved out of Cheriton to trade in Exeter city. What remained of their property in the village had been either sold or passed on to married daughters e.g. Ann Reynold married William Hewish c1650 and continued to farm at Pool Barton.

Only one member of the family with the surname Reynold was still paying Poor rates on a jointly owned property in the parish: 1692 William Reynolds and Augustine Wootton 1d.

Scutt family

1661 June 1st Andrew Scutt married Alice Croydon St Edmunds Exeter

1663 Andrew Scutt, gent 2s.11d. rates for church repair

1664 Andrew Scutt snr, Andrew Scutt jnr 17s.6d., rec of John Scutt 8s.9d. Richard Scutt of Stokaden and Andrew Scutt of Grewe

1664 June 13th Lease between Andrew Scutt the elder and Grace his wife to James Scutt his second son (and wife Margaret) for Grew alias Grewlands

1670 Grace Scutt appears in the rates list

1670 June 27th indenture between James Scutt and Elizabeth Scutt for Grew alias Grewlands

1671 indenture re moiety of Stockparks

1673 Grace Scutt buried

1673 November 26th Indenture between Andrew Scutt the elder and Grace his wife on the first part, Wiliam Jerman of Killand and George Melhuish of Culmstock, clothier on the second part, and Andrew Scutt the younger his son and Alice Croydon his intended wife as a competent marriage portion, Stockadonm Grew, and lands in Romansleigh, Marionsleigh, Kitcott, Upcott and Crediton.

1674 June 24th lease between Grace Scutt, widow and Andrew Scutt her son for Grew alias Grewlands

1675 Andrew Scutt buried

1675 list entry Will of Robert Scutt of CF

1686 Recovery between Andrew Scutt and Alice his wife and John Hawkins, gent for Grew alias Yarncombe and Stockadon

1691 March 15th Mortgage on Grew between Grace Fursdon and Andrew Taylor who married Elizabeth Scutt

1691 October 29th Mortgage for Grew between Andrew Scutt and Thomas Clarke the younger of Exeter, gent determinably on the decease of James Scutt and Margaret his wife

1694 Richard Scutt of Stokaden, Andrew Scutt of Grewe, and Robert Scutt, church sidesman.

1694 list entry Will of Isaac Scutt alias Western of Thorveton

1696 June 7th Andrew Scutt petitioned officials for a women's church seat to be constructed in the space behind his seat for his wife and children.

1697 October 26th and 27th Lease and Release between Rachel Scutt, spinster and George Westron for her 1s.3d. part of Stockadon and Grew

1698 October 8th indenture between Andrew Taylor, husbandman married to Elizabeth Scutt and Abraham Langbridge for Grew

1697 September 28th marriages of three Scutt sisters in Cheriton Fitzpaine to George Western/Westron, 'Charles Avery' (John Davey), and Abraham Langbridge

1697 October Grace Scutt buried

1722 Anna (nee Scutt), last of the three sisters died

1454 William Scutt juror

1494 John Scutt, juror – 1515

1524 Subsidy roll – John Scutt G18, Thomas Scutt G14, Richard Scutt G2

1548 Thomas Scutt juror

1548 list entry Will of Peter Scutt of Cheriton Fitpaine

Andrew and Clement Scutt born in Cheriton Fitzpaine

1559 Clement Scutt married Agnes Reynold

Andrew Scutt married in Cheriton Fitzpaine and held Perryhays and a moiety of Stockparks

1558–1579 Clement Scutt rates paid on property[12]

1558–1579 Chancery Court pleadings: Raynolde v Scutt. Plaintiff William Raynolde, Defendants Clement Scutt and others. Moiety of Stockparks in Cheriton Fitzpaine C3/154/43 National Archives

1590 Sentence of Clement Scutt PROB 11 76

1594 Will of Andrew Scutt

1610 Robert Scutt had daughter Dunes baptised, and Grace in 1617.

1613 Robert Scutt paid 56 for church repairs (Fursden)

1613 Andrew Scutt snr, Andrew Scutt jnr and John Scutt appeared on the church rate list for the village

1617 Anne Scutt buried

1636 Clement Scutt received a bequest from his uncle Roger Isaake of Heavitree and Polsloe

1640/1 Protestation Returns Andrew and Robert Scutt

1642 list entry Will of Robert Scutt of CF

1644 Amias Isaake a Cavalier aged 24 was staying with his Great Aunt Scutt in C F prior to his contentious marriage with widow Gertrude Courtenay Moore of Upcott

1656 Will of Agnes Scutt of Cheriton Fitzpaine PCC Admons Vol 2 p 93

Lower Saunders/Hewish family

1613 Peter Saunders paid Church rates and may have been the first to live in the house, which in part dates from the late sixteenth century. It certainly bears his family name.

1640 Protestation Returns for the parish listed men over the age of eighteen years including Roger Saunders, Roger Saunders jnr, John Sanders [ibid], and John Saunders jnr. 1664 Richard Saunders paid 3/- towards the repair of the church and John Hewish and Richard Hewish paid 2s.6d. each

1670 occupiers of John Hewish tenement paid 10d for repair of the church

1670 John Saunders paid 1/-

1673 John Sanders paid rates of 1½d. on Lower Saunders. A John Sanders had married Mary Guy of Poughill in 1667 and may have made it their family home at the time of their marriage. The couple had John jnr 1670, Jone 1673, Christopher 1675 and Robert 1677. Mary Guy was from the wealthy Gye and Prowse families of Poughill and Dodderidge.

1678 John Sanders paid rates on the property

1685 Morrish Hewish married Elizabeth Oxenham at Puddington and they had their first child John Hewish in 1686.

1691 Morrish Hewish was paying rates for Saunders

1696 and 1702 Morrish Hewish acted as Churchwarden

1704 Morrish Hewish paid 1/6 church rate on Saunders

1725 Morrish Hewish of Saunders (will dated 1723 has not survived)

1727 William Hewish jnr born

c1731 deed for three lives on the property from William Harris to William Hewish on the three lives of William jnr, Abraham and Andrew Hewish

1731 Hugh Payne paid rates for Saunders

1735–9 William Hewish

1744 William Hewish paid 2/- Church rate for Saunders

1744 William Hewish paid 2/- Church rate for Saunders

1752 William Hewish

1753 William Hewish jnr hung for murder

1753 Rates not collected on the property whilst it was unoccupied

1756 John Hewish or Mrs Kingdon paid 2s.6d. Church rate Andrew Hewish

1758–1763 Lawrence Greenslade paid 2s.2d. Church rate Andrew Hewish

1782 William Harris esq with Andrew Hewish

1761 Andrew Hewish and Sarah Stabbick had their son John Hewish (he was married 3 times and had 10 children)

1800 Samuel Wootton with John Barnes tenant

1801–4 William Lake

1804–6 Samuel Wootton and John Brewer

1812 William Lake with John Melhuish

1824 James and Robert Wootton with Robert Manning, tenant

1613 William Hewish 1/10 for Church repairs, John Hewish 6d.

1663 Andrew Hewish for the Mill 4/-

1664 William Hewish 14s.6d, Margery Hewish widow 13/-, Andrew Hewish jnr 4/-, Robert Hewish 3s.3d., Richard Hewish 2/6d., John Hewish 2s.6d., Alice Hewish 1s.6d., Margery Hewish for Mill 12s.6d., Robert Hewish 1/- paying for the repairs of the church (FURS)

1663 church rates (Fursdon) Richard H 1/-, John H 10d., Alice H 6d., Andrew H gent 4s.4., Robert H jnr 1s.4d.

Churchwardens: 1681 Richard H, 1684 William H, 1695 Andrew H, 1679 in the Glebe Terrier land of 8 acres called Sentry of Sanctuary ground mentioned as being bordered on the south side by land of Mr Andrew Hewish and on the north by the highway

1686 Hearth Tax – 13th July William Hewish jnr of Cheriton Fitzpaine has totally demolished one chimney of four which he formerly paid duty on – sworn by officials as being true. (was this at Pool?)

Sellicks 1704 William Hewish, 1737–60 Edward Hewish. 1753 Redyates William Morrish

Perryhayes 1706-9 Andrew Hewish, 1725–37 Mrs Mary Hewish, 1742–45 Mrs Anne Hewish, 1751 William Hewish, 1752 occupiers, 1776 Philip Mogridge 1805 John Hewish

East Coddiford (Little) 1731 Andrew Hewish (1741)

West Coddiford (Great) 1734–9 John Hewish

Barnshill 1723–9 Andrew Hewish, 1744 John Hewish

Brindiwell 1734 William Hewish

Cheriton Barton 1730 Mr Maunder for the Barton of Cheriton,1734 Thomas Parkhouse for the Barton, 1738–40 John Hewish, 1746 Thomas Parkhouse for the Barton, 1752 occupiers, 1753–75 Andrew

Hewish, 1782 William Harris esq with Andrew Hewish, 1788–99 William Harris esq with John Hewish, 1792 Robert Melhuish, Thomas Tucker tenant 1806–8

1765 Andrew Hewish discharged his apprentice Agnes Camp and then prosecuted her for a felony. She was 17.

Cross 1737–9 John Hewish, 1752 John Hewish, 1756–79 Andrew Hewish, 1763–76 William Wootton, 1804 John Brewer, 1782 William Harris esq with Andrew Hewish

Pool 1737 Mr Edward Hewish, 1739–64 Mr William Hewish, 1758 James Chamberlain, 1782 William Hewish and Mrs Harris with Robert Melhuish, 1788 William Harris and Mrs ?Hicks with John

Hewish, 1792 Robert Melhuish, 1799–1805 Samuel Pridham, Cleave and with tenant Samuel Pridham, 1807 Pridham and

In 1781 Daniel Tremlett he took on land around Pool called Stockparks. In 1799 Ann Tremlett married Samuel Pridham and in 1806 her sister Sarah Tremlett married John Brewer, Each had a son named after their father: Daniel Tremlett Pridham and Daniel Tremlett Brewer. Daniel owned Upcott Barton

1745 West Hayne Mrs Anne Hewish

1748 Dovers Hill, Dobles Mrs Sarah Hewish

Grew 1748 John Hewish

Holes 1748 William Hewish, 1788 William Harris with Robert Hodge for one part and Richard Glanville for another part 1840 John Hewish

Morles 1742–56 John Hewish

1762 Workhouse Governor Richard Hewish 'to make and amend at his own cost all the wearing apparel both woollen and linen' of the inmates.

Stockparks 1763 (separate from Perryhayes 1742) Mrs Rebecca Hewish, 1788 William Harris esq with Mrs Tremlett, 1793 John Hewish

Index of Names

Hawkings, Rebecca 148-9
Hawkes, George 203
Hayes, John 76
Heal, Edward 203
Hearndon/Hardin John 12-3
Heard, John 203
Heart, Mary 15
Heathman, Elizabeth 202, George 202,
 Henry 202
Hedge, Mary 15
Hellyons, William 63-4
Helmore, Timothy 111
Hepper, James 224, Thomas 224
Hewish, 215, Abraham 18, 20, 23, 29, 33,
 38, 40, 105, 231, Andrew 20, 23, 29-31,
 33, 37, 78-9, 108, 167, 218, 228, 231,
 263, 278, 314, 325-7, 332, Ann 21-4,
 32-3, 279, 325, Annie Agnes Lavinia
 327, Ben 3-6, 182, Betty (also Westcott)
 39, Charity 33, Edward 30-3, 39, 79,
 279-80, 319, 325, Elizabeth 18, 31, 33,
 35 Emily 35, Emma 33, 36, 39, 322,
 Hannah 33, Henry 327, James 39, 327,
 Jane 18, John 12, 18-20, 28-30, 33, 36-7,
 39, 40, 107, 109, 149, 182, 228, 231,
 242, 244, 249-50, 305, 322, 327, 332,
 334, Lucinda 33, Maria 33, 35, Mary
 18, 21, 30, 40, 79, 327, Mary Ann 33,
 40, Merina 33, Morrish 18-20, Rebecca
 21, 31-2, 327, Richard 10, 18, 33, 35-7,
 39, 107, 232, 326-7, Robert 33, 39,
 Sarah 33, 40, 79, 228, 234-5, Simon 269,
 Susannah 79, Thomas 3, 305, Thomas
 Henry 327, Thomas James 327, William
 18-40, 68, 76, 78-9, 181-2, 217, 231,
 279, 318-9, 325
Hicks, Elizabeth 3, 12, 32, 279-80, 325,
 John 31, Mary 31, 32, Nicholas 31, 67,
 279, Rebecca 31, Thomas 31
Hill, Mary Ann 328, Maud Meta 328-9,
 Sarah 95, William 13, 148, 181

Hitchcock, Faith 142, William Dummet
 142
Hockaday, 108, Ann 199, Thomas 109,
 Richard 109
Hodge, Daniel 191, Florence Emily 202,
 Mary 196
Hodgeland, John 128
Hole, Agnes 79, Ann Pridham 265, Annie
 Harris 265-6, Amy Elizabeth 265-6,
 Edward Albert 265, Elizabeth Ann 228,
 230, Ellen Harris 265-6, Henry Robert
 265, John Duffield Rev 223, 225, 227-9,
 232, 236, Louisa 229, Lydia 227-8,
 Margaret 79, Penelope 228, Sophia 229
Holland, Elizabeth 168, Faith 168, John
 168, Mary 142, 149, 168-9, Sarah 168,
 Thomas Melhuish 142, 149, 169
Holman, Humphrey 218
Holsgrove/Hosegood Mary 145, Thomas
 109, 145
Hookway, John, Mary 150
Hopper, Elizabth 327, Henry 332, William
 160
Horwill, Mark 235
Hoskings, William 246
Hoxland, Mary 155, Roger 126, 234-5
Hucker, Sarah 292
Huckley, Mary 269
Huckwell, Alice 40, Elizabeth 40, Hannah
 40, Lucinda 40, Mary Ann 40, Merina
 40, Reuban 40, Thomas 40
Hullard, Ellen 325, Ernest 325
Hurrell, John 314
Hutchings, Mary 167

Isaac, William 308
Isles, Mrs 209
Jacob, Thomas 3
Jackman, John 322
James, Alice Holmes 333, George 321, Mrs
 A H 327, William Henry 333

Mayne, William 321
Melhuish, Albert 177, Alfred 177, Ann
  20, Bessie 178, Charles Sidney 177,
  Christopher 169, Daisy Frances 178,
  Daniel 191, Edith 177-8, Elizabeth 39,
  192, Ellen 177, Elsie 178, Ernest 178,
  Ethel 177, 333, Faith 33, Ferdinando 20,
  Florence 178, George 333, Henry 37,
  Ivy 178, J 118, James 178, Joan 20, John
  37, 57, 163, 169, Lucinda 333, Margery
  333, Mary 37, 333, Mr 276, Reginald
  326, 333, Richard 37, 224, Robert 202,
  242, 326, 328, 330, 333, Sarah 169,
  Susannah 169, Thomas 149, 168-9, 185,
  232, Thomas Abraham 169, Thomas
  Rev 285, Walter 177, William 177
Middleton, Thomas 147-8
Mildon, Loveday 258-9, Olive 259, Tom S
  258-9, 272
Miller, Doris, 276, widow 117
Mills, Elisha 169
Mitchell. William 317
Mitton, John 149
Mogford, John 203
Mogridge, Grace 142, John Hewish 142,
  Mary 325, Philip 251, 258, 325, Sarah
  325, Thomas 126, 234, 274, 318, 325
Moore, Ernest John 258, Robert 203
Morris, John 218,
Morrish, Alexander 304, Ann 278, Cecilia
  Chamberlain 163, Elizabeth 19, James
  125, 218, Jane 162, Joane 19, John 162,
  Mary 162, Mr 118, Richard 162-3,
  William 278-9
Morrison, Ann 281, Ebener 281,
Mortimore, John 150,
Moxey, Ann 108, 251, Grace 95, Hugh
  196-7, 244, John 108, 251-2, Martha
  244, Mary 252, Matthew 244,319,
  Solomon 244, William 91, 224, 244
Mugg, Walter 3

Murging, Mary 135-6

Nation, William 57, William Hamilton
  Codrington 58
Newcombe, Elizabeth 2, Robert Lydstone
  32, William 32
Newbury/Newberry Henry 209, John 209,
  258, William 200
Newton, William 198
Nichols, Diggory 67
Noble, John 150,
Norrish, John 279, William 150, 280, 319

Oaten, Samuel 108
Ocock, Mary 199
Oldbridge, Elizabeth 196
Oliver, Ann 86, 236, 328, Edward 145, 261,
  269-70, Edwin 270, John 86, 105, 107,
  145, 150, 224, 237, 260-1, 263, 269-70,
  328, Mary 107, 237, 261, 269-70,
  Mary Ann 145, Mr 236, Mrs 260, 263,
  Richard 86, 105, 107, 197, 260-1, 263,
  269, 313, 328, Sally 237, Sarah 237, 261-
  3, 270, Susannah 145, Thomas 184, 261,
  270, William 68, 105, 107, 145,184, 197,
  251, 260-2, 269-70
Orchard, Rebecca 281
Osmond, Anna Maris 263, Bessey Ridler
  263, Hannah 263, Thomas 263
Oxenbere, Richard 195
Oxenham, Elizabeth 21

Packer, Agnes 160, 169, Ambrose William
  160, Ann 160, Charles 161, Ellen 160-1,
  Emma 160-2, James 160-1, 169, 208,
  John 159-60, 169, Mary 160-1, Mary
  Ann 160, Richard 160, Robert 160-1
  169, Sarah 160, Susan 160, Thomas
  161
Paddon, Farmer 185, Mr M 283
Page, Thomas 321

Paine/Payne, Andrew 68, 303, 320, Elizabeth 32, Hugh 19, 320, Joan 303, John 303, Louisa 323, William 303

Parkhouse John 305, Richard 68, 196, Thomas 313

Passmore, William 269

Pawlyn, John 303

Pearce, Elizabeth 327, John 327

Pearcey, William 220

Pearn, Claude 328, Joseph 328, Samuel 328, Sarah 328, Sarah Blake 328

Peasler, George 95, Rose 95

Peaster, Roger 224

Percy, PC 191,

Phillips, Aaron 68, 120, Arundell 28, Charlotte 28, Jane 28, John 28, Maria 28, Samuel 128, Sgt 191

Pierce, Margery 11

Pike, John 104-5, 107

Pine, Joseph 150

Pitt, William 104-5, 107, 254

Please/Pleace, Charlotte 287, Elizabeth 287, Robert 287, William 224

Pole, William 303

Pope, John 90, 141, Joseph 127,197,203, Martha 197, Mary 142, 164-5, Thomas Downing 142, William 127

Poufford, widow 218

Powe, Abraham 150, John 217-8, Thomas 150, William 217

Pownsford, Thomas 303

Prise, Thomas 326

Pridham, Agnes 235, Ann Harris 238, 241, Betty 235, 262, Charlotte 235, Daniel Tremlett 223. Elizabeth 223-4, James 120, 127, 128, 235-6, Joseph 223-4, 238, Louisa 264, Lucy Elizabeth 238, Mary 223, 235, Mrs 97, Peter 235, Samuel 32, 80, 109, 179, 223-4, 232, 238-41, 246, 264, 265-6, 322, Susan 238,

Prince, Rev John 48, 62

Prior, Albert John 246, D 276, Daniel 207, 258, 325, Elizabeth 261-3, 270, Emma 246-8, James 108, 263, 323, 325, John 105, 246-8, 255, 258, Laura 246, Leonard 323, Louisa 323, Mabel Ann 326, Mary Ann 245-7, Mr 102, Mrs 234, Sarah 206, 258, Thomas 236,William 262, 323

Pubb, Richard 313

Pyne/s, John 303, 321

Radford, Nicholas 321

Rashleigh, George 155, Maria 155

Rattenbury, John 244

Raymont, Albert 202, Albert John 259, Amy 178, Annie 177-8, Emily 177, Fanny 178, Frederick John 177, John 178, 191, Lily 177, Louisa 308, Mary 177, May 177, (Myrtle Ada Green) 178, Richard 191, Samuel 178, Thomas 177, William 177

Reed, Roger 286

Rendell, George 279, James 150

Retter, David 184

Reynold, Agnes 49, 58, 72-3, Alice 50, 59, Andrew 75, 187-8, Edmund 49, Elizabeth 49, 59, Heiron (Jerome) 49, 51, 59, James 49, Jane 49, Joan 49, 50, John 48-50, 59, 62, Nicholas 49, Margaret 49, 50, Michael 41, 49-50, 58, Richard 45-50, 53, 54, 58, 63, 187-8, Sarah 48, 62, 78, Thomas 41, 43, 45, 47-50, 53, 54, 58,59, 62, 63, 67, 72, William 49-50, 53-55, 57, 73, 75, 188, 226,

Rich, John 108

Richards, Dr 12, 14, John 217, 219, Silas, 150, 158

Ridge, Grace 108, William 185

Ridler, Hannah 263

Roach, William 274

350

Tanner, George 251
Tapp, (Godbere) Joan 209, Hannah 209,
    Philip 209
Taverner, George, 183, William 183
Taylor, Alice 11, Andrew 11, 156, 204,
    216, 333, Ann 1, 105, 150, Betty 105,
    142, Catherine 6, Elizabeth 16, 95, 216,
    Francis 11, George 105, Herman 1-12,
    16, 182, 197, Jacob 12, James 1, Joane
    11, John 1, 12, 16, 108, 125, 173, 197,
    Joseph 197, Margery 11, Mary 1, 105,
    147-8, 155, 197, Rebecca 105, Richard
    11-13, 16, 105, 333, Robert 7, 11, 197,
    226, Sarah 12, 16, Thomas 12, 105, 126,
    197-8, William 12, 105, 145-6, 150, 333,
    William Cruwys 142
Templeton, James 288
Thomas, Emilia 202, Hugh 188, 202, John
    116, Thomas 188
Thorne, Bessie Ann 257, Arthur James
    257, Edwin 178, 255, 257-8, Elizabeth
    254, G L Dr 267, Granville James 178,
    257, Herbert Edwin 257, James 254,258,
    James Bidgood 255, 257, Mary Ann
    254, Mr 99, Sarah 254, William 171,
    240
Tibbs, John 287
Tincombe, James Kerswell 142, Mary 142
Tolly, Mary 150,
Tom, Catherine 1, (6)
Towker, Thomas 73
Treble, John 236, Mr 280
Tremlett, Ann 240-1, Daniel 79, 132, 170,
    236, 240-2, 244, 252, Elias 79, 240,
    Elizabeth 79, 240, John 79, 240, Mary
    240-1, Sarah 241, 252
Troake, James 321
Trobrigge, Robert 3
Trott Athur 103, Phyllis 97, 103
Trull, George 112
Tucker, Betty 220, Daniel 1, Hannah 220,

Humphrey 313, Loveday 292, Mary
    224, Thomas 109, 220, 232, 325, W J
    264
Tuckett, John 105, 254, 313, Nicholas 262,
    William 103, 283, Susan 103
Turner, John 150, Mr 14, 205, 308, Mrs
    244, William 333
Tyler, Andrew 111

Upham, Davy 203, Elizabeth 198, Grace
    15, Katherine 11, 155-6, Samuel 196,
    200, William 131
Vasper, Selina 292
Veasy, Agnes 133
Vickary, Olive 79, Robert 79, William 200
Vinnicombe, 278
Voisey/Voysey/Veasey, Ellen Kathleen
    328, Jane 329, Humphrey 329, Laura
    Annie 328, Maud Meta 328, Richard E
    328-9, Robert 282, John 68

Wall, Amelia 159
Waller, James 320
Walrond John 27
Ware 106
Ward, Henry 95, Phyllis 103
Warren, Mary 206, Robert 304, Thomasin
    304-5
Waters, Henry 320
Way, Ethel 103, George 97, 103, Nellie 103
Way/Whey, Agnes 161, 169
Waybourne, Elizabeth 165, George 150,
    163-5, Robert 165
Webb, Robert 304
Webber, Bessie Ann 257, John 196, 249,
    334, Mary 333, Mrs 249, 333-4
Weeks, John 117
Wellington, Alice 231, Ann 231, Elizabeth
    15, Judith 231, Mary 30, 228, 231,
    Susanna 231, Thomas 30, 228, 231
Wessen, Mrs 249, 333

Index of Places